A Realistic Blacktopia

A Realistic Blacktopia

Why We Must Unite to Fight

Derrick Darby

OXFORD
UNIVERSITY PRESS

Oxford University Press is a department of the University of Oxford. It furthers
the University's objective of excellence in research, scholarship, and education
by publishing worldwide. Oxford is a registered trade mark of Oxford University
Press in the UK and certain other countries.

Published in the United States of America by Oxford University Press
198 Madison Avenue, New York, NY 10016, United States of America.

© Oxford University Press 2023

All rights reserved. No part of this publication may be reproduced, stored in
a retrieval system, or transmitted, in any form or by any means, without the
prior permission in writing of Oxford University Press, or as expressly permitted
by law, by license, or under terms agreed with the appropriate reproduction
rights organization. Inquiries concerning reproduction outside the scope of the
above should be sent to the Rights Department, Oxford University Press, at the
address above.

You must not circulate this work in any other form
and you must impose this same condition on any acquirer.

Library of Congress Cataloging-in-Publication Data
Names: Darby, Derrick, 1967– author.
Title: A realistic blacktopia : why we must unite to fight / Derrick Darby.
Description: New York, NY : Oxford University Press, [2023] |
Series: Philosophy of race series |
Includes bibliographical references and index.
Identifiers: LCCN 2022023701 (print) | LCCN 2022023702 (ebook) |
ISBN 9780197622124 (hardback) | ISBN 9780197622148 (epub)
Subjects: LCSH: African Americans—Civil rights. |
African Americans—Politics and government. | Race discrimination—
United States—Philosophy. | United States—Race relations.
Classification: LCC E185.61.D266 2023 (print) | LCC E185.61 (ebook) |
DDC 323.1196073—dc23/eng/20220816
LC record available at https://lccn.loc.gov/2022023701
LC ebook record available at https://lccn.loc.gov/2022023702

DOI: 10.1093/oso/9780197622124.001.0001

1 3 5 7 9 8 6 4 2

Printed by Integrated Books International, United States of America

In memory of Charles W. Mills

[E]ven if segregation is gone, we will still need to be free; we will still have to see that everyone has a job. Even if we can all vote, but if people are still hungry, we will not be free. . . . Singing alone is not enough; we need schools and learning. . . . Remember, we are not fighting for the freedom of the Negro alone, but for the freedom of the human spirit, a larger freedom that encompasses all of mankind.
—Ella Baker, "Minutes of the SNCC Executive Committee"

And beware of those who call for the salvation of black males but will not support the rights of Caribbean, Central American, and Asian immigrants, or who think that struggles in Chiapas or in Northern Ireland are unrelated to black freedom.
—Angela Y. Davis, *The Meaning of Freedom*

The same forces that deny health insurance to people with preexisting conditions, the same forces that want to deny women the right to decide when and if they reproduce, the same forces that want to deny protections to transgender people, the same forces that want to roll back voting rights for Black people, the same forces that want to deny each of us the right to live dignified lives are the ones that have invested a lot in making sure you don't understand that discrimination based on race and gender and sexuality and class are all strategies to keep the powerful in power and to deny those without power from accessing it.
—Alicia Garza, *The Purpose of Power*

Contents

Introduction: A Hard-Eyed View of Racism — 1

PART I. THE DEMISE OF SMALL-TENT REMEDIES

1. Affirmative Action — 15
2. Voting Rights — 32
3. Racial Reparations — 47

PART II. THE DAWN OF BIG-TENT REMEDIES

4. Black Liberalism Can't Save Us — 71
5. Postracial Remedies — 103
6. Collective Responsibility — 136

PART III. THE DEMAND FOR DEMOCRACY

7. Power to the People — 161
8. Making Voting Easier — 189
9. The Dignity of Voting — 208

Epilogue: Democracy Born of Struggle — 235

Acknowledgments — 249
Notes — 253
Index — 299

Introduction

A Hard-Eyed View of Racism

A CNN staff writer wanted my thoughts about the Atlanta hip-hop community's impact on the 2020 presidential and senate elections. A big story, at the time, was the pivotal role that Stacey Abrams, Keisha Lance Bottoms, and other black women played in Donald Trump's defeat and the Biden-Harris victory. Elliott McLauglin, who penned a piece on my fellow Queensbridge native, Nasir Jones—arguing that Nas was the greatest lyricist ever—was highlighting hip-hop's important contribution to flipping the White House. During our chat, we talked about Killer Mike, T.I., Big Boi, 2 Chainz, Offset, and Lil Baby, and how they and other rappers from Georgia were using their celebrity and social media platforms to transform American politics and shape the Democratic agenda. During the phone interview, which went well over an hour, my talking points were informed by three themes. Conscious rap lyrics, film, literature, scholarship, and other sources of knowledge about race and racism in America follow a recognizable script: they shed light on past and ongoing racial wrongs, on racial progress (or lack of it) in realizing an imagined blacktopia, and on remedies to right racial wrongs and to make lasting racial progress. This book defends a perspective about how to pursue racial progress despite the persistence of racism and the enduring myth that America is a postracial society.

The standard progressive story about how to achieve racial progress in America is that it demands "small-tent" remedies. Focusing narrowly on what African Americans (usually black males) need and how to get it is an example of a small-tent remedy. To put it crudely, the point of the story is this: "If you want to secure racial justice for *black* people then do shit for *black* people." I will use this illustration of a small-tent remedy throughout the book. When we consider the transatlantic slave trade, black chattel slavery, the old and new Jim Crow, and enduring racial disparities, it seems hard to argue against the claim that African Americans represent the most harmed victims of America's racial wrongs. Yet some people will disagree, arguing, to the contrary, that indigenous populations whose ancestors occupied the land long before Europeans and Africans arrived in North America hold this unfortunate title. They will argue that if small-tent remedies are the way to go, we should focus narrowly on what Native Americans need and how to get it. But once we start down this road—arguing over America's most harmed racial victims—it is easy to see how small-tent remedies rapidly proliferate. And if we frame the argument, more generally, as one about America's most harmed victims of historical wrongs, many more small tents will pop up. There will be small tents for women, black women, women of color, poor women, trans women, religious minorities, persons with disabilities, immigrants, immigrants of color, and so on.

Racial remedies—ones that target a specific race or ethnicity—are a prime example of a small-tent remedy in America. And they are among the most widely discussed and debated type of remedies. Various considerations explain this. Many people self-identify by race or ethnicity. However, as history reveals, such identification is not entirely voluntary in the United States. The nation has long identified people with racial labels, has assigned meanings to these labels, and has treated people in certain ways based on racial and ethnic membership. When focused on African Americans, the standard story places anti-black racism at the center of understanding past and ongoing oppression, subordination, and discrimination against blacks. Anti-black racism and white supremacy have also been central to explanations of why blacks are disproportionately worse off than whites in wealth, health, education, and criminal justice and other outcomes. The prevailing logic of the standard progressive story is that race-specific remedies are required to address racial wrongs and to find a way forward. Or, as I will sometimes put it in this book, the path to racial progress—both new progress as well as holding on to past racial gains—and to corrective justice in America requires flying the race-first flag.

I am a philosopher. And in my field no one has done more to defend this view than Charles W. Mills, author of *The Racial Contract*. During the completion of my book, which is dedicated to his memory, I and many others within and beyond philosophy mourned the untimely death of this innovative and influential critical philosopher of race and racism. He was a dear personal friend and a significant source of inspiration for my work. Challenging the prevailing logic of the standard story is an especially formidable task because Mills—a champion of black radical liberalism—has so vigorously defended it and has persuaded so many people with his arguments. Nevertheless, as I will argue in chapter 4, "Black Liberalism Can't Save Us," Mills's methodological commitment to theorizing about justice while taking seriously the historical and ongoing realities and manifestations of anti-black racism helps to explain why flying the race-first flag is unlikely to secure corrective justice for racial wrongs. If anti-black racism is as entrenched and pervasive in America, as Mills argues, and if whites, particularly well-meaning liberals who might be allies in the struggle for racial justice, are psychologically disposed to deflect and resist charges of racism, the prevailing logic of the standard story will have serious limits.

When focused on black people, the standard story takes different forms depending upon whether it comes from black nationalists—either those calling for emigration back to Africa or ones calling for building a sovereign black government within US borders—or from black liberals—either mainstream or radical ones like Mills. Although their ideologies will vary, these storytellers agree on the importance of rallying around the race-first flag to pursue black progress.

It is important to distinguish two kinds of progress. There is the kind that gets a public apology for slavery, a federal holiday for Juneteenth, another street named after Dr. Martin Luther King Jr., or maybe after Barack Obama or Breonna Taylor, or perhaps more token representation of black people in positions of authority and power. We can call this *symbolic* black progress. And there is the kind of progress that gets a massive influx of tax dollars directed to improving housing, schools, parks, community centers, roads, and transportation in black communities, the kind that supports after-school programs, job counseling and training, and mental health services in these communities, and the kind that results in real police accountability to the communities they serve, criminal justice reform, and equity in schools that serve these communities. We can call this *substantive* black progress. To be sure, both kinds of progress are valuable. It is important for blacks to secure recognition that comes from monuments and demographic representation. And it is important for black communities to secure the material resources and tangible outcomes that come from concrete policy-driven reform. However, we need to pitch a much bigger tent if substantive progress is our goal. And the reason is obvious: the substantive things blacks want for themselves are also things that other marginalized populations want too, and to get them we must unite to fight.

* * *

To appreciate why the race-first logic underlying the standard progressive story about how to achieve racial progress is naive and unrealistic, we must confront America's postracial orientation. I started working on this book in 2008 when Barack Obama was making his historic run for president of the United States. At the time, and in the aftermath of his victory, much was written about "postracialism." One the one side were those who took this historic moment to signal that America was no longer a society that made race an obstacle to progress and living the American dream. Conservatives were not the only group singing this tune. Mainstream liberals also sang it, along with significant portions of the general public. Harvard sociologist Lawrence D. Bobo summed up the prevailing ethos this way:

> To wit, American society, or at least a large and steadily growing fraction of it, has genuinely moved beyond race—so much so that we as a nation are now ready to transcend the disabling racial divisions of the past. From this perspective, nothing symbolizes better the moment of transcendence than Obama's election as president.[1]

On the other side were those including Bobo and myself, who were skeptical that America had achieved this status though it was certainly striving toward it. Social scientists were doing empirical studies linking durable racial disparities in wealth, housing, health, education, and criminal justice to forms of racial discrimination.[2] And this evidence exposed postracialism as mere mythology. Still, the myth prevailed. As I waded through the empirical evidence, I became convinced that whatever story we told about how to achieve racial progress in the United States had to assume this premise. To be clear, the premise is *not* that America is postracial but that, by and large, it takes itself to be postracial.

Some will wonder whether this premise remains valid in post–George Floyd America, where many Americans have experienced a so-called racial awakening. Is it still fair to say that America takes itself to be postracial when so many Americans marched for justice in the aftermath of Floyd's death, when social justice initiatives are proliferating in education, business, and the arts, and when Ibram X. Kendi's book *How to Be an Antiracist* and similar titles are flying off the bookshelves?

I think the postracial premise still rings true. And I am not alone in thinking this. In a recent essay, entitled "Our New Postracial Myth," Kendi proclaims, "The postracial idea is the most sophisticated racist idea ever produced. It keeps resurfacing and mutating and harming in new forms."[3] This myth is believed by many people, regardless of race, says Kendi, because everyone longs for a world without racism and is eager to embrace reasons for believing that this end is in sight. Historian Keeanga-Yamahtta Taylor's aptly titled *New Yorker* piece, "Did Last Summer's Black Lives Matter Protests Change Anything?," observes, "Even the most moderate Republicans still believe in the U. S. as a place where color blindness and unimpeded social mobility allow anyone from anywhere to reach the heights of social acceptance and personal wealth."[4] But the truth is that this view—a core theme of postracialism—is more widely endorsed by partisans across the political divide as well as by their various constituents.

Consequently, the change we have seen in America following Floyd's murder has been largely symbolic. Old statutes commemorating America's Confederate past have been torn down, and new ones, including monuments to Floyd and Breonna Taylor, have been erected (and sadly defaced). Juneteenth was made a national holiday. But a demand for voting rights and full inclusion into American democracy was a core concern during the first Juneteenth gathering by formerly enslaved persons. And, today, numerous states have enacted laws that make it increasingly harder for black people to vote. Juneteenth should be a reaffirmation of the importance of studying American history, and not just parts of it that makes us feel good and patriotic. We must also attend to the abhorrent historical legacy of black chattel slavery, Jim Crow segregation, and systemic racism and their far-reaching consequences for the persistence of black poverty, police brutality against blacks, economic underdevelopment of black communities, and the black–white educational achievement gap among other things. Scholars and educators of critical race theory have been at the forefront of teaching this history. But in post-Floyd America critical race theory is under assault, charged with preaching hatred and dividing Americans, and there are ongoing efforts to ban teaching critical race theory in schools and universities. In addition, conservative publishers are putting out books with postracial counternarratives, with titles such as *Blackout: How Black America Can Make Its Second Escape from the Democrat Plantation*, *Race Crazy: BLM, 1619, and the Progressive Racism Movement*, and *I Can't Breathe: How a Racial Hoax Is Killing America*.[5] These books are also flying off the shelves in post-Floyd America.

Taking the postracial premise seriously is especially important if we want our philosophical ruminations about racial progress and how to achieve it to be grounded in the reality of our lived experience. The most significant implication of postracialism is that it takes certain remedies for continued racial progress, for holding onto racial progress, and for corrective racial justice off the table. I make each point, respectively, in chapter 1 on affirmative action, in chapter 2 on voting rights, and in chapter 3 on black reparations. Although everyone may not believe the postracial myth, many people in power and in high places do, including members of the

US Supreme Court as well as state and federal legislators. And given the significant power the latter have in making law, and the former have in evaluating its constitutionality, we must reckon with the very real constraints this imposes on how to pursue racial progress in America.

* * *

I tell a different story about racial progress in this book. And it is somewhat paradoxical. The best way to pursue racial progress for blacks in America is to pursue "big-tent" remedies. We need to focus broadly on building coalitions among marginalized populations interested in a range of issues that impact them collectively. Blacks, Native Americans, Latinos, women, working-class whites, persons with disabilities, persons identifying as LBGTQ+, DREAMers, and other groups are concerned about jobs, housing, healthcare, education, discrimination, mental health, drugs, criminal justice, environmental pollution, the climate crisis, voting rights, and other pressing matters. And the truth is that they must find ways to work together on solving these problems to make lasting progress, racial and otherwise. When they work together they can pursue big-tent remedies, take collective responsibility for sustaining just and equitable institutions, and fight for making voting easier so that all can have a hand in democratic rule. I make each of these points, respectively, in chapter 5 on postracial remedies, in chapter 6 on collective responsibility, and in Part III with three chapters on democracy and voting rights. The good news is that we need not lament the demise of small-tent remedies narrowly focused on racial remedies. Because if we pursue big-tent remedies broadly focused on a constellation of matters affecting marginalized populations, and we fight for unfettered access to the ballot box, we can secure a realistic blacktopia in racist America.

According to the standard progressive story, we should target the population that has been most adversely affected in these areas, e.g., the one with the highest unemployment rates, greatest residential exposure to toxic pollutants, lowest levels of educational achievement and attainment, highest rates of arrest and incarceration, etc., and pursue targeted remedies on their behalf. Some will argue that because African Americans are the most adversely impacted (and there is ample data to support this), we should pursue race-specific remedies that specifically address their situation. Reparations for descendants of African slaves are the most widely defended remedy of this type today. Not long ago, affirmation action was another example. However, to anyone taking a hard-eyed view of racism in twenty-first-century America, looking at the courts, the legislatures, and surveying public opinion on race matters, it is obvious that such remedies are not viable. And if they yield anything, it will likely only be symbolic. But, at some point, we must refuse to be content solely with museums, murals, holidays, and other symbolic gestures that do not amount to deep and lasting systemic changes. To be sure, these things can be sources of racial pride, but they do not put food on the table, reduce black incarceration rates, improve funding of public schools in marginalized communities, or make it any easier for their residents to vote or to not have their votes neutralized by partisan legislators.

Even after the nation's post–George Floyd racial reckoning, flying the race-first flag is not likely to yield meaningful and lasting racial progress in America. Indeed, as some of us celebrated the guilty verdict in Floyd's senseless murder by the police as well as the tireless efforts of social justice protesters to raise awareness about racial and other forms of injustice, some lawmakers were busy working on legislation to silence protestors and to allow police to sue protestors for financial damages if injured, menaced, or harassed in the line of duty. This is one of many examples of how racial progress in America is swiftly followed by efforts to undo it.

We see similar examples when taking a longer view of US racial history. In 1808, the trans-Atlantic slave trade is outlawed—banning the importation of new African slaves into the United States—but several decades later, amid calls for Southern secession from the Union, an act is passed in 1850 requiring that escaped slaves be returned to their owners. The 13th Amendment to the US Constitution, ratified in 1865, abolished slavery, but not long after Reconstruction ended when the North and South struck a deal over a contested 1876 presidential election that removed federal troops out of the South. This made way for the enactment and enforcement of racial segregation and other Jim Crow laws relegating blacks to second-class citizenship. Observant students of US racial history will notice this familiar recurring pattern. America makes racial progress. It inches closer to embodying exalted ideals of freedom and equality, and to being a genuine democratic nation governed by and for all the people. But before the victory lap is completed steps are taken to either undo this progress or to find new ways of maintaining the racial status quo.

As bad as the pushback to police accountability and reform is, this is not the most troubling example of how racial progress is swiftly undone in America. The ongoing and systematic efforts underway to make voting more difficult for black and brown people and for likely democratic voters in Georgia and other historically red states, as well as controversial laws to shift power away from election officials and to partisan state legislators, empowering them to decide close elections, are examples of rolling back the racial progress clock. And this is a much more consequential endeavor because it seeks to make democracy less inclusive. Although there was not enough time to pursue this point during the CNN interview, it was on my mind. However, before we were done I did shed light on Georgia's dark past, singling out its infamous history of voter suppression. I did this not only to concede that there has been racial progress in the United States of America but also to stress, more importantly, that whatever progress black people have achieved in this country has generally been answered with swift and concerted efforts to undo it.

So, although post-Floyd America is awash in discussion about race and race relations, antiracist books are everywhere, and diversity seminars are hot tickets, many efforts are underway to roll back the racial progress clock, including laws penalizing peaceful protestors, reducing penalties for striking protestors with vehicles, allowing police officers to file civil suits against protestors, and the demonization of critical race theory and teaching it in schools. I had these and other racial patterns in mind when I reminded the reporter of Georgia's dark past. And I had something else in mind that also speaks to the need for big-tent remedies.

*　*　*

The recurrence of such patterns has been, and is likely to remain, America's reality for the foreseeable future. To take a "hard-eyed view of racism," a phrase used by the late legal scholar Derrick Bell, whose work inspires mine, is to start philosophical reflection on how to pursue racial justice and equality from this realistic premise. And this is precisely what I do in this book by arguing for big-tent remedies as a path to a realistic blacktopia.

Growing up in New York City's Queensbridge public housing projects during the 1970s and early 1980s taught me many lessons. My beloved aunt, affectionately known in the neighborhood as grandma hip hop, was the source of many of my most important lessons. When I am wrestling with philosophical questions and problems, trying to figure out what to think, and how to argue for what I think, I often hear her commanding voice in my head admonishing me to "keep it real." This saying means different things to those in the hip-hop community. But my aunt captured the core meaning—it's about truth telling even if it is not always what people want to hear. I had this on my mind too.

On one side are those who are quick to celebrate America's racial milestones, such as abolishing slavery, ending Jim Crow, and passing civil rights legislation, but slow to acknowledge how legally sanctioned apartheid followed slavery, informal segregation followed formal desegregation, and half-hearted commitments to enforcement of black civil rights combined with increased attention to reverse discrimination against whites followed the civil rights era. This group of racial optimists, who fail to take a hard-eyed view of racism, will not want to hear about all the ways that racial setbacks and white backlash follow racial progress in America.

On the other side are those who acknowledge the racial milestones but highlight the ways that America taketh as quickly as it giveth when it comes to race matters. Here we find two groups. Those who insist on pursuing race-specific small-tent remedies even in the face of this reality and those of us who remain skeptical about this strategy. The former will not want to hear about big-tent remedies, worrying that blacks will come up short in securing what they need and that America will fail to overcome legacies of anti-black racism. Those of us in the latter group defend the urgency of taking up big-tent remedies, believing that this is a more viable pathway and that it can secure much of what blacks need right now. To wit, this book makes a case for skepticism about the sufficiency of small-tent remedies to achieve racial progress and urges big-tent remedies as a way forward. It is important to stress that these remedies are tools or strategies that can help secure racial and other forms of justice where postracial mythology prevails.

My big-tent approach to racial progress takes inspiration from the black activist tradition, especially examples set by Ella Baker, Fannie Lou Hamer, and Angela Davis. They taught us valuable lessons about how we must work together to get real power and about how we can only secure substantive progressive change with real power. And this power must be directed toward addressing the problems we all live with. Alicia Garza, co-creator of #BlackLivesMatter, belongs to a younger generation of black women who appreciate this insight and who use it to orient organizing activities on behalf of black lives. The crucial lesson is to link the black struggle with a broader struggle on behalf of the 99 percent. A realistic blacktopia is the just and equitable world we can pursue free from racial subordination and domination by engaging with other marginalized groups in a collective struggle against all forms of social injustice, subordination, and domination. In her book *The Purpose of Power: How We Come Together When We Fall Apart*, Garza writes:

> As organizers, our goal was to get those in the 99 percent to put the blame where it actually belonged—with the people and institutions that profited from our misery. And so, "unite to fight" is a call to bring those of us stratified and segregated by race, class, gender, sexuality, ability and body, country of origin, and the like together to fight back against truly oppressive power and to resist attempts to drive wedges between us. More than a slogan, "the 99 percent" asserts that we are more similar

than we are different and that unity among people affected by a predatory economy and a faulty democracy will help us to build an unstoppable social movement.[6]

A Realistic Blacktopia argues for lowering the race-first flag and moving beyond racial politics. Forget race-based affirmative action. Forget a black voting rights act. Forget racial reparations. If we want to get closer to the elusive ideals of racial justice and equality in twenty-first-century America, and withstand predictable efforts to undo racial progress, paradoxically, we need to fight for big-tent remedies to racial injustice and for more robust democratic rule to realize them. This approach to racial politics and racial progress may not get us the most familiar blacktopia we can dream up. But it can get us closer to one that more effectively addresses our most pressing needs and can endure the volatility and vindictiveness of American politics. To pursue what is effective is not to forsake what is ethical. Seeking a realistic blacktopia is rooted in making our normative commitment to the dignity of all persons more robust. The pragmatism that permeates the argument in this book is principled and not merely strategic.

America is far from being a postracial nation. However, many Americans operate with this myth. This means that in practice securing substantive and lasting racial progress with race-specific small-tent remedies will face legislative and judicial dead ends. The way to move forward is to build big-tent coalitions among marginalized populations interested in a range of issues that impact them. This is principled because it is rooted in valuing the dignity of all persons. And it is strategic because it takes seriously the very real limits on small-tent remedies such as ones that focus exclusively on race. Many of the issues that blacks care about are also ones that concern other marginalized groups dogged by a predatory economy and a faulty democracy. To address this we need to build coalitions among marginalized groups to tackle the problems we face collectively. Lowering the race-first flag, and pitching a bigger tent, is a means to doing this. To echo Garza's prescient words, we must "unite to fight."

PART I
THE DEMISE OF SMALL-TENT REMEDIES

1
Affirmative Action

More than five decades after the US Supreme Court ruled in *Brown v. Board of Education* that racial segregation in education was unconstitutional, there remains a crisis of black student educational underachievement relative to white students in America. This sobering fact may have been on candidate Barack Obama's mind during a 2007 presidential primary address in South Carolina when he remarked, "I think the reparations we need right here in South Carolina is investment, for example, in our schools."[1] He was certainly not suggesting that no blacks have fared well since *Brown*. Indeed, many blacks have obviously excelled in both educational achievement and attainment. Many have also enjoyed positive labor market outcomes and have garnered a share of power, prestige, and influence in American society—as Obama's unprecedented success in running for and being elected president of the United States for the first time in 2008 so vividly illustrates. However, whatever the facts about America's racial history that account for the black–white educational achievement gap, and despite there being exceptions to this general pattern, the way forward was something that all parents could support, especially parents from marginalized black, brown, and poor white families, namely, putting more resources in schools to improve education for all kids. This is an example of a big-tent remedy. And I will have much more to say about such remedies as the book's argument unfolds.

Make no mistake about it. There has clearly been racial progress in America. Yet the familiar racial pattern of retreat following racial progress rings true here as well. The crucial point Obama was flagging is that blacks in general remain grossly overrepresented in the ranks of underachieving students and underrepresented in the ranks of high-achieving students. That point is supported by various measures of academic achievement and success including, but not limited to, K–12 standardized test scores, grade point averages, graduation rates, and performance on college and professional school entrance exams such as the SAT and LSAT. It is also supported by evidence that blacks are still underrepresented in professional schools, including law schools. So, while there has been racial progress in education and other areas, it is being undone and, many would add, by the persistence of racial discrimination. There was a brief period when affirmative action (a small-tent remedy) was a way to create greater educational opportunities for blacks. But that ship has sailed. And it faces impassable judicial headwinds.

The Postracial Era

Charting a course toward a realistic blacktopia begins with understanding why we must forget about race-based affirmative action to secure racial progress in America going forward. To understand why this small-tent remedy is no longer viable, and what the alternative is, we can attend to lessons from *Grutter v. Bollinger*.[2] In this 2003 ruling on a race-conscious law school admissions policy, a liberal majority of Supreme Court justices accept the demise of race-based affirmative action and pragmatically pursue a path forward on racial progress by lowering the race-first flag.

Crafting a race-specific legal remedy that addresses the role of racial discrimination (even if it turns out to be a relatively small role) in creating educational and other persistent inequalities between blacks and whites has become increasingly difficult in America's contemporary post–civil rights, or as I prefer to say, postracial era. First, many Americans believe that the United States has largely realized its dream of being a free and equal society with equal opportunity for all citizens, including black descendants of persons that endured the brutality and dehumanization of chattel slavery and American racial apartheid under Jim Crow segregation. Consequently, many citizens believe that a person's life prospects in the United States are no longer meaningfully determined (or hampered) by the color of their skin, but largely by the content of their character, their values, their work ethic, their success in taking advantage of opportunities, and their level of education.

Many people would say that at long last—particularly in the aftermath of electing the first African American US president—we are living the American dream envisioned and so eloquently articulated by Dr. Martin Luther King Jr. more than four decades ago during the historic 1963 March on Washington. Indeed, it is easy to agree with one historian's observation that perhaps "no figure more fully embodies the notion that racial equality is a US national imperative than Martin Luther King Jr."[3] It is certainly true that Dr. King is also widely read as holding not only that civil rights reforms were "urgent matters of national redemption and moral regeneration that would open up a world for individual black achievement (the content of our character) beyond the barrier of race (the color of our skin)."[4] He is also read as holding that the passage and enforcement of civil rights reforms would enable the United States to live up to its normative promise by extending its cherished founding normative ideals of freedom and equality to all of its citizens—particularly those descending from individuals characterized in the infamous *Dred Scott v. Sandford* decision as being "so far inferior, that they had no rights which the white man was bound to respect."[5]

Another crucial and related aspect of what has been aptly called a "King-centric"[6] account of the civil rights era is the idea of shared citizenship, which is, in an important sense, post-ethnic or postracial.[7] By extending the scope and protection of universal normative ideals to include blacks, the civil rights movement—according to a widely held understanding of racial progress—brought us the final way toward being a unified people living under a common rule of law equally applied to and protecting all persons living under shared normative ideals of freedom and equality. This universalizing picture of citizenship associated with King, and characteristic of a postracial understanding of American society, is aptly summed up by US Supreme Court Justice Antonin Scalia as follows: "In the eyes of the government, we are just one race here. It is American."[8]

With the watershed *Brown v. Board of Education* decision in 1954, the formal undoing of American racial apartheid was fully underway. With President John F. Kennedy's 1961 signing of Executive Order 10925, which established a Committee on Equal Employment Opportunity and is famously remembered for invoking the phrase "affirmative action," and with President Lyndon B. Johnson's Great Society reforms—the Civil Rights Act of 1964, the Voting Rights Act of 1965, and the Fair Housing Act of 1968—America had seemingly provided blacks all that they were owed after having endured the legacies of slavery and Jim Crow and having been formally excluded from free and equal citizenship in American society.

Of course, there were many challenges associated with the implementation of *Brown* and the civil rights reforms in the face of widespread public resistance to the formal imperative of racial integration. And there were many challenges associated with making the case that realizing equal opportunity for blacks would ultimately demand not only implementing and enforcing anti-discrimination laws, but also dealing with widespread socioeconomic racial inequalities, which arguably placed blacks at a considerable disadvantage in taking full advantage of the removal of de jure barriers to equal civil and political participation in American society.

These challenges notwithstanding, the doors of American society were deemed to be fully open for all citizens to do business and make a life of their own choosing without being hampered on account of their race. From this vantage point, some critics of race-conscious social policy and legal remedies have insisted that government should not intervene to elevate, to assist positively, or to enable blacks individually or collectively who were coming up short as a group, relative to whites, according to many measures of well-being, including educational achievement. Rather, they argue that blacks should be left to bear the full burden of their poor choices when it comes to education, or that they should be provided with various incentives, both positive and negative, to make better choices so that they can fully partake of King's American Dream. This charge that poor choices are the main source of black disadvantage has typically been directed at blacks who are among the least well off. Moreover, it has been further argued that failure to acknowledge the impact of black choices and values on black disadvantage has served to widen the gap between blacks and whites along various measures of well-being, and it has resulted in misplaced emphasis on government intervention in the form of affirmative action and welfare policy, which have contributed to the problem of black disadvantage rather than solved it.[9]

The foregoing sketch captures the spirit of what I am calling the "postracial" era in the United States. This is a recurring motif throughout this book. Here are its main characteristics:

1. affirmation of the inclusive nature of the American ideals of freedom and equality;
2. affirmation that the greatest legacy of the Civil Rights Movement—understood from a King-centric perspective—was extending the scope of these ideals to previously excluded blacks, which resulted in a single "race" of Americans, blending whites and blacks into a common nationality; and
3. affirmation that the creation of a "single" and "racially integrated" America has rendered the need for further government intervention on behalf of blacks, in particular, unnecessary and, moreover, that further intervention would not only be unfair and unconstitutional when secured at the expense of non-minorities but would also be detrimental to further black progress against persistent racial inequalities.

Part of what gives this postracial outlook purchase is that old-style racism, or what has been called "Jim Crow racism," is no longer with us.[10] It has been argued that the relative infrequency of overt bigotry, of segregationist demands, of public support for government-sponsored racial discrimination, and of open and widespread adherence to the belief that blacks are biologically inferior to whites, rather than marking an end to racism, has instead marked a shift to a new form of racism aptly called "laissez-faire racism."[11] Aspects of this new racism are said to involve "persistent negative stereotyping of African Americans, a tendency to blame blacks themselves for the black-white gap in socioeconomic standing, and resistance to meaningful policy efforts to ameliorate US racist social conditions and institutions."[12] Hence, the power of this new form of racism lies in acknowledging the persistence of disparities between blacks and whites but locating their source in black agency (that is, choices that blacks themselves make or fail to make either individually or collectively), which undermines the legitimacy of government-sponsored intervention to decrease racial disparities.

Social theorists and social scientists wishing to argue that racial discrimination is alive and well in postracial America (though in the form of laissez-faire, not Jim Crow, racism) face several challenges, two of which are particularly relevant for present purposes. In addition to demonstrating empirically the ways in which blacks are disadvantaged relative to whites, they must establish causal links between current racial inequalities (e.g., in education) and historic racial discrimination during slavery and Jim Crow. Moreover, they must demonstrate that current racial inequalities are being maintained, or in some cases even worsened, by contemporary racial discrimination. Proponents of this thesis need not hold that racial discrimination is the only factor constraining black opportunity in the modern period or that race is as central a factor in the life chances for any given black individual as it was in the pre–civil rights era. Meeting both challenges, however, is particularly difficult when overt acts of racial discrimination are, on the one hand, admittedly less prevalent than before but, on the other hand, remain in the eyes of many people the only way of showing that racial discrimination operates to undermine black freedom and equality.

The main problem for advocates of the persistence-of-racism thesis in the current postracial era is not that the possibility of racial discrimination playing a vital role in accounting for the existence of racial inequalities in education and other areas is summarily dismissed. Rather, the main problem is with the burden of proof placed on persons advancing explanations for the persistence of racial inequalities that include a racial discrimination component.

This burden of proof demands a particular causal accounting of racial inequalities, by establishing racist motives or racist intent, or old-style Jim Crow racism, as the basis for any statistical disparities between blacks and whites. In the absence of such proof, some people have been tempted to dismiss racial inequalities as merely the effects of agent-driven economic transactions in response to various needs, wants, liabilities, and incentives in a free market economy rather than the unhappy results of bad or racist intentions.[13]

The main problem is that there is no serious acknowledgment of the shift from Jim Crow to laissez-faire racism in the postracial era. Consequently, any appeal to racial discrimination accounting for the causes of racial disparities or proscribing legal or policy decisions faces the constraint of providing evidence of racist intent or motive. Although it is widely acceptable to presume that racial disparities in education, wealth, health, housing, and the criminal justice system are largely due to certain agent-relative factors, in the postracial era, we cannot presume that they are due to agent-neutral factors such as racial discrimination. Any efforts to link these disparities to racial discrimination are compelled to show evidence that racial bias or motive accounts for the racial disparities in question.

Indeed, one can find evidence of this in the courts. Consider the criminal law case, *McCleskey v. Kemp*, in which Warren McCleskey, a black man sentenced to die in Georgia for killing a white police officer, challenged the law as a violation of the Equal Protection Clause.[14] The petitioner's defense relied upon a statistical study on death penalty cases in Georgia showing that "defendants charged with killing white victims were 4.3 times as likely to receive a death sentence as defendants charged with killing blacks."[15] A five-to-four US Supreme Court decision ruled against McCleskey's equal protection claim without challenging the data showing that he was at a higher risk of being put to death because of the race of his victim.[16] Instead, the court set aside the statistical evidence as irrelevant in capital punishment cases unless there was proof of intentional discrimination or proof that racial bias had tainted the defendant's trial.[17]

In the next section I will consider how this inflexible constraint on proving racial discrimination has also shaped the pursuit of greater equality of educational opportunity between blacks and whites in the courts. Specifically, I consider how the University of Michigan School of Law sidestepped the burden of proving that past or present racial discrimination caused statistical racial inequalities between blacks and whites in adopting a race-conscious but not race-specific admissions policy.

The Diversity Argument

On the recommendation of a faculty committee,[18] the University of Michigan Law School adopted a multi-criteria admissions policy calling for each applicant to be evaluated individually based on the entire admissions file, which included a personal statement, letters of recommendation, undergraduate grade point average, LSAT score, and an essay describing ways in which the applicant would contribute to the life and diversity of the Law School.[19] In making clear that grades and scores were not assigned enough weight to guarantee admission in the case of high grades and scores or rejection in the case of low ones, the Law School emphasized the value of so-called soft variables, such as the quality and content of the personal statement and essay. These variables were taken to provide valuable information about how potential applicants might usefully advance the Law School's general educational objectives.

A vital educational objective of the Law School was to "enrich everyone's education and thus make a law school class stronger than the sum of its parts." The Law School maintained that achieving student body diversity, which would contribute to the intellectual life, social life, and the overall character of the Law School, was instrumental in achieving this purpose. Although the Law School stressed that various types of diversity considerations were weighted in the admission process, it nonetheless reaffirmed its long-standing commitment to a particular type of diversity, namely, "racial and ethnic diversity with special reference to the inclusion of students from groups which have been historically discriminated against, like African-Americans, Hispanics and Native Americans." With the adoption of this admissions policy, the Law School asserted an interest in using racial classifications to realize the educational benefits it associated with having a racially diverse student body.

Barbara Grutter, a white Michigan resident with a 3.8 GPA and 161 LSAT score, who was denied admission to the Law School, challenged the legality of this policy in 1996. Grutter subsequently filed suit in the US District Court for the Eastern District of Michigan alleging that the Law School's admissions policy discriminated against her in violation of the Fourteenth Amendment of the Constitution. Agreeing with the petitioner that the policy was unconstitutional, the District Court ruled that the Law School's asserted interest in realizing the educational benefits of a racially diverse student body was not compelling, and even if it had been compelling, the policy had not been narrowly tailored to further this interest.[20] On appeal, a divided US Court of Appeals for the Sixth Circuit reversed this judgment, holding that Justice Powell's opinion in *Bakke* was a binding precedent and established diversity as a compelling state interest. Moreover, it found that the Law School's use of race was indeed narrowly tailored since race was merely a "potential 'plus' factor" in a multi-criteria admissions policy. Upon granting certiorari, the pivotal issue brought before the US Supreme Court in *Grutter v. Bollinger* was "[w]hether diversity is a compelling interest that can justify the narrowly tailored use of race in selecting applicants for admission to public universities."[21]

By finding that the Law School's interest in attaining the educational benefits that flow from a diverse student body was compelling, the Court ruled by a narrow five-to-four margin that the Law School's use of race passed the compelling interest requirement of the strict scrutiny test established by the Court in *Adarand Constructors, Inc. v. Peña*.[22] By finding that the school's policy of considering an applicant's race as a "plus" factor along with other individual academic and nonacademic factors, and by considering each applicant individually rather than merely as a member of a racial group, the Court ruled that the Law School's use of race in a highly individualized and holistic review of each applicant's file was narrowly tailored. The Court concluded that because the Law School's race-conscious admissions program was narrowly tailored and asserted a compelling interest in gaining the educational benefits of student body diversity, the admissions program survived strict scrutiny as required by the Equal Protection Clause.

Not since *Bakke* had the Supreme Court taken up the issue of whether using race as a criterion for admission to an institution of higher learning violated the Fourteenth Amendment.[23] Although *Bakke* did not result in a majority opinion, Justice Powell's opinion has served as the "touchstone for constitutional analysis of race-conscious admissions policies."[24] Given the heavy reliance on this opinion by the majority in *Grutter*, it is reasonable to interpret *Grutter* as making Powell's opinion in *Bakke* settled law.[25] Furthermore, several insights first expressed by Powell—and later by the *Grutter* majority—are paradigmatic instances of judicial thought about racial discrimination in the postracial era that embody a clear endorsement of the prevailing King-centric perspective. The first insight is that equal protection of the law applies to individuals (not groups), and for the protection to be truly equal it must apply to all persons (including whites) who are asked to bear a burden because of race. The second and related insight is that this understanding of equal protection proscribes any government use of race designed to reduce disadvantages suffered by historically disfavored minorities. Describing such uses as "racial balancing," Powell contends that using race to set aside positions for minorities in professional school would place undue burdens on innocent third parties "who bear no responsibility for whatever harm the beneficiaries of the special admissions program are thought to have suffered."[26] A further insight, which presumably makes up for the loss incurred by restricting the scope of backward-looking or remedial justifications of race-conscious admissions policies, is permitting uses of race to advance a forward-looking interest in student body diversity provided that it encompasses a broader array of qualifications and characteristics of which race is but a single element. Although all uses of race must be subject to strict scrutiny in the postracial era—and no uses can be deemed benign absent such scrutiny—not all uses of race will fail this test. Powell's opinion in *Bakke* and the *Grutter* majority allow for uses where racial diversity is part of a larger project of advancing legitimate educational objectives.

The general outlook captured by these insights is that there can be no presumption that racial disparities are due to past or current race-based discrimination against historically disfavored groups. In the postracial era, we must allow that other factors might account for these things given the racial progress that has been made since the civil rights era and the subsequent Great Society programs. In the postracial era, to establish that discrimination is the cause of racial disparities and to justify a race-conscious remedy one must demonstrate that there was intent or bias operating to burden someone because of race.

Given the great difficulty of establishing this finding, and not merely due to the conservative bent of many federal judges and the majority of Supreme Court justices, but due to the very complex and subtle ways in which race operates in contemporary America—as many social scientists have observed—the respondents in *Grutter* justified their race-conscious admissions policy by making an end run around race, as it were. This was accomplished by relying upon a general diversity argument, which defended a race-conscious admissions policy (though not exclusively or even principally race conscious) as part of a larger strategy of building a more diverse student body to secure the educational benefits that flow from such diversity, including: promoting learning outcomes; better preparing law students as professionals; and better preparing law students for an increasingly diverse workforce, society, and global marketplace. As the Court notes, with this policy the Law School aspired to "achieve that diversity which has the potential to enrich everyone's education and thus make a law school class stronger than the sum of its parts."[27]

This worthy aspiration notwithstanding, perhaps the greatest practical virtue of the Law School's strategy was skillfully adapting the justification for its policy to the Powellian insights, which reflect the current paradigm of judicial thought about racial discrimination in the postracial era. Most importantly, the Law School made sure that the central argument for its race-conscious admissions policy—the argument that carried the day—was a forward-looking argument. It was an argument focused not so much on historical injustice—that is, what America has done wrong to blacks and what they are owed and by whom—but instead on bringing about the commonly desired good of improving educational outcomes for the benefit of law students, the Law School, and society in general. Surely, even the justices who dissented in the case (Justices Kennedy, Rehnquist, Scalia, and Thomas) could appreciate the way in which this argument plays into the ideal of one nation, one "race" (namely, American), striving to achieve a common and positive future that does not turn on laying blame for past wrongs or historical injustices and their lingering effects.

To be sure, the Law School was aware of the legacy of historical injustice toward racial and ethnic minorities in America. Indeed, it stressed that the admissions policy reaffirmed the Law School's long-standing commitment to "racial and ethnic diversity with special reference to the inclusion of students from groups which have been historically discriminated against, like African-Americans, Hispanics and Native Americans, who without this commitment might not be represented in [the Law School] student body in meaningful numbers."[28] Yet by making this kind of diversity just one among many types of diversity it sought to achieve, by not giving it greater or special weight, and, most importantly, by not defending its policy as an effort to take affirmative action in favor of racial minorities to overcome the disadvantages and exclusions rooted in past wrongs, the Law School rendered its argument immune to the obvious objections. A backward-looking argument in favor of a race-conscious admissions policy, namely, one that defended a policy to reduce the deficit of historically disadvantaged minorities, would be deemed an unlawful instance of racial balancing and unfair to innocent third parties forced to bear the burdens of such a policy.[29]

The Science of Diversity

Some critics of *Grutter* will question whether, in the final analysis, justifying the adoption of a race-conscious admissions policy as a way to achieve certain educational outcomes is better than a more direct justification of racial diversity as a way to remedy the legacy of past racial wrongs. And of course other critics of *Grutter* will question whether the justification for racial diversity—however indirect it may be—is nonetheless a blatant attempt to remedy past racial wrongs and is thus unlawful (in violation of the Equal Protection Clause) as well as unfair.[30] But apart from these concerns some persons who are sympathetic to the outcome of the case and the general goal of achieving a racially and ethnically diverse student body (setting aside whether it be justified on backward- or forward-looking grounds) may raise concerns about another aspect of the argument that carried the day in *Grutter*.

Perhaps the most striking aspect of the forward-looking argument for racial diversity in *Grutter* is the prominent role played by social scientific research in this argument.[31] The *Grutter* majority not only acknowledged this role, but it also gave deference to the judgment supported by this research. Justice O'Connor observes, "The Law School's educational judgment that such diversity is essential to its educational mission is one to which we defer. The Law School's assessment that diversity will, in fact, yield educational benefits is substantiated by respondents and their *amici*."[32] And she further observes, "In addition to the expert studies and reports entered into evidence at trial, numerous studies show that student body diversity promotes learning outcomes, and 'better prepares students for an increasingly diverse workforce and society, and better prepares them as professionals.'"[33]

As the amici curiae noted, *Grutter* would not be the first time the Supreme Court relied upon empirical evidence in an equal protection case related to race, and to determine whether promoting "educational diversity in higher education is a compelling government interest."[34] In addition to being a landmark decision in Supreme Court constitutional history for taking the monumental step of dismantling racial segregation in public schools, *Brown v. Board of Education* is also heralded for having begun the era of reliance upon modern social scientific research in judicial decision-making.[35] In footnote 11 of the *Brown* decision, which has been described as "at once the most celebrated and infamous footnote in Supreme Court history,"[36] Chief Justice Earl Warren's opinion for the unanimous Court cites several social scientific studies addressing the harms of segregated schools on black children.

Following in the footsteps of *Brown*, the *Grutter* majority also affirmed the value of social science in assessing the constitutionality of using a race-conscious policy to achieve diversity in higher education. But in *Grutter*, unlike *Brown*, the Court did not relegate the social scientific findings it relied upon to a footnote. This time, the various sources of empirical authority that were introduced in the lower courts and in amicus curiae briefs were explicitly discussed in the decision and used to support the ruling that student body diversity was a compelling interest and that the Law School admissions policy was indeed narrowly tailored, thereby surviving the strict scrutiny test and thus proving to be lawful under the Equal Protection Clause of the Fourteenth Amendment. While reliance upon empirical research has many virtues, including affording the decision a measure of empirical authority, it also has potential drawbacks, including concerns that the Court is not the proper venue for screening and filtering scientific evidence speaking to such matters as whether student body diversity promotes positive educational outcomes.

On a related note, some sympathetic critics of *Brown* worried that tethering the desegregation decision to the prevailing social science of the day left open the possibility that the vital decision could be undermined or even reversed by alternative social scientific research or by discrediting the empirical findings cited in *Brown*.[37] Of course, this is precisely what happened in *Brown*, where the segregationists, seeking to undo the decision, not only called the empirical findings cited by *Brown* into question but also recruited their own social scientists and marshaled their own empirical findings to argue that a segregated learning environment would produce the best learning outcomes and that desegregated schools actually cause more harm than good, all things considered.[38]

By embracing an even more thoroughgoing commitment to empirical research findings than *Brown*, the *Grutter* Court leaves its decision vulnerable to a similar line of attack, which would draw upon alternative research findings seeking to show that diversity does not produce the claimed educational benefits or that it causes educational harms or causes more harm than good, all things considered. Indeed, this is precisely one of the strategies employed by Justice Thomas in his lengthy dissenting opinion, where he maintains,

> The Constitution abhors classifications based on race, not only because those classifications can harm favored races or are based on illegitimate motives, but also because every time the government places citizens on racial registers and makes race relevant to the provision of burdens or benefits, it demeans us all."

According to Justice Thomas, "an interest in remedying general societal discrimination," or racial disparities, is a seriously inadequate justification for using racial classification.[39] Indeed, such classification can only be justified, as he says, "to provide a bulwark against anarchy, or to prevent violence . . . 'rising to the level of imminent danger to life and limb.'"[40] Moreover, Justice Thomas has frequently insisted that when it comes to the meaning of the Equal Protection Clause we cannot distinguish between benign and suspect uses of racial classification (a point that Justice Powell emphasizes as well in *Bakke*, although Powell seems to allow strict judicial scrutiny to determine whether a use of race is benign, whereas Justice Thomas seems to rule out all but very limited uses as benign in advance of such scrutiny).

Setting up one of his challenges to the majority ruling in *Grutter*, Justice Thomas maintains, "The Court's deference to the Law School's conclusion that its racial experimentation leads to educational benefits will, if adhered to, have serious collateral consequences. The Court relies heavily on social science evidence to justify its deference."[41] He then takes issue with what he takes to be a crucial oversight. Justice Thomas contends, "The Court never acknowledges, however, the growing evidence that racial (and other sorts) of heterogeneity actually impairs learning among black students."[42] He then cites two studies, one published in the *Journal of College Student Development*, "concluding that black students [at Historically Black Colleges (HBCs)] experience superior cognitive development . . . and that, even among blacks," the more diversity they are exposed to the more moderate the effects of attending an HBC.[43] The other study, published in the *Harvard Education Review*, finds that blacks "attending HBCs report higher academic achievement than those attending predominantly white colleges."[44] In addition to suggesting that racial diversity might actually impair learning among black students according to these and other studies, Justice Thomas notes that social science has not discredited the views that affirmative action "engender[s] attitudes of [racial] superiority or, alternatively, provoke[s] [racial] resentment among those who believe that they have been wronged by" race-conscious policies.[45]

We see that by relying on empirical findings to support its ruling that an interest in achieving educational diversity is compelling, the *Grutter* majority ruling is vulnerable to Justice Thomas's attack, which challenges the decision by taking on—at least in part—the conclusiveness of the studies cited, which are at odds with the alternative empirical findings that Justice Thomas elicits. Although my present purposes do not require me to take issue with the studies that Justice Thomas cites, and I am certain that those better informed about the empirical debate on the issue would have much to say, it is nevertheless important to note that social scientists have certainly disagreed about the educational benefits of racial diversity. So, even if these studies are found lacking, or if Justice Thomas's use of them is unconvincing, his objection raises a real concern. What do we make of competing empirical findings that challenge the authority of the findings to which the majority in *Grutter* defers? There are many competing empirical explanations of the racial achievement gap and the benefits and burdens of segregated schools. There are also competing explanations for why black students are underrepresented in our nation's law schools. And there is no doubt that some of these explanations would undoubtedly lend support to Justice Thomas's objections.

We see, therefore, that the appeal to social science in judicial rulings comes at a cost: it opens the door to reliance on contrary empirical findings to take issue with rulings that we are otherwise sympathetic to. Of course, this is not a deep objection to social science per se, as we could believe that some empirical explanations of the facts are simply incorrect, or that some are simply much better than others. Accordingly, one way to proceed in response to Justice Thomas would be to take on the empirical findings and conclusions directly that he presumes to raise against the ones relied upon by the *Grutter* majority. For this purpose, we will certainly need much more input from social scientists. Moreover, the Court will need a reliable way to adjudicate the debate.

In the absence of a resolution to this debate, the courts must be mindful of how legal reasoning informed by empirical explanations is susceptible to challenges that reject the proffered explanations in favor of others. By the same token, philosophers of race must be mindful of how prevailing normative arguments for other race-based remedies such as reparations, which similarly rely upon empirical findings regarding the causes of racial disparities in education and in other areas, are vulnerable to similar challenges. I shall have more to say about this lesson and its bearing on the black reparations debate in chapter 3. The next chapter takes up another Supreme Court ruling to illuminate related reasons for skepticism about maintaining the racial progress secured by the 1965 Voting Rights Act.

2
Voting Rights

The US Supreme Court, in 2013, removed an obstacle to making voting more burdensome in *Shelby County v. Holder*.[1] It invalidated a key provision of the 1965 Voting Rights Act (VRA) that imposed a statutory requirement on certain states to secure federal permission before changing their voting laws.[2] The states affected by section 4(b) of the VRA, the "coverage formula,"[3] not only wanted to be free from federal oversight of their sovereignty, but they also wanted to be treated "equally" with other states and have their "dignity" affirmed, or so the *Shelby County* majority would have us believe. Far from denying that states, like persons, can actually have dignity or claims to be treated equally, the Court conjured a "fundamental principle of equal sovereignty" to support giving them what they wanted.[4] This principle, as applied, demands that any departures from the presumption of equal treatment for equal states requires a "rational" relationship between the statute's exceptional allowance of unequal treatment (e.g., preclearance for covered states) and the problem being addressed (voting discrimination). As the Court puts it, "a departure from the fundamental principle of equal sovereignty requires a showing that a statute's disparate geographic coverage is sufficiently related to the problem that it targets."[5]

Chief Justice Roberts, writing for the 5-4 majority, agreed that this relationship once existed in areas affected by section 4(b). Back in 1966, for instance, there was evidence of tests and devices historically used as tools of voting discrimination, *and* the voting rate in the 1964 presidential election was significantly below the national average in the covered areas. But the Court argues that was then. This is now. In an opinion joined by the other conservatives and Justice Kennedy, Roberts presents a *racial progress argument* to deny that this rational relationship still exists, to conclude that the departure from the principle of equal state sovereignty is no longer justified, and to strike down section 4(b) of the VRA as unconstitutional.

Critics have taken the Court to task for appealing to the principle of equal sovereignty. Some have complained that the principle does not exist in legal precedent,[6] while others have argued that it does but has a dubious pedigree in the *Dred Scott v. Sandford*[7] decision denying black citizenship.[8] Some argue that the Court conflates "sovereignty" and "autonomy" in understanding the states' authority under the Elections Clause.[9] Others have sought to vindicate the Court by defending the principle of equal sovereignty and assigning it a more respectable pedigree.[10] But neither critics nor defenders have considered the racial progress argument the majority offers for why this controversial principle now prevails.

In this chapter I reconstruct the Supreme Court's racial progress argument in *Shelby County* and raise some concerns about ways of answering it that merely replace a conservative narrative about racial progress with a liberal one. Although I am partial to the latter narrative and believe that the Court's overall argument for striking down the coverage formula is deeply flawed, it seems unwise to rest the entire case for saving the VRA and defending the right to vote—moving forward—on winning the racial progress argument, especially in a nation so smitten by the view that we have reached the "postracial" promised land, and where this fanciful outlook is arguably now entrenched in Supreme Court equal protection doctrine.[11] This chapter proves further evidence of the limits of race-first reasoning—this time to stave off a retreat from racial progress—when faced with a conservative judiciary. I conclude with brief and very speculative remarks about where we might turn to safeguard the right to vote post *Shelby County*, particularly in cases where vote denial rather than vote dilution is chiefly at issue.[12]

The Racial Progress Argument

In *Shelby County*, the coverage formula of the VRA and for all practical purposes the preclearance requirement are the immediate casualties of the majority's narrative of racial progress in America. While they concede that the nation has a tarnished racial history, and is far from perfect, the majority makes a big deal of the fact that "history did not end in 1965."[13] They rest their novel argument against the coverage formula on the claim that the "entrenched racial discrimination in voting" in covered states in 1965 that justified exceptional legislation back then is no longer prevalent or flagrant.[14] This perspective can be summed up with the motif "that was then, this is now." On the basis of this, and two further grounds—a concern with fair elections and equal state sovereignty—the Supreme Court invalidates a primary federal statutory obstacle to selected jurisdictions imposing requirements on voting, including but not limited to, voter ID laws.[15]

From the majority's perspective, the need for exceptional voting rights legislation was more obvious prior to 1965 than it is today.[16] They contend that significantly fewer blacks than whites were registered to vote in states throughout the South before the enactment of VRA. Writing for the majority, Roberts notes that only 19.4 percent of eligible black voters were registered to vote in Alabama prior to the enactment of the VRA.[17] Moreover, he points out that the coverage formula was warranted given the plausible assumption that this low percentage (nearly 50 percentage points below comparable rates for whites at 69.2 percent) was linked to the long history of Alabama and other states using tests and devices as a tool for perpetrating the injustice of racial discrimination in voting. Due to the long history—well before 1965—of these tools being used to disenfranchise black voters in Alabama and other covered jurisdictions, Roberts concedes that the rational relationship between their use and the lower black voting rates at the time was impossible to argue with.

The regions singled out by the coverage formula shared two features: they relied upon tools that had been used historically to disenfranchise black voters, *and* in these areas the black voting rate in the 1964 presidential election was well below the national average. Thus, in 1965, it was reasonable to assume that the use of these tools was a cause of low black voter turnout in these areas. This position explains why Roberts concludes that the VRA coverage formula was "rational in both theory and practice" when it was first enacted in 1965.[18] But that was then, and this is now, or so the Court claims.

America has undoubtedly come a long way since Bloody Sunday in Selma in 1965. Citing voter registration data from House and Senate reports compiled prior to the 2006 reauthorization of the VRA, Roberts notes that black voter registration in Alabama had increased dramatically by 2004, and the gap between black and white voter registration rates in the state virtually vanished, at 72.9 percent and 73.8 percent, respectively.[19] And he considers similar data for other covered states. Although he does not make the point, which would have further strengthened the majority's hand, Mississippi—the state with the largest gap between white and black registered voters—was the state that made the most significant racial progress in voter registration outcomes by 2004, with the percentage of registered black voters (76.1) exceeding that of whites (72.3) by 3.8 percent.[20] However, Roberts does note that Selma now has an African American mayor, before concluding, "Problems remain in these States and others, but there is no denying that, due to the Voting Rights Act, our Nation has made great strides."[21] Roberts thus calls attention not only to increases in black political representation in covered jurisdictions but also to increases in black voter registration and a shrinking gap between black and white voter registration rates to support a racial progress argument.

Dissenters and critics argue that singling out states and jurisdictions—excepting those that satisfy a bailout provision—with a past history of voter discrimination against blacks for a special preclearance burden remains rational in theory and in practice. However, as Roberts puts it, "Nearly 50 years later, things have changed dramatically."[22] America has made progress in combating the kind of voter discrimination against blacks that was prevalent back then. And he contends that Congress has not adequately taken this into account in crafting the VRA, nor have the dissenting members of the Court in objecting to the majority ruling.

Being out of step with what it views as clear national progress in combating first-generation voter discrimination—access-to-the-polls problems of the sort that were commonplace in 1965—is not the totality of the majority's case against the coverage formula. Assuming further that statutes should reflect current, not past, conditions and arguing that the coverage formula does not do this, Roberts concludes that this formula, an exceptional legislative measure not otherwise appropriate, must now be scrapped given other weighty constitutional values and principles. Among these include the legitimate interests of states in maintaining the integrity and fairness of elections, and in retaining the broad power bestowed upon states under the Tenth Amendment to control voter eligibility requirements, qualifications for office, and determining congressional districts. Respecting these powers, according to the chief justice, is essential to respecting the dignity of the states. Moreover, this ensures that the "fundamental principle of *equal* sovereignty" is upheld given that each state is equal in dignity. Roberts concludes that upholding these basic principles of federalism is also vital to the "harmonious operation of the scheme upon which the Republic was organized."[23]

Hence, with this multilayered argument rooted in a narrative of racial progress in America, the Court affords the Southern states and other covered jurisdictions a momentous opportunity to get out from under the burdensome preclearance requirement imposed upon them by the now significantly diminished VRA. This argument places the burden squarely on the federal government to show a rational relationship between uses of certain voting tools and their effects on voting patterns and outcomes. While it could do this in Alabama and other states in 1965, it cannot do so today, according to the Court, unless it dubiously relies upon decades-old data. Failure to establish this relationship, Roberts argues, is fatal to the cause of upholding the VRA status quo because only extraordinary circumstances can justify legislation violating the principle of equal sovereignty and contravening the states' interest in running fair elections.

Polarization about Racial Progress

Even though some may have been surprised that the Supreme Court struck down section 4 and not section 5 of the VRA, it is no surprise that this ruling generated much controversy and disagreement. Many people anticipated that the outcome would have a direct impact on voter access to the polls. States free from the constraint of the preclearance requirement would have more leeway to enact regulations to make voting more burdensome.

Liberals wanting to make access to the ballot easier lament this ruling. Conservatives wanting to make voting impervious to fraud applaud it.[24] And here too, in the political and the public realm more broadly, we find sharply different views about racial progress in the United States since the civil rights era. The Right generally argues that racial progress has been considerable, voting discrimination of the kind that existed in 1965 is ancient history, and so the oversight of state autonomy to regulate elections should be removed to reflect current conditions. The Left generally rejects this argument, noting that there is still work to be done and that voting discrimination still exists, and it further argues for keeping the VRA fully intact to guard against rolling back the gains for black voting rights.[25]

A cursory review of Supreme Court cases involving voting rights, affirmative action, school desegregation, and disparate impact in employment reveals that conservative members of the Court are more inclined than liberal ones to endorse and promulgate narratives of racial progress that paint a blissful picture of current conditions in post-civil-rights America.[26] And there is general evidence from political sociology and political psychology for thinking that the opposing sides will not agree on a single narrative about racial progress anytime soon.

One study finds that liberals and conservatives often do not see eye to eye on the relationship between a group's current conditions and its past mistreatment.[27] Whereas liberals are more likely to posit such a link and attribute current inequality or disadvantage to persistent discrimination, conservatives are more inclined to downplay it and look to choices, character, effort, and other factors unrelated to discrimination or prejudice to explain a historically disadvantaged group's current conditions.

Another study finds that where the Left is more likely to take a long view of history when assessing these conditions, the Right often takes relatively recent events as the reference point for assessing racial progress.[28] A recent case bears this out. In a voter ID case, a panel for the US Fifth Circuit Court of Appeals draws this distinction in discussing why the lower court striking down Texas's strict voter ID law erred by not appreciating the Supreme Court's focus in *Shelby County* on "relatively recent" history rather than on "long-past" history in claiming that there has been racial progress in America since 1965.[29]

With respect to voting rights, polarization on the Supreme Court is evident in how conservative and liberal justices construe the scope of the VRA, as well as in what kind of voter discrimination they consider to be its target. We can distinguish between narrow and broad interpretations of the VRA. Conservatives on the Court, such as Justice Thomas, have endorsed the former. As Thomas sees it, the requirements of the VRA "reach only state enactments that limit citizens' access to the ballot or the processes of counting a ballot. The terms do not include a state's or subdivision's choice of one districting scheme over another."[30] On this narrow interpretation of the VRA, structural schemes such as at-large voting and racial gerrymandering, or schemes that have a disproportionate impact on certain groups such as racial vote dilution, are not ruled out.

In contrast, liberals on the Court such as Justice Ginsburg have favored a broad interpretation of the VRA. Partly conceding and qualifying Thomas's point, she observes, "Whatever the device employed, this Court has long recognized that vote dilution, when adopted with a discriminatory purpose, cuts down the right to vote as certainly as denial of access to the ballot."[31] She further argues that Congress's 2006 reauthorization of the VRA made clear that it aimed to address these second-generation barriers as well. Quoting Congress, she notes,

> without the continuation of the Voting Rights Act of 1965 protections, racial and language minority citizens will be deprived of the opportunity to exercise their right to vote, or will have their votes diluted, undermining the significant gains made by minorities in the last 40 years.[32]

Ginsburg makes a sensible point here, though more evidence of polarization lurks in the background. Her point is that distinguishing between a narrow or broad interpretation of the VRA, or between first-generation and second-generation barriers to voting, is inconsequential. Both barriers have essentially the same effect: they deprive the targeted community (in this case, black Americans) of an equal opportunity to participate in the electoral process by having a fair chance of electing their desired candidates. Denying blacks access to the ballot, making their access to the ballot more burdensome, and giving them access but watering down their votes all have this result.

There is an important philosophical question at issue, which the Court does not take up, namely, how should *equal opportunity* to participate in the electoral process be understood?[33] Some liberal philosophers have taken for granted that appealing to an antiprejudice interpretation of equal opportunity can command the assent of both liberals and conservatives. Even if we suppose this to be so, applying this standard to the voting rights case will expose their divide about racial progress and the persistence of discrimination. Thus, as we will see, by attending to Ginsburg's *Shelby County* dissent, substituting a liberal for a conservative narrative of racial progress will not avoid the problem of polarization. Not heeding the depth of polarization about racial progress and the continued significance of racial prejudice raises trouble for the liberal dissent in *Shelby County*.

Problems with the Dissent in *Shelby County*

Chief Justice Roberts's presents a multilayered argument for striking down the coverage formula that relies, in part, on a racial progress narrative. Any response to the argument, committed to working from more realistic assumptions regarding the depth of disagreement over racial progress and prejudice, should take seriously the futility of convincing a conservative court (or a general public that is increasingly skeptical of racial prejudice and racial-discrimination-based explanations of black disadvantage) to disavow this narrative.[34]

It is tempting to reply—as Justice Ginsburg does writing for the dissent[35]—by distinguishing two kinds of voter discrimination against blacks, firstgeneration and second-generation discrimination, and arguing that even if the former is less pronounced, the latter is ubiquitous. After the VRA was enacted, it has been well documented that Southern states found other ways to achieve the ends of diminishing black participation in the political process. Rather than imposing barriers to voting such as polls taxes, literary tests, and other tools designed to make access to the ballot more difficult, they increasingly relied upon tools such as racial gerrymandering and at-large voting designed to dilute the black vote, thereby making it more difficult for blacks to get representatives they favored into office.

Thus, the objection is that the majority's racial progress narrative falls flat if we consider second-generation voter discrimination. And we should certainly consider this since both forms of discrimination have the same intent and effect, namely, to undermine equal participation of blacks and other minorities in the democratic process made possible by the right to vote. One line of response by the majority is to quibble over whether Congress intended to include this kind of discrimination in the original VRA. Another is to argue that subsequent congressional action expanding the law to proscribe these forms of discrimination, and Supreme Court rulings supporting this, were misguided. But these replies take a back seat to their most effective response.

Making the case for scrapping the coverage formula of the VRA turn on taking a stand on the status of racial progress in America is an ingenious trap. Unfortunately, critics of the decision, including the dissenting justices, have taken the bait. I say that this is "unfortunate" because none of the replies to this argument currently on offer seem destined to get sufficient traction.

If one accepts Roberts's way of framing the issue, then a position *must* be taken on whether there has been racial progress on voting rights in America. And the answer to this question has to be a simple "yes" or "no," notwithstanding whatever qualifications might be added about the degree of progress. The unrelenting cynic might reply that nothing at all has changed since the VRA was enacted in 1965. Blacks are still second-class citizens, and they still face both barriers to accessing the polls and to electing persons of their choosing, which effectively prevent them from participating in the democratic progress on equal terms with their fellow citizens. Among these current barriers include burdensome registration requirements, restrictive voting times, voter purges, and felon disfranchisement laws, all of which have a disparate impact on black voters.

But this "no-progress" reply is implausible. Furthermore, it is a hard sell to both liberals and progressives, not to mention conservatives and moderates. Even the dissenting liberal justices in *Shelby County* give the VRA credit for bringing about racial progress in America, particularly with respect to diminishing firstgeneration voting discrimination against blacks. Furthermore, some progressives have also canvassed evidence of progress in black voting and representation since 1965. And historian Manning Marable, a radical democratic socialist, has persuasively argued that we cannot make sense of the evolution from first-generation to second-generation barriers to black voting in America unless we see this as a response to the success of the VRA.[36] The no-progress reply can also be countered by looking at 2012 election numbers.[37]

Yet the most serious problem with the no-racial-progress-since-1965 thesis is that if we take this route, then the hand for scrapping the VRA seems stronger still. Why should we keep fully intact a law that has been utterly ineffective for fifty years? It is not clear that we should. Moreover, if true, this might be reason to undo the law altogether and go back to the drawing board. I believe that this is the majority's most forceful reply to the no-racial-progress thesis.

The majority relies upon empirical data to establish its case for racial progress. Consequently, one can certainly argue that they fail to consider other empirical findings, which undermine the racial progress narrative. There is, for instance, evidence that the observed trends in racial progress in voting, particularly in recent elections, is skewed by various contributing factors, including the exclusion of prisoners[38] and disenfranchised felons[39] as well as the disproportionate impact of voter ID requirements on black youth (ages 18–29) not voting. A recent study finds that lack of proper ID is a common explanation for 17.3 percent of black youth not voting compared with 4.7 percent of white youth.[40] Such evidence suggests that public reports of shrinking voting gaps between blacks and whites may be grossly overstated due to the exclusion of large segments of would-be black voters from the calculations.

If this is the case, the problem is that Roberts relies upon some of the same data Ginsburg relies upon to affirm that some racial progress has indeed been made, and that Congress relies upon in defending the need for reauthorization of the VRA in 2006. She uses this data to support her argument that the coverage formula should be kept intact to guard against backsliding and rolling back the racial progress that has already been made. Roberts uses it to support the claim that there has been racial progress even if some voting problems persist.

So, if more accurate data on shrinking voting gaps undermines the majority's narrative of racial progress, it will likewise undermine liberal and progressive affirmations of racial progress based on similar data. The crux of the problem, then, is that taking this evidence seriously, as I believe we should, can only support one of two positions on the racial progress question—either that there has been no racial progress or that there has been some, though not enough. The-no-racial-progress conclusion would be fatal because it would suggest that the VRA has been entirely useless and should be scrapped.

Moreover, it would remove the rationale for being worried about backsliding, and for using this worry to justify maintaining the legal status quo. The other conclusion—that there has been some, though not enough, racial progress—gives the majority all that it needs to justify scrapping the coverage formula.

To complete its case, and to put the dissent in a "catch-22," the majority does not need there to have been significant progress, complete parity, or even the elimination of all first-generation and second-generation barriers to black voting. All it needs is the claim that things now are better than they were back then, and frankly I find this difficult to argue with. If things are even somewhat better than they were back then, and the law should indeed be updated to reflect current conditions, then some modification of the VRA is clearly in order by this reasoning.[41]

To be sure, one might rightfully insist that functionally equivalent barriers to blacks fully participating in the democratic process (e.g., photo IDs) have replaced older ones (e.g., poll taxes). But if the majority grants this point for the sake of argument, they might plausibly reply that these tools do not *only* target blacks. If these barriers to voting do make it harder to vote, they do so for a much broader class of citizens, namely, those who would have trouble procuring the requisite ID, which most certainly includes not just blacks but other minorities as well as some whites, the poor, students, the disabled, etc. Of course, some will say that this is precisely the problem; however, the majority might add—though perhaps not with a straight face—that this counts as some kind of "racial" progress in America, that barriers to voting are more evenly distributed across the population and not directly tied to suspect racial classifications.

Here we might complain that Republicans have largely favored these newer strategies to gain and maintain a political advantage over Democrats by making it harder for citizens to vote who have historically supported Democrats at the polls. While this may be true, the majority will claim that this does not impugn the racial progress argument for scrapping the coverage formula. And they might add that if this diagnosis is correct, the most pressing need may be to craft laws that prevent Republicans in covered *and* non-covered states from disenfranchising voters who would support their Democratic rivals.

Where Do We Go from *Shelby County*?

Justice Ginsburg and many others feared that weakening the VRA would open the floodgates to jurisdictions looking to reverse the civil rights gains in voting rights made since 1965. And from the looks of things—the proliferation of voter ID laws in Kansas, Mississippi, North Carolina, and other places making it more burdensome to cast a ballot[42]—these fears were not unfounded. A liberal narrative about racial progress supports the dissent and the case for keeping VRA at full strength, coverage formula and all.

Persons with more optimism than I can muster might try to convince those who hold the "that was then, this is now" view—including conservative members of the Supreme Court—to abandon this perspective, to follow Justice Ginsburg's call to heed the words of Shakespeare that "what's past is prologue,"[43] or the words of Santayana that "[t]hose who cannot remember the past are condemned to repeat it,"[44] and to affirm the continued need for the VRA and other civil rights era legislation meant to secure the full blessings of citizenship to blacks and other historically disadvantaged and vulnerable groups.

However, if the divide between liberals and conservatives on how to understand current racial conditions proves to be as deep and intractable, as I fear, it will be attractive to have in hand reasons for affording the right-to-vote protection that does not hinge on embracing the liberal or the conservative perspective on the racial progress matter. Indeed, particularly in voting denial cases such as *Crawford v. Marion County Election Board*,[45] where the concern is with an individual's right to vote, it will be useful to have a defense that allows us to avoid any debate whatsoever over the role of prejudice or discrimination in altering existing electoral outcomes to the detriment of voters from certain racial or ethnic groups.

One consequence of appreciating the limits of efforts to contest the racial progress argument, in a society deeply polarized about race matters, is that this forces us to attend to the various interests at play, more carefully, in upholding the VRA status quo. Many of the regulations the critics feared would come to pass, leading to "backsliding," are ones that affect an individual right to vote rather than group interests. As vote denial becomes more of an issue in the United States—post–*Shelby County*—we must consider novel arguments for saving the VRA from further damage, and for protecting the right to vote. Such arguments need not begin with the question of how much progress has been made in advancing the interests of certain groups, e.g., African Americans, the disabled, or the poor. Rather, they would ask whether the weighty substantive equality and dignity interests every individual citizen has in voting and having his or her vote counted, which have long been protected by the VRA, have been afforded sufficient judicial protection by being duly balanced against competing state interests.[46] I will say more about the relationship between voting rights and dignity, drawing on Martin Luther King Jr.'s ideas, in chapter 9.

Some scholars, who are otherwise champions of the VRA, have expressed concerns that reviving the coverage formula, or a similar device, is not the way to go. While they do not deny the persistence of voting discrimination, they worry that such formula will be too static to accommodate rapidly changing conditions.[47] Others worry that because voting discrimination is shifting from vote dilution back to vote denial, any geographically restrictive formula will exempt places—such as Kansas or Ohio—that may have records of voting rights discrimination.[48] In view of these and other concerns, many of these commentators have observed, and I agree, that *Shelby County* creates an opportunity for federal legislators to enact voting regulations that aim to ensure that no eligible citizen is denied the right to vote.[49] Of course, given the depth of political polarization, this will not be an easy feat. Democrats and Republicans will likely have to reach a "Grand Election Bargain."[50] Whether they can do so, and save this "superstatute" from dying, remains to be seen.[51]

In 1965, Martin Luther King Jr. made the point that America's march toward his dream of a truly equal society must not be halted by "the myth of exaggerated progress."[52] We can apply his cautionary warning to our present circumstances because this myth still holds sway over many people (including conservative members of the Supreme Court) who mistake a bud on the plant of equality for the whole flower—to paraphrase King. As we come to terms with *Shelby County*, his words still ring true: "[s]o while we talk of the progress let us realize that we still have a long, long way to go."[53]

The VRA emerged out of America's lamentable voting rights history. It sought to permanently end racially discriminatory state practices that undermined the right to vote. In *Shelby County*, the Supreme Court struck down a provision of the VRA that singled out for special attention states with particularly egregious histories of voting rights abuses. The Court did so by relying, in part, on an argument rooted in a peculiar narrative about racial progress in the United States. Although we should give lie to the myth of exaggerated racial progress, as Justice Ginsburg does in her *Shelby County* dissent, we must not underestimate the challenge it raises in a deeply polarized society for defending the right to vote. This challenge may ultimately call for a more universalistic approach to safeguarding this fundamental right, one that is more in line with the non-race-specific remedies defended in this book. Arriving at an approach that is politically achievable and able to withstand constitutional scrutiny will not be easy. But the importance of voting rights to publicly affirming the dignity of democratic citizens certainly warrants the effort. Racial realists are skeptical about flying the race-first flag to secure racial progress in contemporary America. They are skeptical about doing so to maintain the racial progress secured by the 1965 Voting Rights Act. And, as the next chapter argues, they are skeptical about doing so to secure corrective justice for historical wrongs perpetrated against blacks in the United States.

3
Racial Reparations

From when the first recorded black African slaves arrived on the shores of Jamestown, Virginia, in 1619, black chattel slavery was practiced and protected until its demise in 1865 with the ratification of the Thirteenth Amendment following the deadliest war in US history. And more than 140 years after the abolition of slavery, the debate over whether living descendants of black slaves should receive reparations for the heinous legacy of slavery and its aftermath is one of the most hotly contested debates in the public sphere. This debate is often situated within the larger international context of nations coming to terms with different legacies of historical injustice in the aftermath of World War II, most notably Germany coming to terms with the legacy of the Holocaust, Japan coming to terms with its treatment of so-called comfort women, and the United States coming to terms with the internment of Japanese Americans.[1] Yet, the movement for black reparations has a much longer history than casual observers typically assume. Indeed, it predates the Holocaust reparations movement by many years.[2]

The black reparations movement has garnered increased public and scholarly visibility in recent years as demands for redress of various historical injustices—and long overdue formal apologies for them—have increased in frequency and prominence worldwide, and as unprecedented municipal and state slavery-era commerce disclosure laws in the United States have forced financial, insurance, and other companies to disclose slavery-era-related business, exposing them to legal liability as well as moral condemnation. Moreover, the visibility of this debate was heightened when the United States seated its first black president, who, ironically enough, is not a descendant of black African slaves.

Of course, this modern black reparations movement invites the provocative questions of whether a public apology for slavery issued by President Barack Obama would be taken seriously, and whether his election (as some have suggested) renders the continued pursuit of black reparations passé. Yet, it should come as no surprise that the debate over reparations for slavery is most spirited in response to demands for monetary reparations—or the so-called 40 acres and a mule—for the living descendants of black slaves, as opposed to calls for greater black representation in prominent political offices and positions of power, and as opposed to calls for public formal apologies or other purely symbolic measures such as a National Slavery Museum on the Mall in Washington, DC.

Indeed, it is telling that the unprecedented apology to black Americans for wrongs committed against them and their ancestors who suffered under slavery and Jim Crow issued by the US House of Representatives on July 29, 2008, made no explicit mention of reparations, though it did commit the House to "redressing the lingering consequences of these misdeeds." Although this purely symbolic step is quite remarkable in its own right and should not be taken lightly despite the fact that the resolution was nonbinding and passed on a voice vote, it is certainly less threatening and less contentious than passing a binding resolution to provide material reparations to rectify the lingering consequences of slavery and its aftermath, which, many would argue, includes persistent black-white inequalities in education, wealth, health, and many other areas. Such a measure certainly would have garnered much more prominent headlines the day after passage than the measure adopted. Furthermore, as some scholars have argued, it is far from clear that anything short of this—including the election of a black president—will be adequate atonement for the legacies of black chattel slavery and Jim Crow segregation.[3]

In addition to there being evidence that many people are willing to accept providing black people with some form of symbolic reparations for slavery (such as a formal apology or a slavery museum or national monument) but that fewer people are willing to endorse monetary reparations, there is also survey data indicating that pro-reparations and anti-reparations supporters can largely be divided along racial lines. Brophy cites a poll of Alabama citizens conducted in 2002 by the *Mobile Register* in which only 5% of white people supported reparations for slavery from the federal government, in stark contrast to 67% of black people who supported them.[4] The poll also showed that a marginally higher percentage of black people, 73%, and a considerably higher number of white people, 24%, believed that the federal government should apologize for slavery. And anticipating the objection that Alabama is way out of step with the mainstream American society, Brophy also cites an empirical study conducted by Harvard University and University of Chicago researchers in 2003 in which only 4% of white people believed that the federal government should pay compensation for slavery and 67% of black people believed that it should, whereas a marginally higher percentage of both black people, 79%, and considerably higher percentage of white people, 30%, believed that the federal government should apologize for slavery.[5]

Numerous scholars, including social scientists, historians, political scientists, critical legal studies scholars, and philosophers, have been arguing for years that America and Americans remain deeply divided by race and that these divisions usually show up when "race" matters become a topic of public concern and debate.[6] And from this vantage point any empirical survey data suggesting that the division between advocates for and critics of slavery reparations follows along racial lines will not be a surprise. Indeed, some people will say that this is precisely what we should expect to discover. Although such public opinion surveys have merit and cannot be entirely dismissed, we should not presume that the black/white racial divide is always a reliable way to track the pro- /anti-reparations divide. It has been well established that black political thought is complex and diverse, with black people holding a variety of political ideologies along the spectrum of available options, including nationalism, liberalism, conservatism, Marxism, and so forth.[7] Moreover, it has been shown that black political thought yields further complexity and diversity when viewed through the prism of a comparative lens offering a more global view of the black world.[8]

Hence, when taking stock of what individual black people think about reparations, affirmative action, rights, freedom, justice, solidarity, equality, and other political ideals or public policies, we must consider how their perspectives are profoundly shaped by their background theories and norms, which may serve to distinguish their perspective not only from white people but from other black people as well. Indeed, one implication of the current discussion is that racial membership may not be the most reliable or most telling way to sort defenders and critics of black reparations.

Several questions commonly raised by the reparations debate include: Who is owed reparations? Who owes reparations? And what form should reparations take? Recent philosophical treatments of the topic also invite us to consider the following question: What is the relationship between the historical injustices of slavery and Jim Crow and current racial inequalities in wealth, health, housing, crime, and education in the normative argument for black reparations? Some ways of answering this question seek to undermine the prevailing normative argument for black reparations, namely, the argument from corrective justice. Influential versions of this argument turn on a particular explanation of the "root" cause of racial inequalities. This is a serious source of concern, however, given the depth of disagreement in the social science literature about why black–white inequalities persist in the postracial era. This chapter develops the concern to vindicate skepticism regarding a race-first approach to securing reparations for racial wrongs.

The Corrective Justice Argument

Although historical injustice is not a straightforward matter, a common point of agreement is that this is a wrongdoing that occurred in the past, and there is a moral presumption that it be rectified where possible and where defeating conditions do not obtain. Hence, in defining the nature of historical injustice, we will find ourselves taking not only a specific conceptual stance on what kind of wrongdoing it amounts to, but also a normative stance that it be redressed. And here we will most certainly find ourselves disagreeing—perhaps even sharply—about the reasons that historical injustice ought to be redressed and about what exactly this demands.

Before considering one of the main normative arguments for readdressing the historical injustices of slavery and segregation, we should note that one of the things that redressing historical injustice obviously demands is looking back to these past wrongdoings and bringing them into sharper focus before the public eye. The nation and its citizens must be reminded of these infamous institutions as an essential aspect of coming to terms with their legacy. And, as others have observed in related discussions, this creation of a common collective memory is an essential element of any reparations movement:

> A chief function of reparations movements is to create and hallow a particular set of memories, to restore to collective consciousness events otherwise obscured by official histories and "common sense" as defined by dominant groups.[9]

With respect to the black reparations movement in particular, the history of black chattel slavery and Jim Crow segregation must continue to be recollected in our schools and universities as well as in our films, books, theatrical productions, music, museums, and monuments to the past. Moreover, it must be performed in a way that reflects the wide diversity of perspectives on this past and not merely the perspectives of those who paint a flattering portrait of slavery and segregation.

Of course, some people—especially in the aftermath of Obama's election as president—will disparage the value of looking back to the past in this way as well as the wisdom of seeking reparations for past wrongdoing. Indeed, one such critic, sociologist John Torpey, presses the concern this way: "The preoccupation with past crimes and atrocities mirrors the eclipse of more visionary modes of imagining the future."[10] Not only does he credit the Holocaust for stimulating competition for recognition of various historical injustices as "Holocaust-like" or "worse than the Holocaust," in what Barkan describes as an era of the unfolding of guilt around the globe,[11] but Torpey also blames the Holocaust for what he takes to be a not-so-progressive focus on the preoccupation with the past rather than a focus on the future as the space in which to seek improvements in the human condition. Thus, he contends that looking back to the so-called historical injustices undermines ongoing efforts to realize certain visions of the ideal moral community in which diverse peoples can live together in a nation as citizens beholden to the common normative ideals of freedom, equality, and justice for all. And to the extent that the pursuit of racial reparations demands that we look back to our infamous past, then this pursuit undermines efforts to realize a particular idealized vision of a common future of unified citizenship.

But we need not deny that a common future of unified citizenship is an admirable aspiration to wonder whether we can reasonably hope to realize such a future without adequately coming to terms with past historical injustices, especially when we are arguably still living with their legacy. With regard to the legacy of slavery and segregation, although there is some debate about whether to make the case for reparations by looking all the way back to slavery rather than to Jim Crow and the period leading up to *Brown v. Board of Education* and the Great Society and civil rights reforms during the middle of the twentieth century, it has been argued that persistent racial inequalities between black and white people in wealth, health, housing, crime, education, and other areas are the most visible marks of the past on the present, whether they can be linked all the way back to slavery or only to more recent post-slavery governmental actions and institutions. And these visible marks of racial inequality have informed some of the most recent normative defenses of black reparations in the philosophical literature.[12]

Underlying the prevailing normative argument for reparations is the moral intuition that corrective justice supports racial reparations. The pursuit of corrective justice, which will be familiar to readers of Aristotle's *Nicomachean Ethics*, demands that if one party (the victim) is wronged by another party (the perpetrator), then the perpetrator has a prima facie moral obligation to make the victim whole by restoring the status quo ante, as far as possible, for the wrongful harm. When applied to the case of black chattel slavery, a simple version of the corrective justice argument for racial reparations goes roughly as follows: black chattel slavery was a wrongful harm against slaves perpetrated by slaveholders. Slaveholders had a prima facie moral obligation to make slaves whole by restoring the status quo ante, as far as possible, before this wrongful harm. Some form of reparations to slaves would accomplish this. Therefore, slaveholders owed slaves some form of reparations for the harm of enslavement.

Of course, some critics will object that this argument does not establish that present-day black people are owed reparations for the obvious reason that they were not enslaved. So even if this is a strong argument for reparations, it has no applicability today, as there are neither black slaves nor slaveholders in the United States, and therefore no parties that rightfully stand to benefit and none that are obliged to make amends. Obviously, if some black people could indeed trace their roots back to slaves who were harmed by some enduring corporate or collective agent, then their case would be stronger. Yet, some critics will add that this will not be sufficient to establish that *all* present-day black people are owed reparations but only ones who can firmly establish their claims. The most compelling line of response to these criticisms of the simple corrective justice argument has been to shift the focus away from individual victims and individual perpetrators to empirically demonstrable patterns of black–white inequalities along various measures of well-being, and to take the closing of these gaps attributable to past wrongdoing as the basis for a more compelling corrective justice argument for reparations.

Reparations for Racial Inequality

Defenders of reparations have certainly appreciated the force of criticisms that challenge the moral or legal standing of present-day black people to press claims associated with past wrongs to their ancestors. But they deem these criticisms ineffective in derailing the corrective justice argument for reparations. For one thing, they maintain that it is a red herring to take the case to turn on whether there are slaves or slaveholders alive today. Rather, they contend that the strongest corrective justice argument takes account of the direct and indirect role of the US government in supporting and facilitating a system of black subordination and disadvantage long after slavery's demise, a system that has had an enduring and disproportionate impact on black people in general. To be sure, both defenders and indeed most critics of black reparations admit that slavery was a wrongful harm to enslaved black people and their immediate descendants. Yet differences of opinion emerge, as we get further away from slavery, with many critics suggesting that claims of later descendants to have suffered continuing harm become increasingly dubious with the passage of time and changing circumstances.

For example, by considering the histories of injustice surrounding white settlers' dealings with aboriginal peoples of Australia, New Zealand, and North America, legal philosopher Jeremy Waldron offered a perspective on our obligations to rectify previous injustices that generated considerable debate in the subsequent legal and philosophical literature on reparations.[13] Observing that efforts to redress historical injustices proceed in the name of principle—the principle of justice—Waldron claimed that we cannot lose sight of the demands of justice in these efforts or, more precisely, that we must realize that justice cuts both ways. Accordingly, we must question the judgment that rectification of past injustice generates a nonnegotiable or absolute demand for more than symbolic reparations: transfers of land, wealth, and other resources. Hence, when considering claims to reparation, such claims must be considered alongside competing and conflicting claims to the resources in question. Arguably, these claims may also be made in the name of justice and, in many cases, may have greater weight and priority, as they are current claims and not ancient ones tied to distant wrongs that took place generations ago or that impacted people who are long dead, or claims whose force has faded with the passage of time. Although Waldron's suggestion that some historical injustices can thus be superseded by time and changing circumstances has been widely criticized,[14] it has clear implications for the reparations debate, and it has been utilized to challenge the normative case against reparations for the so-called ancient wrong of slavery.

The main way of dealing with the foregoing worry regarding the passage of time has been to turn our gaze back not to the "ancient" wrong of slavery but to much more recent wrongs that have disproportionately harmed present-day black people. For instance, one case study that has received considerable attention in several important articles is the role of the government in supporting and sustaining racial discrimination in housing and lending practices in the post–World War II era.[15] It has been argued that housing discrimination, and the resulting residential segregation of black and white people, has had far-reaching negative consequences for black people as a group, leaving them with less wealth,[16] poorer health,[17] greater exposure to crime,[18] and inferior education[19] relative to white people as a group. And for these reasons, this is an especially pernicious form of discrimination, with much more recent roots and a more demonstrable and quantifiable impact on present-day black people.

According to defenders of reparations, this recent case study and other similar ones have various virtues: (i) they avoid taking us all the way back to slavery and thus avoid certain objections; (ii) they focus on empirically demonstrable and quantifiable harms; (iii) they shift our focus from an individual-centered perspective, in which we look for specific victims and perpetrators, to a group-centered perspective, in which we look for discernible patterns of racial inequality; and (iv) they suggest that the most fitting reparations, if the case can be made, should be aimed at yielding greater equality between these groups across a wide range of measures of well-being.

This shift in focus to more recent wrongs and to real patterns of racial inequality is captured in modified versions of the corrective justice argument for reparations. Assuming that the US government played an active role in supporting and sustaining black subordination and disadvantage (e.g., in home ownership opportunities and home equity wealth accumulation) long after the demise of slavery and well beyond the World War II era, and assuming that such practices have been harmful to present-day black people and their immediate descendants, then corrective justice demands that the US government has a moral obligation to redress the visible marks of the harms attributable to its own actions, namely, demonstrable and quantifiable inequalities in which black people are overrepresented in the ranks of the least well off and underrepresented in the ranks of the most well off. And insofar as some sort of reparations program would accomplish this, and insofar as these continuing effects of past wrongdoing constitute a continuing harm, the United States ought to pursue such a program.[20]

One important aspect of this argument is that it focuses our attention on the concrete effects of past wrongdoing, and it presumes that but for this past wrongdoing these particular harmful effects would not obtain. A defender of the corrective justice argument puts the point this way:

> Although, laudably, America enacted national antidiscrimination laws in the 1960s, wide disparities between blacks and whites persist across virtually every indicator of social and economic well-being. Indeed, as the twentieth century came to a close, the condition of many poor blacks had worsened in many respects.... Given the history of discrimination against blacks in this country, the persistence of substantial disparities reflect, at least to some degree, effects of past discrimination. That is, these conditions would not exist to the same extent but for American's history of racial discrimination against black Americans.[21]

This focus on more recent harms, which do not require us to go all the way back to slavery, presumes that comparisons between the actual circumstances of black people and counterfactual circumstances are much less difficult. But even ardent supports of black reparations have been critical of such counterfactual reasoning in reparations arguments.[22]

Another important aspect of this argument is that it presumes the existence of a causal connection between practices of racial discrimination and patterns of racial inequality. In other words, it adopts a particular view of the causes of persistent racial inequalities, one that roots them variously in both overt and subtle past discrimination. To wit, this strategy anticipates two important concerns often raised by critics of reparations. How can the purported harms that present-day black people are alleged to suffer collectively as a result of past wrongdoing be empirically articulated and quantified? And what are the prospects for connecting these present harms with past wrongdoing so as to establish the claim that present-day black people suffer enduring injury? To address these questions fully, advocates of this modified corrective justice argument have deferred to social scientific research findings that empirically articulate and quantify persistent racial disparities, and they offer an empirically grounded explanation of why these disparities can arguably be linked back to governmental practices that subordinated and disadvantaged black people long after the demise of slavery. Although the turn to social science is a welcomed development in advancing our understanding of the normative case for racial reparations, it comes at a price.

Debating the Science of Racial Inequality

Black chattel slavery as practiced in the United States until slavery's demise in 1865 was a historical injustice. So too was the legacy of post-slavery, forced racial segregation of blacks and whites under local, state, and national law, as well as public policies that prescribed and permitted the separate and unequal treatment of blacks and whites in the public and private spheres. These historical injustices have left enduring marks on contemporary American society, foremost of which are the enduring inequalities between blacks and whites along various measures of well-being, including, but not limited to, inequalities in education, wealth, health, housing, and the administration of criminal justice. The persistence of these empirically demonstrable racial inequalities—long after the demise of slavery and Jim Crow—has been at the center of the public debate about reparations as well as more general debates about social justice.

Consider the congressional hearing on bill H.R. 40 to study slavery and its impact on American society and subsequent generations of slave descendants.[23] This bill, which Representative John Conyers of Michigan has reintroduced every year since first proposing it in 1989, seeks to do four things: (1) acknowledge the fundamental injustice and inhumanity of slavery, (2) establish a commission to study slavery and the subsequent racial and economic discrimination against freed slaves, (3) study the impact of this legacy of discrimination on contemporary African Americans, and (4) make recommendations to Congress on appropriate remedies to redress the harm inflicted on living African Americans.[24] After almost two decades, this bill finally got a hearing on December 18, 2007, during a meeting of the Congressional Subcommittee on the Constitution, Civil Rights, and Civil Liberties. During this historic hearing the issue of persistent racial disparities and black disadvantage relative to whites figured prominently in some of the testimony by supporters as well as critics of the bill.[25]

During the hearing, Representative Conyers cited empirical data that he contended linked current racial disparities in education and in the poverty rate to the legacy of slavery, namely, that the black high school dropout rate is 50 percent compared with 23 percent for whites; that the national average scores in math, science, and reading for black seventeen-year-olds are comparable to the scores for white thirteen-year-olds; and that the poverty rate of blacks, at 24 percent, is twice the national average.[26] But critics of reparations rejected this explanation of the racial achievement and poverty gaps.

One critic of the bill, Roger Clegg, a former deputy in the US Department of Justice's Civil Rights Division from 1987 to 1991, testified that the proposals in H.R. 40 are an unnecessary, hopeless, and divisive task "ill-suited" for a government commission.[27] During his testimony Clegg contended,

> The principal hurdle facing African Americans today is the fact that seven out of [ten] African Americans are born out of wedlock. Just about any social problem that you can name—crime, drugs, dropping out of school, doing poorly in school and so forth—has a strong correlation

with growing up in a home without a father. And it is very hard to argue that this problem is traceable to slavery or Jim Crow, since illegitimacy rates in the African American community began to skyrocket just at about the time that Jim Crow was starting to crumble.[28]

Another critic, Stephan Thernstrom, adopted essentially the same explanation of enduring economic disparities between whites and blacks.[29] He contended,

> The principal source of black poverty today, for example, is African American family structure. One-paycheck families (or zero-paycheck families who are dependent upon public assistance) are far more likely to fall into poverty than two-parent, two-paycheck families. Blaming African-American out-of-wedlock births and absent fathers upon an institution that disappeared 142 years ago makes little sense.[30]

These critics opt for what might be called *black agent-relative* explanations of persistent racial disparities, namely, ones that locate their root causes in the action (or inaction) of blacks themselves.

In contrast, Tommy Wells, then president-elect of the American Bar Association, was present at the hearing to indicate the ABA's support, in principle, for H.R. 40.[31] In addition to citing Justice Ginsburg's concurring opinion in *Grutter v. Bollinger* as an authority for the claim that "rank discrimination based on race" remains alive and continues to impede the nation's realization of its highest values and ideals, Wells cited Justice Kennedy's address before the ABA in 2004 as support for the persistence of racial disparities in the criminal justice system in particular.[32] Furthermore, he added to Kennedy's findings by noting the following:

> Even though African-Americans comprise only 13% of the American population, over 44% of the 1.4 million persons incarcerated in 2003 were black[.] A report released by the Bureau of Justice Statistics found that a black male had a 1 in 3 chance of being imprisoned during his lifetime, compared to a 1 in 6 chance for a Latino male and a 1 in 17 chance for a white male. Nearly 10% of black males age 25 to 29 are incarcerated

compared with 1.1% of white males in the same age group, and black females are five times more likely to be incarcerated than white females.[33]

To be sure, Wells admits that there is serious disagreement about the causes of these enduring racial disparities in the criminal justice system, but they certainly lend themselves to an explanation that grounds these disparities in some sort of systemic discrimination based on race.[34] This is an instance of what might be called a *black agent-neutral* explanation of persistent racial disparities, one that locates their root causes in something other than the actions (or inactions) of black agents.

The foregoing explanations of racial inequalities in the public debate draw or rely upon empirical scholarship. Social scientists, including sociologists and economists, have compiled and analyzed data pertaining to racial disparities that now figures prominently not only in academic discussions of reparations but also in the halls of Congress and in the courts as the legislative and judicial branches of government labor to determine what—if anything further—the United States must do to come to terms with the nation's legacy of slavery and segregation.

Empirically Informed Corrective Justice Arguments

Establishing the connection between these past wrongs and persistent racial inequalities in education (and in other areas) has been vital to recent scholarly arguments for black reparations. I want to raise a concern about a commonplace normative argument for black reparations—an argument that forges a strong causal link between the past wrongs of slavery and Jim Crow and present-day inequalities between blacks and whites. Not surprisingly, many reasonable people sharply disagree about how best to explain the widely accepted empirical facts pertaining to persistent racial inequalities between blacks and whites. Furthermore, many of these people disagree about how best to redress the historical injustice suffered by previous and current generations of black Americans in a liberal democratic society with a deep and abiding commitment to the normative ideals of freedom, justice, and equality. Careful consideration of the opposing arguments reveals that in many instances these empirical and normative perspectives are interrelated, such that the empirical perspectives on the root causes of ongoing racial inequalities in education, wealth, health, and crime strongly correlate with normative perspectives about what a liberal democratic society owes the racially disadvantaged. For some time now, this general relationship between empirical and normative perspectives on racial inequality has figured into scholarly and public policy debates about welfare, affirmative action, education, crime, and healthcare reform. But with increasing frequency it now figures into the current debate over the controversial question of whether the United States owes blacks reparations for slavery and its aftermath.

For example, within moral and legal debates about reparations we see that social science is increasingly called upon to support the claim that present-day black descendants of slaves in the United States suffer the effects of harms that are traceable to the past wrong of slavery perpetrated against their ancestors and are therefore entitled to redress. This general relationship between the empirical and the normative is salient in the corrective justice argument for black reparations, which is arguably the most common and influential normative argument for reparations.

The basic idea underlying the pursuit of corrective justice, a moral idea that can be traced back to Aristotle's *Nicomachean Ethics*,[35] demands that if party A wrongfully harms party B, then A has a prima facie moral obligation to repair or make amends, so far as possible, for the wrongful harm to B. There can, of course, be debate about what exactly discharging this objection amounts to. Does it amount to A making B whole for the losses suffered? Or does it amount to A or some other party creating conditions for A and B to have good future relations despite the history and legacy of injustice between them? However we articulate the precise nature of this obligation, the general point—which seems sensible to most people—is that corrective justice demands taking concrete steps to right past wrongs. This normative ideal seems well suited to make the case for reparations, particularly if one accepts the presumption that previous racial disparities and black disadvantage relative to whites and current disparities are due to similar causes rooted in the past wrongs of slavery and segregation.

But various objections have been raised against applying this idea to reparations. Some critics contend that facts having to do with mixed racial ancestry and the resulting mixed racial identities make it virtually impossible to determine who is owed and who should pay reparations, pointing out possibilities in which particular blacks may owe reparations due to having slaveholding ancestors while particular whites may be owed reparations due to having slave ancestors.[36] Other critics contend that if upholding justice is really at issue in corrective justice arguments for reparations, then we must consider that the passage of time can result in the normative claim for repairing past wrongs being in competition with more recent competing normative claims that preclude—on grounds of justice—taking certain reparative courses of action that will impact current or future generations.[37] Perhaps the most frequently pressed objection, however, is that the perpetrators of the past wrong and its victims are long dead, in which case there are no parties that rightfully stand to benefit and none that must make amends. Some critics of reparations believe that this objection poses a fatal problem for defenders of black reparations, preventing them from firmly establishing that any parties are morally or legally responsible for slavery and its aftermath.

We find a version of this objection in a recent Seventh Circuit Court of Appeals decision on reparations. In this decision, the Court concluded that not only do descendants of slaves lack moral standing for any redress on corrective justice grounds, but they also lack legal standing. Writing for the Court, Judge Posner puts the point this way:

> [T]here is a fatal disconnect between the victims and the plaintiffs. When a person is wronged he can seek redress, and if he wins, his

descendants may benefit, but the wrong to the ancestor is not a wrong to the descendants. For if it were, then (problems of proof to one side) statutes of limitations would be toothless. A person whose ancestor had been wronged a thousand years ago could sue on the ground that it was a continuing wrong and he is one of the victims.[38]

So, when applied to the historical injustice of slavery and its aftermath, the corrective justice argument is that certain parties are said to have perpetrated past wrongs against slaves and consequently have a moral and legal obligation to repair these wrongs and make the victims whole. However, the argument faces obvious objections in this form, most significantly that present-day blacks lack the moral and legal standing to be owed redress.

Defenders of reparations have not abandoned the case in view of this objection. Instead, they have modified the corrective justice argument. One modification has been to focus more on past harms associated with Jim Crow racial segregation and the period immediately following the demise of segregation rather than the harms associated with slavery.[39] Here the presumption is that comparisons between the actual circumstances of blacks and counterfactual ones are much less difficult if we concentrate on this more recent period of time.[40] Along with this, defenders of reparations have proposed more nuanced accounts of who constitute the perpetrators and victims of the past wrongs, and who is ultimately responsible for righting these wrongs.

The most crucial amendment to the corrective justice argument has been to establish that descendants of slaves suffer continuing harm. For this modified version of the corrective justice argument to go through, it must be demonstrated that the past wrongs associated with slavery and its aftermath have harmed—or are continuing to harm—present-day blacks whose ancestors were slaves, so as to make clear that the victims due redress are not only those individuals who have long since died but also individuals who are living today. Within the scholarly literature on reparations the most compelling way of meeting this requirement has been to establish a causal connection between the past wrongs of slavery and racial apartheid under Jim Crow, and the current racial inequalities in which blacks are statistically overrepresented in the ranks of the worst off and underrepresented in the ranks of the better off when it comes to educational achievement, health, income, wealth, entanglements with the criminal justice system, and so on.

So, for instance, with respect to racial disparities in health it has been recently argued that

> A large gap in health exists between Blacks and Whites, and it is inextricably linked to the history of race and racism in the United States. Racial differences in SES and health are the predictable results of the successful implementation of residential segregation, a policy that was deliberately set up to create separate and unequal living conditions for Blacks. It and other aspects of racism remain central determinants of racial differences in health. Thus, the legacy of slavery and legal discrimination still matters for African Americans in the 21st century.[41]

Here the authors conclude that these current racial disparities in health, traceable to racial segregation, provide a basis (on corrective justice grounds) for black reparations. In the scholarly literature we also find powerful complementary arguments linking the legacy of slavery and post-slavery racial segregation to other persistent racial disparities. Some argue that housing discrimination itself, as practiced during and immediately after Jim Crow—setting aside the health-related problems—provides a basis for black reparations. Others have explored the connections between residential segregation during and after slavery in tracing the roots of educational inequalities between blacks and whites, taking the latter inequalities to provide an independent basis for black reparations. And yet others have examined the relationship between differential racial patterns of violence and residential racial segregation as a basis for some form of reparations.

For those of us sharing a particular explanatory narrative regarding the history of race relations in the United States—both prior to and after the civil rights movement—this causal connection seems to be relatively obvious and does not require much effort to prove. However, for reasons that I will now sketch, establishing this causal connection between the wrongs of the past and present-day racial inequalities in education, crime, health, housing, and in other areas is a considerably more daunting task than one might expect, especially when it comes to persuading a person to embrace a corrective justice argument for reparations who does not share our explanatory historical narrative, or our understanding of the empirical causes of persistent racial disparities. This obstacle to linking the racial wrongs of the past with current racial inequalities is endemic to the postracial era in America.

The Limits of Corrective Justice Arguments

In these newly fashioned corrective justice arguments for reparations—where the empirical meets the normative—social scientific research is called upon to establish the causal connection between past wrongs and current inequalities. The normative arguments are tethered not only to empirical findings, but also to particular empirical explanations of the phenomena, say, black agent-neutral rather than black agent-relative explanations.[42] Hence, we find defenders of reparations challenging critics who seek to ground the causes of black disadvantage in facts about blacks themselves (e.g., propensities to engage in violent behavior or to shy away from studying and hard work) by contending that

> Those who blame the victims of hypersegregation for the culture of hypersegregation are *getting the causal story backward*. The institutionalized, federally sanctioned and implemented discrimination that was instrumental in creating the black ghetto and the black underclass was largely the work of individual and corporate agents of the white majority, which was thereby continuing through transforming the institutionalized domination over blacks it inherited from slavery. And now, it appears, those ghettos and that underclass are self-reproducing, linked in a causal feedback loop of race and poverty. They will not disappear

themselves, without the political will to repair the damages of slavery and segregation.[43]

Putting considerable weight on this causal story to complete the argument will not only require the input of the social sciences, but it also makes the corrective justice argument vulnerable to critics who question the empirical findings. To be sure, some of these critics are somewhat more sensible than ones who suggest that defenders of reparations, positing such causal connections, are relying upon ideology (in a pejorative sense), not science.[44] A more sensible and charitable critic might elicit empirically grounded reasons for thinking that the plight of blacks on the short side of inequalities today has much more to do with their own choices rather than older (or even newer) forms of racial discrimination. Indeed, with respect to the educational inequalities between blacks and whites mentioned in chapter 1, some of these critics might add that black underachievement relative to whites need not be construed as evidence of black cultural dysfunction (as some less charitable critics have suggested). Instead, it could be construed as the result of very rational decision-making.

For example, according to an increasingly popular economic explanation of persistent and quantifiable racial disparities in educational achievement between black and white students, the impact of the social environment of black students—particularly racial peer group influence—on their choices is taken to be the primary empirical explanation for blacks performing more poorly than whites on a variety of measures of educational achievement.[45] From this vantage point race does indeed matter when it comes to understanding the racial achievement gap, but not in the way that many people think. From this economic perspective, race matters in understanding why the racial achievement gap is first and foremost a problem that stems from strategic black student choices in response to their black peers, rather than one that stems from racial discrimination or institutional racism in the delivery of education.

Hence, a more sophisticated and more charitable critic who focused on the question of whether blacks are owed reparations for educational inequality might draw on these and similar research findings to undermine an empirically informed normative argument for reparations that embraces a black agent-neutral explanation of educational inequality. I am not interested in trying to adjudicate this disagreement here. Rather, my concern has been to highlight the fact that empirical work is called upon both to defend and challenge corrective justice arguments for reparations in both scholarly and public debates, which brings us to the main lesson of this chapter.

A Crucial Lesson

The foregoing demonstrates that corrective justice arguments for black reparations seeking to forge a link between past racial wrongs and present racial inequalities are vulnerable to the kind of attack launched by Justice Thomas in *Grutter*.[46] In *Grutter*, the Court upheld the use of race as an admissions criterion for purposes of achieving educational diversity but rejected the use of race as a means of remedying past societal discrimination. Had it pursued this remedial strategy, the University of Michigan Law School would have been asked to demonstrate how past discrimination, understood narrowly, was operative and why it required such a remedy. This would have been a hard sell given the unreasonable burden placed upon parties seeking to establish racial discrimination in this postracial era.

By opting to look forward to the benefits of racial and other kinds of student diversity, the Law School anchored its case in a particular empirical take on the educational benefits of diversity (racial and otherwise) and managed to sell the argument to the Court. But this created an opening for Justice Thomas and others not sold on the argument. It invited these critics to challenge the argument by taking issue with the Law School's empirical analysis of the educational benefits of racial diversity. Although this counterattack was underdeveloped in many respects, one can certainly imagine a much more formidable attack being advanced along these lines. By the same token, one can also envision a much more formidable challenge being mounted against corrective justice arguments for reparations tethered to black agent-neutral explanations of the causes of racial inequality. To my mind, what makes these challenges particularly worrisome is that insofar as they are grounded in black agent-relative explanations of racial inequality, they will have considerable appeal in this postracial era where laissez-faire racism or racism without racists prevails.[47]

Some scholars will contend that we should simply fight it out by showing that the competing empirical explanations relied upon by these critics are flawed, ideological, or do not provide the best explanation of the data. Alternatively, others might contend that these critics have not identified the root causes of racial inequality. These may prove to be profitable strategies and are well worth pursuing. However, philosophers, political theorists, legal scholars, and anyone else who has an interest in these matters will certainly have to leave it to the social scientists to fight this battle, though it is far from clear how we will declare a winner. But what is clear is that insofar as corrective justice arguments turn on a black agent-neutral explanation of the root causes of racial disparities, which is characteristic of a race-first approach, they will not be able to make the case for black reparations to large segments of the American population operating with a postracial mentality. The good news is that we need not despair the demise of small-tent remedies. We can pursue a realistic blacktopia by pitching a bigger tent.

PART II
THE DAWN OF BIG-TENT REMEDIES

4
Black Liberalism Can't Save Us

> Won't you help to sing
> These songs of freedom?
> 'Cause all I ever have
> Redemption songs
>
> —Bob Marley

This chapter builds upon the concerns I raised in the previous one about the dim prospects for pursing corrective justice by using race-first appeals. I believe that these prospects remain dim even when they are dressed up in liberal ideology to recruit philosophical liberals as allies. A prominent proponent of this strategy, philosopher Charles Mills, does this by attacking the dominant liberal theory of justice in contemporary philosophy and offering alternative principles to transform liberalism into a better tool for pursuing small-tent racial justice remedies. I express my doubts about this project in what follows.

Charles Mills thinks that contemporary liberal political philosophy has a race problem. Its most celebrated theory of justice cannot rectify the shameful American legacy of white wrongs against black rights. This explains why he has been so critical of John Rawls. Mills argues that Rawls has produced principles of justice that are utterly unfit for racial justice duty. The publication of *Black Rights/White Wrongs: The Critique of Racial Liberalism*[1] marks the twentieth anniversary of Mills's contemporary classic, *The Racial Contract*.[2] This new book, mainly a collection of previously published essays, lays out his evidence—most of it historical, sociological, and psychological—for why liberalism has a race problem. It explains why he refuses to reject liberalism wholesale or retain it unmodified, and why he wants to transform liberalism into a useful normative tool for racial justice. The present chapter reconstructs Mills's case for the redemption of liberalism. It argues that his alternative principles of justice may rectify racial wrongs but are unlikely to gain sufficient support to facilitate the move to a racially just society. I worry that Mills offers a solution that is not silent about the race problem but is powerless to fix it given what we know about the social psychology of race and racism.

Liberalism's Race Problem

Given his well-known reputation as a critic of Rawls and Rawlsian liberalism, Mills makes a surprising concession at the end of his book. He writes, "Rawlsian political philosophy could at last become a real player in the righting of the historic and current white wrongs to black rights."[3] What's going on here? Is the Rawls slayer having a change of heart? Does Mills now believe that Rawlsian liberalism is not so bad after all? Well, not exactly. To resolve the puzzle, let us begin with his understanding of liberalism, a conjecture about the primary audience for his book, and reflection on the meaning of racial realism.

After observing that liberalism, understood as a political ideology, comes in different variants, Mills contends that all varieties are "committed to the flourishing of the individual."[4] However, this does not suffice to individuate the ideology, or to register meaningful differences in thought between those who espouse it, whether we are thinking about liberals in American politics or in the analytic philosophical tradition. For example, Barack Obama, Bernie Sanders, and Hillary Clinton all want individuals to flourish. However, they have different views about what this looks like, and about what obligations government, the private sector, and individuals have to realize this aim. The same can be said about George W. Bush, Rand Paul, and Donald Trump—all are committed to individuals flourishing—but it would be bizarre to describe them as liberals (though non-Americans might have a different take on this). Likewise, it may seem strange to call John Rawls, Robert Nozick, and G. A. Cohen liberals, though each was undoubtedly committed to individuals flourishing.

The problem here, as Mills realizes, is that if we have mundane political discourse in mind, say, from the Fox News perspective, liberalism represents a leftist ideology and liberals lean left. And the worst of the bunch, we are told, lean left on both social and economic issues. These critics say that liberals defend abortion, attack gun rights, want basic income for the poor, and seek reparations for black people and Native Americans. Then there are the public debates about differences between classical and contemporary liberals, with the former—the "true" believers in unfettered freedom from serfdom—proclaimed by some observers to be the original liberals, who represented liberalism before welfare and egalitarian liberals allegedly tarnished the ideology. Hoping to avoid these matters, by relying on what he calls a sense of the term found in political philosophy that transcends the left/right and classic/contemporary dichotomies, Mills tells us that liberalism is a celebrated "anti-feudal egalitarian ideology of individual rights and freedoms that emerged in the seventeenth and eighteenth centuries to oppose absolutism and ascriptive hierarchy."[5] But this definition does not solve the worry, especially if it entails that libertarians such as Robert Nozick and Ayn Rand are liberals too—a claim that has been contested.[6]

Mills may insist that we not get hung up on semantics. What's really at issue, on his view, is a fundamental difference between dominant or exclusionary variants of liberalism and nondominant or inclusive variants. The villain in his story is the former. According to Mills, exclusionary liberalism is an ideological tool that white philosophers have crafted, which is—by design—unable to undo white supremacy and black domination. Mills holds that Rawlsian liberalism, with its distributive principles of justice as fairness, represents the state-of-the-art modern version of this ineffective tool. While Nozick, Dworkin, and Cohen have also said much about justice, Mills's response has to be that their silences about race and white supremacy have left them no better off than Rawls when it comes to providing principles that can solve the race problem. So, we can quibble about which theorists are liberals. We can also argue for expanding the language to describe libertarians and egalitarians. But the real issue is whether political philosophers attend to race and its legacy, and whether this informs their normative theorizing to yield the emancipatory principles needed to undo past racial wrongs.

Mills's grand philosophical project has been to remake the liberal apparatus, so that it can better serve radical egalitarian white and black liberals, and their allies, seeking a theoretical tool to rectify the white wrongs perpetuated by this shameful legacy of transgressing black rights. However, leaving unsettled the question of how liberalism is understood and whether Mills's argument for the redemption of liberalism is pitched to everyday liberals, ivory tower liberals, or liberal radicals raises additional concerns. Mills operates with a peculiar conception of racial justice: he means by it "not preemptive measures to prevent racial injustice but corrective measures to rectify injustices *that have already occurred*."[7] But few liberals in American politics, including Obama and Sanders, or everyday liberals on the street will support this radical view of racial justice—no matter how beautifully crafted of an essay Ta-Nehisi Coates writes in defense of black reparations. A larger number of egalitarian white liberal philosophers might get behind this, though hardly enough to fill up an American Philosophical Association reception, and for ones who support black reparations they will have widely varied views about what form this should take. Many will likely opt for symbolic forms of reparation, a far cry from 40 acres and a mule, and not nearly as radical as Mills might deem necessary for rectification.[8]

So, one wonders whether Mills is trying to convince everyday liberals, academic liberals, or radical liberals that liberalism needs a makeover. Who is the primary audience for the book's argument and its black radical liberal solution to the race problem? Of course, he can target an audience that disagrees sharply with him such as right-wing liberals, hoping to convince them of the merits of his view. But, as will become clear, we still need to know whom the argument is primarily crafted to persuade to fully assess it. And, unfortunately, we do not get a straight answer to this question. My best conjecture comes largely from evidence in chapter 7, where Mills offers racial exploitation as a useful construct for framing racial injustice as a systemic structural problem. By foregrounding the view that whites wrongly benefit from past and present practices of racial domination of blacks, which makes the question of whether whites are "racist" inessential, we can say that the goal of racial justice is twofold: ending existing racial exploitation and equitably redistributing the ill-gotten gains of the past.[9]

The closing pages of this chapter present the virtues and drawbacks of the racial exploitation framework for selling the racial justice project to allies. So long as Ben Carson, Condoleezza Rice, and Clarence Thomas are not the first black people that come to mind, it seems sensible to suppose that black people are the natural audience for this book's argument and solution. But if something like material reparations for past white wrongs is on the table as a solution to the race problem, then some blacks may not join this party. Some will have other ideas about what is needed, including making better use of one's bootstraps. Others will worry about Obama and Oprah collecting reparations checks. And still others may raise philosophical objections to reparations. And all of this may happen even if they agree with Mills about the basic history of white supremacy and black domination.

Mills might say that this all sounds fine until blacks find themselves on the wrong side of a racially biased police arrest, or trying to secure a bank loan, or having their children disciplined more harshly in schools than their white peers. His reasonable point is that all black people have an interest in ending racial exploitation. And if redistributing illicit white benefits is minimally about rearranging things so that blacks are treated fairly and with dignity, then black conservatives should also get on board with this modest form of reparations. But if the racial justice bus is loaded with black people, who are drawn from across the political spectrum, according to Mills, this is not enough to steer it to the racial promised land. So, his targeted audience is certainly not black folks exclusively. Mills says, "Given their minority status both in straightforward quantitative terms, and, more important, the qualitative dimension of access to social sources of power, they will clearly not be able to do it on their own."[10] Blacks will need white people to navigate the freedom bus with them. This suggests that some subset of whites is the primary audience for the book. His argument aims to convince some class of white people to help pilot the freedom bus toward corrective justice land. But which white people?

Mills lays out a number of possibilities: mainstream white liberals, the majority white population as a whole, and the white working class. And in an illuminating footnote to the final chapter, he offers three more finer-grained possibilities: left-wing liberals, centrist liberals, and right-wing liberals.[11] The difficulties with this unruly list of options should be obvious. Just to list a few, these groups (if they can be neatly individuated) have very different interests, values, beliefs, and so on. They obviously have different thoughts about the race problem in America. Whites who voted for Obama, those who voted for Trump, and even those who first voted for Obama and then voted for Trump may have vastly different interests and concerns.

Mills cannot possibly think that his critique of Rawlsian liberalism and the case for its redemption will suffice to get all these folks on the racial justice bus and rally their support for race-specific policies such as reparations for black people. It seems, then, that the white population as a whole cannot be the primary audience for this book. But deciding between mainstream white liberals and the white working class still seems like too tall of an order. I know members of the latter group in parts of Michigan, Kansas, Texas, and other states who are miles apart on race matters from people I know in the cities of Ann Arbor, Lawrence, and Austin. And I seriously doubt that a crash course on the racial contract and racial exploitation will be enough to close the gap. We need to hear much more from Mills than we get in this book to convince us otherwise.

Evidence we get in this chapter and other places throughout the book suggests that "mainstream" white liberals are really his primary audience. But it is unclear what work this qualification is doing for Mills. Also, if this bunch includes liberals on the left, right, and center, then there still seems to be too much variation in interests when it comes to race matters. So, does "mainstream" mean centrist and left-wing liberals, or does it include right-wing liberals too? If his pitch is, in the end, really to left-wing liberals, then a further puzzle arises. Presumably, what it means to be "left wing" is to be in favor of, or open to, radical policies that aim to uplift the worst off. So, one wonders, does this group of liberals really need a long lecture about the vices of Rawlsian liberalism and the virtues of black radical liberalism?

Not only would this be an obvious case of preaching to the choir, but it also overlooks the possibility that left-wing liberals (black, white, and other) may see considerable radical potential in Rawls's conception of justice as fairness as it currently stands. After all, Rawls's interest in egalitarian distributive justice, which distinguishes him from Nozick, is grounded in reconciling basic individual liberty with substantive socioeconomic inequality manifested in the operation of society's basic structure, so that the worst off do not get left behind by our economic prosperity. But then the debate would hinge on the question of what counts as "radical," and Mills must take care not to assume an answer that clearly loads the dice against this possibility. If, for example, he takes it to be about ending current social oppression, that's one thing, but if he says that it requires this and the rectification of past racial wrongs, that's another thing.[12] The latter is obviously a much stronger claim in need of justification, which, as far as I can tell, is never offered in the book.

Mills could say that this line of questioning is misguided because it presumes that diversity of interests among members of these groups is a problem. All one needs to assume, he might add, is that there is some common core interest that they share, such that if radical racial justice warriors can appeal to that, then we are well on our way to getting these diverse groups of white people to join the cause. He offers a thought about what this interest might be, at least when it comes to appealing to liberals on the left, right, and center spectrum. Mills writes,

> I am claiming that even centrist and right-wing liberals, if they are genuinely morally committed to racial justice, and willing to acknowledge

how white supremacy has shaped modernity and the historically dominant forms of liberalism, should be open to a corrective black liberalism far more "radical" than the current mainstream variety.[13]

This seems like a really big "if." It also shows that Mills is indeed doing some work in criticizing Rawlsian liberalism with his rather strong definition of what counts as radical while allowing that radicalness admits of degrees. The trouble with this is that those who might applaud Mills's making black reparations a demand for racial justice may also charge that his case for this is far less "radical" than one that eschews liberalism entirely. Some of these critics will say to Mills that if you really want to be a radical, then ditch the liberal redemption project and push the corrective racial justice agenda under a black Marxist or black nationalist banner.[14] And the minute Mills says we can't do that because blacks need mainstream white allies, he will lose these radicals immediately—as Martin Luther King Jr.'s troubles with Black Power advocates during the civil rights movement remind us. These radical critics will write Mills off as too damn liberal!

Lastly, Mills's response assumes, unconvincingly in my view, that if white liberals acknowledge our racial past, they will conclude that rectification is in order. The case for doubting that this will happen is related to empirical considerations drawn from social psychology. Mills puts these considerations on the table with a nod to racial realism, which has long shaped his thinking about race. Calling the racial exploitation framework a structural approach to the race problem, which follows Rawls instead of Cohen in taking the basic structure to be the subject of justice,[15] Mills says, "Another signal virtue of approaching things this way is that it would provide a more realistic sense of the *obstacles* to achieving racial justice."[16] He then tells us that a strength of the Left tradition, which takes a materialist approach to social problems, is that it aims for more than articulating normative ideals. It also aims to say how they can be made real, and it does this, Mills says, "by identifying both the barriers to a more just social order and the possible vehicles for overcoming these barriers."[17]

Racial realism identifies "rational white perception of their vested group interest in the established racial status quo"[18] as a primary barrier to realizing racial justice. And racial realists take seriously the importance of appealing to white group interests as well as morality in ending black exploitation and securing racial justice. My work on racial inequality and injustice also takes racial realism as a point of departure, and I worry that Mills fails to appreciate the seriousness of the challenge that in-group psychology poses for rallying mainstream white liberals—both garden variety and academic—around his solution to the race problem.[19] I will make my case in the sections "The Instability of Justice as Rectification" and "Rectification without Redemption" in this chapter. And, to be clear, my claim is not that Mills contradicts himself. It is that he fails to appreciate the problem these psychological considerations pose for his backward-looking principles of rectificatory justice.

If "ideology, like halitosis, is," as Terry Eagleton tells us, "what the other person has," then defenders of *white liberalism* have a bad case of it, according to Mills.[20] It is the ideological nature of *white liberalism*, a term he uses to describe Rawlsian liberalism, that makes it unfit for racial justice duty. But one need not be so harsh. After all, one can also say that *black radical liberalism*, the term he uses to characterize his view, is also ideology without meaning to denigrate it. If we describe ideology generically, not pejoratively, as a package of ideas—both descriptive and prescriptive—that are used to understand the social world and our ethical obligations, then both kinds of liberalism count as ideology. By this neutral definition, both conceptions of liberalism—the one that is blind to race (Rawlsian) and the one that is not (Millsian)—are constituted by a package of descriptive and normative claims. Thus, the uselessness of Rawlsian liberalism, according to Mills, is not due to an immutable fact about the ideology of liberalism itself. Rather, it is contingent on a certain way of developing the package of descriptive and normative elements of the ideology in ways that whitewash the racial history and thereby avoid the rectificatory principles needed to address its implications.

Mills concedes that Rawls condemns racism and racial discrimination but takes him to task for the "marginalization of race in both his explicit normative theory and his (usually more tacit) underlying descriptive theory."[21] The link between descriptive and normative theory is absolutely crucial for Mills. One cannot produce a satisfactory normative theory, with suitable principles for addressing the race problem, unless one starts with an adequate descriptive theory that puts racial domination front and center. Rawlsian liberalism runs into trouble, he argues, precisely because it engages in the wrong kind of idealizing. So, to be clear, Mills is not against idealizing per se. He is against idealizing that confounds the pursuit of racial justice. When theorizing about a just society, we can start from the premise of a society without any history of racial injustice, which he accuses Rawlsians of doing, or from one with such a history that needs to be rectified. Only the latter ideal, which he labels the *rectificatory ideal*, can help establish what is required to remedy past racial injustice or help us choose the right public policy options.[22] Race-based affirmative action, targeted basic income for blacks, and black reparations are examples of the types of proposals that could be justified by this more radical liberal vision of justice. Because of the emphasis on rectification, I shall call Mills's alternative conception justice as rectification.

To be fair, in his closing pages Mills stresses that he is only prepared to offer an outline of his alternative theory of justice as rectification, saving for future work a more detailed brief of the "project of articulating a black radical liberalism that is true both to the (idealized) liberal tradition, the liberalism that *should have been*, and respectful of the black diasporic experience in modernity, victims of the liberalism that actually was and is."[23] My critical remarks are meant to provide food for thought for this future work. And I hope that one lesson extracted from them may be especially useful for Mills and his disciples within and outside of philosophy: if black radical liberalism takes the psychological obstacles to ending racial injustice seriously, as racial realism requires, then to have any hope of radicalizing liberalism for mass consumption in white America, its normative prescriptions must be forward looking, not backward looking. They must take us beyond past white sins in generating support for a society with less racial injustice.[24] With white social psychology being what it is, justice as fairness may offer us a surer, steadier, and stabler route to making reasonable headway on the race problem than justice as rectification.

Mills's Redemption Song

It is one thing to criticize Rawlsian liberalism and another to offer a competing theory of justice that is as comprehensive and illuminating as justice as fairness. Ironically, while Mills condemns Rawls for never getting around to giving us principles for rectificatory justice, in the twenty years since the publication of *The Racial Contract* Mills has yet to produce an alternative systematic conception of justice. Anyone familiar with his work (and famous lecture handouts!) knows that criticizing social contract theory, Rawls, and Rawlsian liberals has been Mills's calling card over the years. But fans of his work, of which I am one, are entitled to expect more from him this many years after he first exposed the racial contract. A major disappointment, especially for those of us working on race in the tradition of analytic political philosophy, is that Mills relegates the thing we have all been waiting for to his epilogue (as prologue)—a statement of his alternative nonideal theory of liberalism and its principles for addressing the urgent demands of racial justice.

If a political ideology should be judged by whether it fulfills normative promises, we should celebrate liberalism only if it delivers the goods. Mills distinguishes two conceptions of liberalism: *ideal theory liberalism* and *nonideal theory liberalism*. The former instructs us about what justice demands in a make-believe, perfectly just society not blemished by group exploitation, domination, and oppression. This is the kind of liberalism that Mills attributes to Rawls. The latter variety, which Mills favors, offers us guidance on what is required in nominally liberal real societies with histories of injustice. He then draws on the actual history of race, racism, and racial injustice in the modern world to argue that ideal theory liberalism fails to deliver the normative goods of freedom, equality, and respect to blacks in America and throughout the African diaspora.[25] Mills concludes that praising this hegemonic ideology is hardly in order. More fittingly, we should treat liberalism's failure as a public relations nightmare that requires immediate action. He considers three options.

Do we toss liberalism out with the trash and find another critical framework for our emancipatory and rectificatory justice political goals?[26] Do we cry foul and rebut the charge that liberalism in its current form fails blacks?[27] Or do we distinguish between two kinds of liberalism—the kind that is blind to race, racism, and racial injustice (an ideal racial liberalism or white liberalism) and the kind that is not (a nonideal deracialized or black radical liberalism)—and argue that the latter is better suited for generating principles of rectificatory justice to fulfill liberalism's promise and merit our esteem? Mills pursues this redemptive strategy in *Black Rights/White Wrongs*.

Calling attention to the discrepancy between America's liberal proclamations and its illiberal practices places Mills within a venerable tradition of black philosophers. For example, consider these words: "Uprooted from the sunny land of his forefathers by the white man's cupidity and selfishness, ruthlessly torn from all the ties of clan and tribe, dragged against his will over thousands of miles of unknown waters to a strange land among strange peoples," writes Anna Julia Cooper, "the Negro was transplanted to this continent in order to produce chattels and beasts of burden for a nation 'conceived in liberty and dedicated to the proposition that all men are created equal.'"[28]

When we take stock of liberalism's historical legacy as Cooper once did, and as Mills does now, we find that the racial damage tally, which cries out for corrective justice, extends many years backward and forward from when Cooper made her insightful observation at the dawn of the twentieth century.[29] But before this normative goal can be realized and suitable principles of rectificatory justice advanced, Mills maintains that the racial nature of the American polity and ideal theory liberalism have to be confronted and deracialized. Only then can this dominant ideology be transformed to serve the more radical agenda to address past and present racial injustice and finally resolve liberalism's race problem.

So, according to Mills, deracializing ideal theory liberalism is necessary for transforming and radicalizing liberalism for racial justice work. And he utilizes nonideal theory—a methodological approach to ethics and political philosophy that takes its cue from real-world experiences of racial injustice—to get the job done. According to Mills, "The best way to bring about the ideal [of a more just society] is by recognizing the non-ideal [actual injustice of society], and that by assuming the ideal or the near-ideal, one is only guaranteeing the perpetuation of the non-ideal."[30]

Mills is the foremost champion of radicalizing liberalism for realizing racial justice. Yet black philosophers have been keenly aware of liberalism's race problem for generations. Some say "To hell with liberalism" and look elsewhere (e.g., Marxism, pragmatism, prophetic Christianity, critical theory, existentialism, intersectionality, and other traditions) for a political philosophy of black emancipation and radical social transformation (*Rejection*). Others recommend retaining mainstream liberalism as is and demonstrate that it already contains the principles it needs to uplift blacks and complete the unfinished journey to emancipation in liberal America (*Retention*). Another strategy, more controversial than Rejection and more ambitious than Retention, is to view race as part of the conceptual architecture of liberalism, to revise how we think about liberalism in the light of this observation, and to produce an alternative conception of liberalism better suited to deliver the necessary principles for addressing the legacy of racial injustice in the United States.

In pursuing this third strategy, what distinguishes Mills from those who came before him and from his contemporaries is his claim that the whitewashed liberalism that Western political philosophy has sold to the world—with its origins in the social contract tradition—is not really color-blind at all, contrary to appearances. It is *racial*, and so the apparent contradiction between liberal pronouncements about the freedom, dignity, and equality of all men and the practices of racial exploitation, domination, and oppression is merely apparent. Thus, the key to reclaiming liberalism's true emancipatory potential is to deracialize it—to see it for what it really is, a *white* liberalism, and to replace it with a *black* radical liberalism. I shall call this strategy *Redemption*, because if liberalism could sing a song after Mills got done with deracializing and thus radicalizing it, it would likely sing this well-known gospel verse: "If you run across anybody that used to know me / tell them I'm doing fine / The last time that you saw me / I was lifting up holy hands / I'll tell them I've been redeemed." Although Mills has done more than any other philosopher to call our attention to liberalism's race problem, his case for its redemption remains a work in progress.

According to Mills, a troubling consequence of Rawls's philosophical construction of an ideal society, which mistakes an ideal norm for actual reality, is that it obscures the need for principles that can adjudicate "the merits of competing policies aimed at correcting for a long history of white supremacy" and black domination.[31] While distributive justice supplies principles that regulate how we divide and distribute the benefits and burdens of our social cooperation and the goods essential to citizenship, justice as rectification provides principles to remedy the legacy of wrongful distributions associated with the racial contract. Throughout his work Mills makes the point, time and time again, that Rawlsian justice is concerned with how to distribute goods and not with how to correct the wrongful past distributions that have resulted in our actual circumstances where we find unjust racial inequality and black disadvantage.

Thus, as he puts it, Rawls neither supplies nor leaves us a way to derive "the principles of transitional justice necessary to move us from our actual ill-ordered racist society, characterized by structural subordination (where races do exist), to the well-ordered society where his two principles of ideal distributive justice apply (and races do not exist)."[32] One could say that Rawls and Mills are engaged in two very different philosophical projects. Mills might wish for Rawls to pursue another project, but that he does not hardly seems like a serious philosophical objection to the project itself.

Mills has done more to develop his criticisms of Rawlsian justice than he has to work out and defend his positive alternative. Yet the basic essentials of his nonideal conception of justice, which takes the racial contract as a point of conceptual departure, include at least three distinct principles:[33]

1. racially unequal citizenship;
2. racial exploitation; and
3. racial disrespect.

Principle 1 reflects the actual history of treating blacks in America first as noncitizens and then later as second-class citizens. Principle 2 captures the historical systemic distribution of the burdens and benefits of social cooperation, including the primary social goods, in ways that have worked to realize and reproduce white advantage and black disadvantage. Principle 3 calls attention to the historical stigmatization of blacks as inferior, and how this, in turn, has rationalized treating them in accordance with principles 1 and 2 simply because of their racial membership. Hence, Mills's general conception of justice as rectification calls for the rectification of inequality of status, exploitation and its enduring consequences, and group-based disrespect. And he maintains that acting to bring about the social reform and resource redistribution that his conception requires is necessary to move us from our actual ill-ordered racist society to a well-ordered one.[34]

Rawls says, "However attractive a conception of justice might be on other grounds, it is seriously defective if the principles of moral psychology are such that it fails to engender in human beings the requisite desire to act upon it."[35] This observation raises a worry about justice as rectification. The worry is that it is unable, given what we know from research in social psychology, to secure a requisite desire in whites en masse to act upon it, which renders this conception incapable of securing the stable scheme of social cooperation over time needed to transition from an ill-ordered racist society to a well-ordered one.

Rawls defines society as a fair system of mutual social cooperation over time, and he tells us that this is the most fundamental idea in the theory of justice.[36] He further distinguishes the point of a philosophical conception of justice from its broader consequences. For Rawls the point of distributive justice is to specify what rights and duties individuals possess, and how the burdens and benefits of their social cooperation should be distributed. One important consequence, which he takes up, is how a conception of justice contributes to stability. So, when assessing a conception of justice, not only must we ask what principles of justice should determine appropriate distributive shares in a fair system of social cooperation, but we should also ask whether prospective principles of justice (whether distributive or rectificatory) make the scheme of social cooperation more or less stable. If they make it more stable, the conception of justice will be obeyed more often than not, citizens will carry out their required duties willingly, and they will feel guilty when transgressing these principles or standing in the way of their realization within the basic structure of society.

After drawing this distinction between the point and consequences of principles of justice, Rawls claims that a conception of justice must also be evaluated by its broader consequences, and that "one conception of justice is preferable to another when its broader consequences are more desirable."[37] If we follow Rawls on this point, considerations of stability supply an important yardstick for measuring the attractiveness of a conception of justice. I will use this yardstick to take issue with justice as rectification. Mills's work is congenial to philosophers who want to talk about race, history, and reparations. And it demonstrates the value of reading widely in history, sociology, psychology, and other disciplines to get a better handle on race and racism. Yet Mills and his followers must nonetheless take great care in spelling out the philosophical implications of this for a theory of justice. Egalitarian-minded political philosophers who have been brought up on Rawls, Dworkin, and Cohen (who, by the way, seem more like allies than enemies in the radical struggle for racial justice to some of us despite their relative silence about race matters) will be especially interested in this. Some will wonder whether the broader consequences of justice as rectification are more desirable.

Mills believes that once we set the racial record straight, the need for modifying a liberal theory of justice to include principles of rectificatory justice will become apparent. Not only is this not obvious, but it is also unclear whether such a modification would be a good idea, particularly if some nonideal theorists are also committed racial realists. As I will argue in the "Rectification without Redemption" section in this chapter, drawing on evidence from social psychology, when we take account of what we know about dominant in-group psychology, incorporating such principles seems like a bad idea if we are concerned with securing the social cooperation of the dominant racial group (whites) in the collective project to address white wrongs and advance black rights.

Stability and a Sense of Justice

Charles Mills's redemption of liberalism does not come cheap. In fact, as I shall argue, justice as rectification may do more harm than good for advancing the cause of realizing racial justice within a multiracial progressive coalition that includes a significant number of white mainstream liberals.

Mills's observations about the whiteness of the social contract notwithstanding, Rawlsians will say that maintaining a fair system of mutual cooperation over time requires principles of justice that can support a stable scheme of social cooperation.[38] And this seems to me right whatever the racial demographics of the contracting parties—presumably even the Wakandans would insist on this! Stability is essentially a matter of ensuring that persons bound by principles of justice reliably act as they require, or at the very least do not impede changes to the basic structure that these principles demand. So, stability is neither realized nor guaranteed by persons merely appreciating the rational force of an argument for why they would or should choose particular principles of justice under certain idealized conditions.

For instance, Rawls demonstrates the rational force of his principles of justice as fairness using the original position thought experiment. But he does not believe that this analytic construction suffices to establish that persons will behave as directed by these principles. As he puts it, "How persons will act in the particular circumstances when, as the rules specify, it is their turn to do their part is a different question altogether."[39] Rational persons will concede that the derivation gives grounds for why they ought to acknowledge and be bound by the principles of justice mutually. However, rationality does not dictate that they feel bound by these principles, where this is something that must happen if they are to do what justice requires. For this to happen, reason must give way to emotion: persons feel bound to do what principles of justice prescribe when they possess what Rawls calls "a sense of justice," which he follows Rousseau in describing as "a true sentiment of the heart enlightened by reason, the natural outcome of our primitive affections."[40]

It is this sense of justice, which persons possess, that supports the stability of a fair scheme of mutual cooperation over time. But the continued existence of this scheme of cooperation is not guaranteed. For it to realize the freedom and equality of persons who form the social contract, the principles of justice ordering it must be able to generate a sense of justice. And because persons participating in this scheme are, by and large, strangers to one another, having a sense of justice does not require that persons have natural ties of affection, trust, or loyalty to those with whom one is cooperating—ties that typically exist between friends and family. So, in a large scheme of social cooperation, such as within a modern state where there will typically not be such ties between cooperating citizens, the sense of justice must on its own accord be able to maintain the scheme of mutual cooperation.

Of course, over time, as certain bonds of association develop, such as bonds rooted in treating one another as fellow citizens, the stability afforded to existing social arrangements by the sense of justice will be enhanced. What Rawls calls "association guilt," which stems from the desire to be a good sport in dealings with others, will reinforce what he calls "principle guilt," which stems from the desire to be a just person in dealings with other people with whom one is cooperating. When this happens, both kinds of guilt will jointly add to the inherent stability of the cooperative scheme. But the crucial point is that for persons mutually cooperating to maintain or bring about fair social institutions and to sustain them over time, principle guilt and a sense of justice are indispensable for maintaining a stable scheme of social cooperation.

It might be that merely recognizing that one is benefiting from social injustice without feeling guilty suffices to engage some people to join the social transformation project and to support corrective justice goals such as black reparations. In this case such recognition would have a motivating force, though one might certainly feel guilty for trying to retain the benefits of injustice. And we may certainly question whether guilt is the appropriate moral affect to move persons to comply with principles of justice and to transform unjust social arrangements into more just ones. Furthermore, some may even wish to argue that emotions with positive valence (e.g., love, humility), rather than with negative valence (e.g., guilt, shame, resentment), are also suitable for this purpose.[41] However, my argument against Mills does not turn on settling these matters. I am simply assuming that insofar as Rawls makes guilt a central factor in explaining the stability of a well-ordered society governed by justice as fairness, it may also be one in explaining the instability of an ill-ordered society governed by justice as rectification. There is no reason to think that Rawls's observations about the sense of justice, guilt, and stability only have purchase when considering well-ordered societies. When dealing with actual ill-ordered societies (such as our own) that we wish to move closer to the ideal of a well-ordered society, this also requires the cooperation of free and equal persons over time.

Hence, whatever conception of justice we call upon to facilitate this transition from America's actual ill-ordered society, where racial inequality, racial exploitation, and racial disrespect prevail, to a well-ordered society must also be able to arouse a sense of justice and elicit feelings of guilt in persons required to comply with its demands. Without this, the scheme of social cooperation will be unstable, and the conception of justice will be seriously defective.

Although we can grant Mills's point about the importance of seeking principles of justice suitable for effecting the transition to a well-ordered society, the content of such principles is not the only thing we must pay heed to if we want to achieve this larger goal. Even nonideal theorists of justice—or better, especially such theorists[42]—must also ask whether a prospective conception of justice can generate a stable enough consensus so that persons bound by it endeavor to act as it demands. And this inquiry requires that we turn our attention to social psychology, which Mills has made central to his case for why liberalism's race problem has been so intractable.

In this book Mills does not bother with an elaborate, original, position-style thought experiment to show that citizens of a nonideal society will select his principles of justice as rectification.[43] But it cannot be taken for granted that a consensus on them will emerge, that they will be complied with, and that the move from an ill-ordered racist society to a well-ordered nonracist one will proceed without fuss. Given some of what we know about racial group differences in beliefs about injustice and inequality,[44] as well as the extent to which justice and equality have been realized for blacks in America,[45] it is highly improbable that consensus will emerge on Mills's preferred principles of justice as rectification any time soon, and certainly not across racial lines.[46]

But even if we suppose that there would be such consensus—that is, we suppose that blacks and whites would equally accept the need for principles of rectificatory justice and perhaps also accept that Mills's preferred principles are the best available ones for transitional justice—it is still highly doubtful that whites en masse in the actual world (as we know it) will do what these principles demand. And this entails that a scheme of mutual social cooperation rooted in a conception of justice as rectification will be inherently unstable. In other words, it will be unable to arouse a sense of justice, and to engender feelings of guilt, for infractions against the social institutions proscribed by its rectificatory principles, or for failures to pursue the resource redistribution that they demand. To see why this is so, we must turn to evidence from social psychology.

The Instability of Justice as Rectification

Social conditioning is an obvious barrier to seeing white privilege for what it is, namely, when social institutions, arrangements, and practices are set up to confer illegitimate advantages on whites and disadvantages on nonwhites. Such conditioning, which can happen in a variety of ways, in the family, in schools, and in the public domain, often teaches that society is a meritocracy and that everyone's lot in life is essentially determined by their work and effort, and in these post-*Brown*, post–civil rights, and, dare I say, "postracial" days it is hardly ever determined by arbitrary factors beyond a person's control, such as their racial, ethnic, or family background. To think otherwise, so the story goes, is nothing more than an excuse to deflect personal responsibility for an individual's disadvantage or shortcomings. This social conditioning often proclaims the importance of charity and goodwill toward those who are needy and less fortunate. But this too can deflect attention away from the ways in which whites are overprivileged to how blacks are underprivileged, only to reinforce the general message that blacks are where they are as a group— substantively unequal and relatively disadvantaged— largely as a result of failure by blacks to take advantage of formal equality of opportunity, goodwill, and charity.[47]

Social conditioning is one instance of an informational basis for masking the reality of white privilege. It operates by communicating information, explicitly or implicitly, which paints a certain picture of how our social world functions and the role that race plays within it. Socialization is a familiar example of how individuals can receive information that can make them oblivious to their own privilege or can afford them heightened awareness of the privilege of others. The personal experience of privilege, or lack of such experience, clearly can have the same effect.[48]

A less familiar though equally powerful way of accounting for racial group–based differences in our beliefs about injustice, inequality, and disadvantage is linked to differences in the content of background knowledge about the history of race and race relations. For instance, there is evidence that racial group differences in perceptions of racism are rooted in differences in historical knowledge, which leads blacks to see or exaggerate racism and whites to deny or diminish racism.[49] The content of a person's background knowledge seems as though it should indeed make a difference to their judgments about racism in current events.

This evidence supports the conjecture that a black person more familiar with the history of excessive police force against blacks in America (e.g., Rodney King, Amadou Diallo, Eleanor Bumpurs, Bloody Sunday in Selma) and a white person without this knowledge might have different takes on the fatal shooting of Michael Brown by law enforcement in Ferguson, Missouri. The black person will be more likely to see racism, while the white person will be more likely to deny it. And if we further suppose that such differences in perception are not simply one-off instances of blacks having read the racial news and whites not having read it on a given day but, rather, part of more systematic differences in the historical events that blacks and whites are taught, then we can see how such differences in background knowledge might explain the epistemological basis of racial group-based differences in the perception of racism in current events.

This psychological evidence establishes a simple point in very general terms—persons who know more about the history of racism are better positioned epistemologically to perceive racism in the present. So, if the average black person generally knows more than the average white person about the history of racism, then the average black person is better positioned to perceive it in the present. The evidence further establishes that correcting for this historical knowledge deficit in whites contributes to closing the gap between black and white perceptions of racism in current events. By enlightening whites about the racial injustices of the past, they will be more likely to see racial injustices of the present for what they are, or so that is the hope.

Mills might be tempted to seize upon this evidence to claim that this is one of the chief virtues of bringing the racial contract to light. He may contend that by unmasking the actual exclusive nature of the social contract, as an agreement among whites to privilege themselves and to subordinate blacks in legal, social, and political relations for white benefit, the hope is that whites will perceive the racial injustices of the present, have their sense of justice aroused, feel guilt, and be moved to join with blacks in undertaking the necessary reforms of the basic social institutions to correct for these injustices, moving us toward a well-ordered nonracist society. But I am afraid this is wishful thinking.

Modifying social contract theory along the lines proposed by Mills to capture the actual, nonideal history of white oppression and black subordination in America could indeed have significant social psychological benefits, particularly for liberal white Americans. In addition to reducing racial prejudice, which may, in turn, improve race relations, removing blinders to the systemic dimensions of "white privilege," that is, making the racial nature of the social contract explicit, might even elicit white support for social change and encourage whites to embrace responsibility for mitigating racial inequality and addressing black disadvantage.[50] However, there is social psychological evidence that whites must come to feel collective guilt if such historical consciousness raising is to yield these and other benefits.[51] Collective guilt, which is a valuable moral response according to this research, amounts to one's group (in this case, whites) feeling remorse or distress upon realizing that group members have unjustly or illegitimately harmed another group (in this case, blacks) without rectifying the damage.[52]

If one could make whites aware of the racial contract and engender in them feelings of collective guilt for their privilege, the undeserved benefits associated with it, and the harms done to blacks in creating and sustaining white privilege, then perhaps getting whites to sign on to—or not press for renegotiating—a theory of justice that includes principles of rectificatory justice to correct these past wrongs would be a simple task. But the problem is that there are substantial barriers to removing white blinders to appreciating the racial contract and its consequences for present-day racial inequalities and black disadvantage, as well as equally substantial barriers to eliciting white guilt for them.

When focused largely on the epistemological barriers to these outcomes, it is tempting to think that merely enlightening whites, say, by having them do a serious study of the racial contract, may suffice to remove white resistance to signing on to justice as rectification. But this is shortsighted. One could argue that the problem is not merely one of misinformation or insufficient enlightenment about America's racial past and its ramifications for today but, rather, a problem having to do with whites being motivated to maintain a positive group image.

There is considerable empirical evidence that whites (as with any social group) are motivated to maintain a positive conception of their group identity, which supports the belief that they are where they are supposed to be in the social hierarchy.[53] This phenomenon poses a considerable psychological barrier to whites acknowledging the contemporary consequences of the racial contract, including present-day racial inequalities. Moreover, it is a barrier to whites having their sense of justice aroused by racial inequality and black disadvantage and to feeling collective guilt for them.[54]

Therefore, conceding white privilege or buying Mills's racial contract story would threaten whites' positive conception of their racial group. For one, it would open whites up to the distressing feeling that where they are in the social order, their current allotment of distributive shares, is not exclusively due to their individual merit or talent but instead due in large part to the privileged status historically accorded their racial group in the distribution of burdens and benefits within the basic structure of American society with its dark history of racial injustice.[55]

To be sure, whites that more strongly identify with their whiteness, ones who are heavily invested in this identity, will be even more resistant to efforts to enlighten them about the racial contract and its contemporary consequences.[56] Indeed, these individuals will be strongly motivated to resist efforts to remove their epistemological blinders to white privilege. And in the absence of genuine feelings of collective guilt for white group privilege, these persons, as well as those not nearly as invested in their white identity, may to varying degrees harbor some resentment and other negative sentiments to being confronted with the racial contract and its modern-day legacy. So, while it may seem that the solution to the race problem is simply to somehow get whites to feel collective guilt for their white privilege, this is easier said than done. Here, too, there will be both informational and motivational barriers to confront.

Defensive mechanisms to protect their positive white identity and to assuage white collective guilt for existing racial inequality and black disadvantage include such things as minimizing the alleged harm done to blacks, legitimizing inequality, victim blaming, and denying white privilege. A particularly powerful defense is when whites create distance between themselves and the past harm done to blacks. An example of this would be to claim, "It wasn't me, us, or my family that did those things to blacks back then."[57] And this can obviously be a way of deflecting white guilt. However, those wishing to keep white folks on the hook for past and present racial injustice and black disadvantage might respond, "But you *are* responsible and should feel guilty because the perpetrators were white just like you and thus you inherit their racial sins."[58] This tactic might prompt a distinction between two kinds of white people, the good ones and the bad ones. With this distinction in hand, whites might create distance from the past harms by claiming that the harms of the past such as the racial contract, black chattel slavery, and post-Reconstruction Jim Crow segregation were perpetrated by atypical whites, indeed bad or perhaps even evil whites who were really monsters and not good white people at all.[59]

Coming to terms with the ways in which whites have benefited and continue to benefit from white privilege requires that whites— middle- and upper-class liberal whites in particular—give up the idea that they are more enlightened and are morally superior to the whites of the past (who they may or may not be related to by blood) who owned, whipped, starved, raped, and abused black slaves.[60] So long as distancing and other defenses to project positive white identity are at work, the prospects for arousing a sense of justice and feelings of white guilt for the racial contract and its legacy and the prospects for getting whites to cooperate in (or not to impede) the collective political project of transforming social institutions as prescribed by justice as rectification are bleak, to say the least. And this seems true even if emotions with positive valence, such as love, can do some motivational work, and if, for some white folks, the mere recognition that they benefit from racial injustice can move them to act.

A final but especially powerful way in which whites protect their positive group identity pertains to how they frame injustice and inequality, which influences what, if any, action they are willing to take to address them. So, for example, when considering existing racial injustice and racial disparities, individuals can choose to frame them as instances of white advantage or black disadvantage. The latter framing might call attention to overt or implicit discrimination against blacks, which deprives them of liberty or fair equality of opportunity. The former framing may call attention to how the basic institutions of society are arranged so as to afford whites undeserved advantages and an unequal share of primary social goods. Framing inequalities as white advantage or white privilege not only predicts white guilt but also predicts white support for certain forms of affirmative action for blacks.[61]

Some evidence supports the claim that whites are motivated to adopt the black disadvantage framing of racial injustice and racial inequality to protect their positive group identity and to assuage collective guilt for it.[62] Thus, this evidence identifies a powerful defensive strategy whites can select for resisting Mills's story of the racial contract and its legacy, which in his hands is a story of white racial domination. Rather than viewing this dark past as a story of undeserved white privilege, whites—especially strongly identified ones—might be motivated to frame this legacy in terms of anti-black discrimination.

One consequence of this weaker, less threatening, framing of racial injustice and racial inequality is that it will not be sufficient to generate a groundswell of white support for policies designed to effect radical structural changes in the institutions of society to dismantle undeserved white privilege. At most, anti-black discrimination measures, and perhaps milder forms of affirmative action, both of which fall far short of the demands of Mills's conception of justice as rectification, might gain some support when racial inequity is framed as black disadvantage. But even this hope for modest forms of affirmative action might be squashed if whites perceive that affirmative action for blacks will come at their expense, by unjustly curtailing whites' chances of access to opportunity. All bets may be off if whites think that righting white wrongs must come at the expense of white rights.

So, if rectification amounts to taking an unjust situation rooted in past wrongs and setting it right, in this case by reforming ill-ordered social institutions to rectify inequality of racial status, black exploitation, and black disrespect, then given what we know from social psychology, rectification for blacks is unlikely in our nonideal world as we know it. If such reform involves making a transition from an ill-ordered racist society to a well-ordered nonracist one, and this transition is to be guided by a public conception of justice, then norms of rectificatory justice will render the required scheme of social cooperation unstable insofar as they are unlikely to arouse a sense of justice and to engender white guilt.

Mills and I may ultimately have sharply different views about the prospects for overcoming the psychological barriers discussed here, now or in the future. I suspect that I am more cynical about this than he is. But supposing that the blinders to white privilege could be lifted and whites could be made to feel collective guilt, it is far from clear that this would be sufficient to get them to rally around his call for rectificatory justice and black reparations. While the social psychological evidence supports thinking that these things may indeed reduce white prejudice against blacks and increase white support for antidiscrimination measures and even for affirmative action,[63] it is largely silent on the issue of increased white support for racial reparations.[64] And one of the recent exceptions to this silence raises further worries about Mills's leap from awareness of the racial contract and past injustice against blacks to support for rectificatory justice and black reparations. As it turns out, the issue of reparations for historical injustice against blacks is as complicated on the psychology terrain as it is on the philosophical one. Some of the same mechanisms discussed earlier—desire to preserve positive group identity, victim blaming, distancing, and framing inequity—apply here as well in accounting for why policies falling short of reparations may be endorsed while reparations may not be.

Mills's conception of justice as rectification—with its backward-looking principles—will not be able to generate its own support under nonideal circumstances. The psychology of white resistance to rectificatory racial justice, as we have examined it, suggests that his principles will not arouse a sense of justice in whites en masse and a corresponding desire to act on these principles in our actual nonideal world. Moreover, failure to work toward (or at least not to oppose) bringing about the reforms that justice as rectification requires will not engender a sense of principle guilt in whites en masse. A conception of justice as rectification is therefore bound to be unstable. And insofar as a conception of justice must be evaluated, as Rawls tells us, at least in part, by its consequences for maintaining the stability of a scheme of social cooperation among persons not joined by blood or friendship but simply by just principles, justice as rectification proves to be seriously defective.

Rectification without Redemption

Charles Mills has been a pioneer in the analytic political philosophy tradition when it comes to illuminating the psychological barriers to moving the white majority to undo racial injustice. Some of his earliest reflections on this, as well as unmistakable evidence of his racial realist orientation, appeared in the pages of *Ethics* many years ago, where he writes,

> From this perspective—doubly "realist," as I have argued elsewhere—it is an unfortunate but quite unsurprising fact that people's moral psychologies are shaped by their social situation in such a way as to make it generally unlikely that any but a few will perceive the necessity for antisystemic change of a fundamental kind. So there will be a general conservative bias, by which moral theory will tend to adjust itself to material structures rather than vice versa. But in addition, as earlier

claimed, in the United States the white majority's moral psychology will be shaped not merely by class but by racial structure, and this racialized identity and psychology ("Herrenvolk ethics") will be characterized by "settled expectations" of racial privilege as a baseline, and a blurred moral vision and diminished affect where the plight of blacks is concerned. Thus it is doubly unlikely that they will recognize, and be moved purely by, considerations of justice—as, in fact, the history of the black civil rights struggle has shown.[65]

In chapter 4 of *Black Rights/White Wrongs*, on white ignorance, Mills returns to this theme, drawing on social psychology to document how white supremacy is secured from moral challenges and how this explains why racial exploitation has been so difficult to undo.

There is, of course, a difference between claiming that white people cannot be moved to pursue racial justice on moral grounds alone and claiming that racial justice cannot be justified on such grounds. Here I agree with Mills that endorsing the former does not entail endorsing the latter.[66] We both agree that ending racial exploitation and achieving a more just society is the end goal, and that one can make a moral case for this. And we both agree that appealing to the white majority's sense of political morality does not suffice to move them to join the struggle to transform the unjust basic social structure where the dominant place of whites in the socioeconomic order is at stake. This will be true of whites across the right, center, and left of the political spectrum, and even more true of white people that strongly identify with their racial identity over other aspects of their social identity. Where we disagree is whether his backward-looking principles of rectificatory justice can command a sense of justice given the counterproductive effects of the white majority's moral psychology. If they cannot, his solution to liberalism's race problem brings us no closer to achieving racial justice in the real world.

In reply, Mills may mention virtues of his effort, such as opening up dialogue about race and racism in philosophy, contributing to the un-whitening of philosophy, and expressing moral condemnation of mainstream liberals who ignore white supremacy and racial injustice. He can say that even if putting rectificatory justice on the philosophical agenda does not have the real-world impact that he hopes, these virtues nevertheless constitute a significant intramural contribution to philosophy. I do not disagree with any of this. But Rawlsians can also mention the virtues of their approach to justice within the broader intramural exercise of political philosophy, which includes demonstrating how egalitarian liberals can reconcile the apparent conflict between protecting basic liberties and promoting egalitarian goals within a coherent theory of distributive justice better than competing theories. They too can certainly say that this is an important philosophical contribution, even if the resulting theory does not offer principles of corrective justice that can move us from the actual world of racial injustice to a more just world. So, what's good for the goose is good for the gander.

The trouble is that Rawls, unlike Mills, did not set out to defend his approach to justice by demonstrating its real-world impact or by claiming such impact. Mills's project is based on reworking the liberal tools (some might say the "master's tools") to make them suitable instruments for ending racial exploitation and achieving racial justice. So, for Mills, trumpeting the intramural philosophical virtues of his solution simply will not cut it. He needs to convince us that the barriers to getting the white majority to use these refashioned tools are not insurmountable. To be sure, principles of justice can set a moral vision that people find attractive. And whether justice as rectification does this and can move the white majority to act in the right way is certainly an empirical question. Yet the evidence marshaled here, and that has been central to Mills's reflections on white social psychology over the years, paints a dim picture of this prospect.

Mills's redemption song is one that he hopes mainstream white liberals will join him in singing. I have claimed that they are the main audience for *Black Rights/White Wrongs*, though he clearly has a message for black mainstream liberals, whom he criticizes for thinking that unmodified Rawlsian liberalism can support a radical racial justice agenda. If conscientious white liberals are really serious about eliminating the scourge of historical racial injustice and its legacy from the American landscape, and they are willing to be cured of white ignorance, Mills's message for them is that they should cast aside white liberalism and become champions of black radical liberalism. And with as much soul as they can muster, mainstream white liberals should sing the black radical liberal redemption song too!

As Mills sees things, black radical liberalism "should be accepted (though not uncritically, of course) by conscientious white liberals who are presumably also committed to such a correction, purging, and reconstruction of liberal theory."[67] It would be interesting to know whether Mills thinks that a rejection of black radical liberalism, or a refusal to sing this song, tells against the goodness of a white liberal, or whether it immediately opens them up to the charge of white ignorance or white blindness. If so, this would be an all-too-easy way out of confronting critical worries about his liberalism redemption project. With this focus on conscientious white liberals, it is fair to ask: What assumptions are we making about this group? What other assumptions can we make as we deracialize white liberalism? What other things are mainstream white liberals committed to when they think about and evaluate theories of justice, and how might these commitments interact with assumptions about them, including their psychology, to preclude their endorsement of black radical liberalism's principles of rectificatory justice? Assessing the prospect of black radical liberalism to yield the progressive agenda sought by Mills requires attending to these questions too.

In this chapter I have argued that the answers give us reason to worry that white mainstream liberals may be reluctant to join in the singing of Mills's redemption song, especially if this means supporting black reparations, affirmative action, and other race-specific policies. The same epistemology and psychology of white ignorance that explains the lack of progress in solving the race problem—by Mills's own reckoning—also dooms justice as rectification. Whites may want to retain their racial advantage and may, consciously or unconsciously, resist embracing principles that appear too threatening to the racial status quo.[68] "It may well be, then, that apart from all the other problems to be overcome," as Mills confesses, "this simple fact alone is powerful enough to derail the whole project."[69] Despite his heroic efforts to solve liberalism's race problem, this worry stands. I am sure that Mills will keep singing his black radical liberal redemption song, but I am also sure that the accompanying choir will be significantly smaller than he hopes.[70] Black radical liberalism cannot save us because it pursues small-tent remedies under a race-first flag. The next chapter offers my big-tent alternative. It pursues racial justice by seeking remedies for issues faced by marginalized populations. I call these "postracial remedies" and believe that they are called for in society that remains firmly within the grip of postracial mythology.

5
Postracial Remedies

Talk of a "postracial" America was widespread after Barack Obama won the White House. To many, electing a black man to the nation's highest office signified that the days of slavery, Jim Crow, and the civil rights movement were behind us and that race was no longer a barrier to achieving the American Dream.[1] Although it is certainly premature to celebrate the passing of racism in America, this postracial narrative is both prominent in our political discourse and deeply entrenched in US Supreme Court doctrine. We must take this fact seriously, along with the reality of stark polarization about race matters, to pursue politically feasible and constitutionally sound remedies for racial inequality. This chapter defends "postracial remedies," as we shall call them, as essential tools for realizing egalitarian aspirations. They represent big-tent remedies. America's real-world circumstances require big-tent remedies for issues faced by marginalized populations and around which they can build broad coalitions to address them. The specific coalitions are not set in stone and will vary depending upon the issues. However, forming them is the way forward because we must unite to fight.

By "postracial remedies," we mean remedies that seek pragmatic solutions for the economic, social, and structural problems that disproportionately burden African Americans without treating people differently because of their race. Postracial remedies are "race sensitive" but not "race specific."[2] They are race sensitive because they recognize the salience of race in American society, including *both* the existence of racial disparities and the reality of racial polarization. They are not race specific, however. Instead, they operate with the faith that effectively targeting underlying problems such as low wages, underperforming schools, and impoverished neighborhoods will benefit all Americans, especially ones in marginalized populations. Even if such interventions are motivated in part by the desire to ameliorate racial disparities, they are not mere proxies for race-specific benefits if they genuinely address such problems without regard to race. Creating a rising tide to lift all marginalized populations can help mitigate racial disparities in America.

Postracial remedies encompass, but are broader than, some other approaches that have been advocated to combat racial inequality. For example, one type of postracial remedy may substitute class (or "place") for race,[3] such as a recent initiative in New York City that establishes admission preferences at seven elementary schools for students who qualify for free and reduced lunch, English language learners, or students in the child welfare system.[4] Another type of postracial remedy is universalistic, insofar as it aims to protect all citizens rather than a particular group of them.[5] Enhanced investments in public education or free college tuition would be examples of universalistic responses to educational disparities. Many other pragmatic approaches that do not neatly fall into these categories may help to improve educational achievement for students or schools that lag behind, including improved early childhood education or before- and after-school programs, programs to enhance parental involvement or encourage students to take more responsibility for their own education, or changes in curriculum or teaching methods. We are agnostic as to whether such remedies come from the progressive left or the conservative right, whether they emphasize public or private initiatives, and whether they rely primarily on public assistance or personal responsibility or some combination of the two. The question of greatest importance is: "What works?"

A postracial remedy "works" if it remedies the problem that it is meant to address and consequently helps those in society who are adversely affected by the problem. Thus, for example, a remedy that targets underperforming schools "works" if it improves achievement by the students at such schools. A central premise of our approach is that pragmatic solutions that work to ameliorate the underlying social and economic problems that disproportionately burden blacks will, over time, reduce racial disparities. Our pragmatic commitment to what works is not merely strategic. It is also principled, in the sense that it is rooted in a normative objective of promoting social consensus, or at least minimizing social divisiveness, in pursuit of effective ways of realizing our common aims as a community. For instance, if a particular remedy such as a higher minimum wage is proposed to address income inequality, low-wage workers of various races and ethnicities may form a consensus in support of it. Similarly, if a particular remedy such as a civilian review board is proposed to address police discretionary stops and arrests, persons of various races, ethnicities, and class may achieve consensus in favor of it.

It is tempting, though mistaken, to assume that advocating postracial remedies implies acceptance of the premises of the postracial narrative. To the contrary, it is precisely because we are conscious of the ways in which race still matters, and pessimistic about overcoming the postracial narrative, that we advance a non-race-specific (not race-blind) approach to addressing racial inequality. Relatedly, we propose postracial remedies out of a genuine concern with minimizing the social divisiveness shaped by the ideological polarization over race matters in America. Thus, this view is also consistent with "antibalkanization" perspectives associated with "race moderates" whose civil rights equal protection jurisprudence is motivated, in part, by a concern with preserving social cohesion.[6]

The United States is hardly a postracial nation. Tragic police encounters with blacks in Baltimore, Ferguson, New York, South Carolina, Texas, and elsewhere remind us that race still matters and that we have a long way to go to achieve the goal of having a postracial society.[7] So, too, does evidence that job applicants with black-sounding names like Jamal and Lakisha get fewer callbacks than ones with white sounding names such as Emily and Greg,[8] as well as reports that banks are still discriminating against black communities in the home loan–lending market even though redlining is illegal.[9] More broadly, as Dr. Martin Luther King Jr. once observed, "Of all the good things in life, the Negro has approximately one half those of whites. Of the bad he has twice that of whites."[10] While the numbers may have changed a bit since Dr. King made this observation in

1967, his point still rings true today: substantial disparities endure between whites and blacks on a wide variety of indicators.

Although the reality of racial disparities is undeniable, their implications for racial justice are matters of deep disagreement. This discord, and its intractability, is consequential for understanding our argument. For most blacks and their allies on the Left, these disparities are compelling evidence of racial injustice. From this perspective, while blacks have enjoyed formal legal equality since the middle of the twentieth century, generations of oppression, and its intergenerational effects, have exacted a heavy toll on black society that has not dissipated. Notwithstanding the hard-fought gains of the civil rights era, moreover, intentional discrimination is an ongoing problem, even if it has been driven largely underground and is therefore difficult to document. Furthermore, aside from overt discrimination, implicit biases and systemic barriers also prevent blacks from achieving genuine equality. In view of these considerations, the Left (especially those pushing small-tent remedies) often concludes that race-specific remedies such as affirmative action—and perhaps even black reparations— are necessary to mitigate enduring racial inequality and to achieve racial justice in America.

This perspective contrasts sharply with the postracial narrative that is advanced by politicians and commentators on the Right and embraced by many whites and some conservative blacks. The postracial narrative acknowledges past racial wrongs but emphasizes racial progress. Slavery was abolished after the Civil War, racial segregation has been unconstitutional since *Brown v. Board of Education*, and civil rights laws in the 1960s outlawed racial discrimination. So, racial disparities can no longer be attributed to America's lamentable history of racial oppression. In short, "That was then, this is now." Under the postracial narrative, even if some intentional discrimination, implicit bias, or systemic barriers remain, racism is no longer a major obstacle to opportunity and success. Nowadays, its proponents argue, unequal outcomes have more to do with personal factors like will, effort, and discipline than with race. Thus, they conclude, it is time for black Americans to take personal responsibility for their own successes and failures and to work their way up the socioeconomic ladder like other minority groups before them. From the postracial perspective, race-specific remedies for racial inequality are not only unnecessary but are also pernicious, insofar as they breed a culture of dependency, foster racial Balkanization, and undermine the ultimate goal of a color-blind society. Thus, as Chief Justice Roberts sums up this perspective in *Parents Involved in Community Schools v. Seattle School District. No. 1*, "[t]he way to stop discrimination on the basis of race is to stop discriminating on the basis of race."[11]

As is the case in other aspects of social and public policy, these diverging accounts suggest that Americans are polarized on matters of race.[12] Blacks and whites, the Left and the Right, and Democrats and Republicans disagree about the causes, meaning, and remedies for racial inequality. Insofar as these divisions have deep philosophical and psychological roots connected with how our social identities shape our perception of race matters, they are unlikely to be overcome in the near future. Notwithstanding this reality, which must be taken seriously in our democratic society, progress can be pursued in a manner that minimizes racial polarization and works toward building coalitions to achieve solutions that work. Of course, getting beyond polarization over race is no guarantee that we can avoid it on other matters, such as class. Still, given the fraught history of race in America, sensitivity to racial exhaustion and disagreements about race are an obvious place to begin our search for less contentious common ground so as to curtail the social divisiveness that obstructs the mutual cooperation required for social progress within a democracy.[13]

Those who, like us, believe that we must take steps to alleviate the sobering reality of racial inequality, and are not naive about the depth and significance of polarization about race matters, face difficult—if not insurmountable—obstacles to race-specific remedies for this purpose. Such remedies are politically divisive and face gridlock at all levels of government. Even when dealing with well-meaning people, they elicit defensive psychological reactions as well as efforts to avoid the collective guilt that can undermine finding common ground and forging productive political coalitions to mitigate racial inequality. Race-specific remedies presume a philosophically contested understanding of the relationship between past racial discrimination and current racial disparities. In addition, and perhaps most significantly, pursuing race-specific remedies for racial inequality faces stiff odds in the courts.

The Supreme Court's equal protection jurisprudence is decidedly postracial, in the sense that decision after decision from the Court rests on postracial doctrinal principles and factual premises. This situation must be acknowledged. The Court has restricted the Equal Protection Clause to intentional discrimination by the government, concluding that the Constitution does not prohibit private acts of discrimination and rejecting challenges based on disparate impact, even when statistical analysis indicates that race is likely a factor.[14] It has held that remedying the effects of past societal discrimination is an insufficient basis for race-specific remedies (i.e., affirmative action).[15] And it has ended remedies of this sort put in place to combat previous state-sponsored racial discrimination, such as court-ordered desegregation measures in schools[16] and the preclearance provisions of the Voting Rights Act.[17]

The Court's postracial orientation limits the pursuit of legal remedies for racial inequality in two substantial ways. First, because the Constitution does not prohibit implicit, systemic, or societal racism, constitutional litigation provides little or no recourse as a means to address racial disparities in outcome that are not demonstrably caused by intentional governmental racial discrimination. Second, race-specific remedies by political actors or governmental institutions are unavailable in practice because they face a level of judicial scrutiny that is difficult to overcome.[18] Even remedies originally put in place to correct intentional discrimination by state actors have been dismantled.

Although we categorically reject the premises of postracialism and recognize the ongoing necessity of confronting those premises with the truth about ongoing discrimination and inequality, there is no denying that the postracial narrative has considerable influence in our political discourse and constitutional doctrine. So, if we take these obstacles to race-specific remedies seriously, and wish to find workable solutions to ongoing racial inequality that are politically and legally achievable, we must answer this pressing question: *What can be done to ameliorate racial inequality in a manner that takes seriously the deep polarization over race matters in America and that does not run afoul of constitutional limits reflecting the Supreme Court's postracial equal protection jurisprudence?* We believe that pursuing postracial remedies provides a promising answer.

It might be objected that our approach is weak, giving away too much to those on the other side who subscribe to vicious racism and are acting in bad faith. We can show up to fight them with the "truth" about racial inequality, its history, causes, and consequences, but if all those who subscribe to the postracial narrative are hell-bent on keeping blacks down relative to whites, then nothing short of a miracle or a successful armed struggle will produce racial progress. We proceed on the premise that this group is the exception rather than the rule, so that it is possible to build alliances in a collective effort to mitigate a social problem with which we all live: racial inequality. Our concern with building strategic alliances resonates with Martin Luther King Jr.'s unifying strategy for addressing economic injustice in America. During the civil rights era, King recognized both the possibility and necessity of building interracial alliances to address social problems that disproportionately affected African Americans.[19]

Postracialism and the Causes of Inequality

Most would agree that America aspires to become a postracial society—one in which race no longer determines life prospects or imposes barriers to equality of opportunity. The racial divide appears, however, when we ask whites and blacks about whether and to what extent this aspiration has been realized.[20] Evidence suggests that white Americans generally have a more optimistic perspective on the existence and achievability of racial equality.[21] In a survey taken after President Obama's inauguration in 2009, nearly two-thirds of whites (61 percent) professed that blacks are now equal to whites and another 21.5 percent said they would be soon.[22] Black Americans were not so optimistic. Less than 20 percent said that racial equality has been realized, nearly half (46.6 percent) said it never will be, and barely half (53.6 percent) believed that blacks would eventually be equal to whites.[23]

The belief that we have nearly achieved our postracial ideal depends on several factual premises related to the causes of racial inequality. First, the postracial narrative assumes that current inequalities are not attributable to past discrimination in the form of slavery, Jim Crow laws, and other forms of intentional racism. While the premise that the effects of past discrimination have completely dissipated in the decades since *Brown* and the enactment of civil rights legislation seems to us unrealistic, we simply cannot take for granted that blacks and whites, or the Left and the Right, will agree that the ongoing effects of past racial wrongs are a more proximate cause of racial disparities than differences in individual attributes such as will, ambition, and effort.

A second and related premise of postracialism is that intentional discrimination is no longer a widespread problem that presents a significant obstacle to equality of opportunity. In *Shelby County v. Holder*, for example, the liberal and conservative justices differed over the prevalence and impact of racial vote dilution or other measures intended to prevent minorities from a realistic chance of getting their preferred candidates in office. Similar issues arise in connection with other areas of racial inequality, for which proof of intentional discrimination is hard to come by.

A third premise of the postracial narrative relates to the significance of implicit biases and systemic barriers. From the postracial perspective, even if such problems exist, they do not constitute "racial discrimination" that would justify race-specific remedies. Every disadvantaged group must overcome implicit biases, which are endemic and cannot be solved by legal remedies. Likewise, postracialists may doubt that implicit biases or structural barriers— as opposed to agent-relative considerations—are the proximate cause of racial inequalities.

In sum, whites and conservatives are far more likely than blacks and progressives to accept the premise that we have achieved (or have nearly achieved) our postracial aspirations. The core premises of this postracial narrative include the following: (1) America no longer practices formal exclusion based on racial membership; (2) the legacy of past racial exclusion was largely rectified during the civil rights era and in the aftermath of the Great Society programs; (3) while overt discrimination in private spaces may still be a reality, it is not widespread and pervasive enough to cause persistent black disadvantage; (4) racial disparities are largely the result of agent-relative rather than agent-neutral factors such as implicit biases and systemic barriers; and (5) race-specific remedies that may once have been necessary to deal with discrimination, segregation, and anti-black animus are no longer acceptable. Postracialists need not endorse all of these premises, of course, and they may even espouse additional ones, including premises that contain agent-neutral considerations. For example, some might deny (2) and add that society must provide greater educational opportunity to rectify past racial injustice. However, they will unequivocally tilt toward placing the onus on black Americans to embrace responsibility for their disadvantage and uplift.

Current events clearly affect public perceptions of racial progress, and survey numbers may change in ways that suggest the prevalence of the postracial narrative is on the decline. For example, recognition of racial issues increased from the Trayvon Martin shooting in 2013 to the Michael Brown shooting in 2014.[24] The general trend, however, is still evident: there remains substantial polarization regarding postracialism. In the aftermath of Ferguson, we remained deeply divided on issues of race. Where postracialists tend to see racial progress and downplay the role of race in social problems such as police violence, critics reject this. A 2014 survey shows that an overwhelming majority of African Americans (80 percent) believed the Brown shooting raised issues of race compared with 37 percent of whites.[25] And nearly twice as many blacks (65 percent) believed that police had gone too far compared with whites (33 percent). It also reveals partisan divisions: 68 percent of Democrats indicated that the shooting raised issues of race compared with only 22 percent of Republicans; 56 percent of Democrats believed the police went too far compared with 20 percent of Republicans.

Recent survey polls indicate that growing numbers of people now characterize racism as a "big problem."[26] The percentage of whites (44 percent) holding this view has gone up 17 points since 2010. Yet here too there remains stark racial polarization, as 73 percent of African Americans hold this view. And a sharp partisan divide remains on the question of whether the country should go further in affording blacks equal rights, with 78 percent of Democrats saying yes, while 51 percent of Republicans say that the nation has done all that it should. The racial gap on this question is even larger, with 53 percent of whites saying the nation has not done enough and needs to continue making changes to achieve racial equality, compared with 86 percent of blacks.

Although these numbers may give reason to hope that some people can be educated about the extent to which racism remains a serious problem, they hardly constitute a sea change in the long-standing trend of racial and partisan polarization about race matters and racial progress. The good news is that the increase in the percentage of whites, Democrats, and Republicans that see race as an issue that merits attention and believe that more progress can be made toward racial equality creates an opportunity to channel this energy into constructive solutions that work to address persistent racial disparities. The cautionary advice, which we take seriously, is that if these solutions prove to be too divisive, they can easily founder on the shoals of polarization. The truth we take seriously in this chapter is that many people accept the postracial narrative notwithstanding evidence to the contrary. So, if we are to move forward in the face of deep polarization about race matters, we should do so constructively, seeking to find solutions, where we can, that promise to lift all boats.

The postracial narrative has deep philosophical and psychological roots that contribute to its influence in political discourse and equal protection jurisprudence. Political or legal advocacy that challenges its premises directly is unlikely to succeed, at least in the near term.

This does not mean that advocates for racial justice should abandon efforts to challenge the postracial narrative, but it does suggest that we should also consider alternative paths to supplement those efforts because race-specific remedies that fly in the face of postracial premises are unlikely to gain broad-based political support or survive the Supreme Court's postracial equal protection jurisprudence.

Postracial Remedies for Racial Inequality

In view of the foregoing considerations, "progressives must retool and think creatively about different approaches to racial justice."[27] Taking this call for action seriously, we argue that postracial remedies, which focus on the manifestations of racial inequality and seek politically feasible and constitutionally sound solutions, offer promise. This is not to say that postracial remedies should replace other strategies for ameliorating racial inequalities but, rather, that they are an essential means to achieve near-term benefits for real people in the here and now. Because postracial remedies are not race specific, they take the philosophical, psychological, and jurisprudential reality of the postracial narrative seriously. Nonetheless, building coalitions will require advocacy that is sensitive to the psychology of race, as well as the legal constraints that limit the use of nominally neutral measures as a pretext for racial preferences.

The search for postracial remedies is, at bottom, a pragmatic one, in the sense that it seeks to build consensus around solutions that work. This pragmatism has both a methodological and a substantive component.[28] Methodologically, pragmatism begins by identifying the problem to be addressed (in this case, black disadvantage) and then takes an incremental, experimental, and evidence-based approach to finding solutions.[29] Substantively, this approach shares pragmatism's commitment to working together to solve problems in pursuit of a common good.

Methodologically, postracial remedies begin with the problems that plague the black community—such as economic disadvantage and poverty, mass incarceration, lagging educational achievement, and residential segregation—and seek to find solutions that will work in the real world. Thus, for example, programs that focus on improving outcomes in underperforming schools hold the potential for helping individual children and, in the process, helping to close the achievement gap, which would tend to increase upward economic mobility.[30]

The causes of racial inequality are complex, interconnected, and disputed. Accordingly, postracial remedies must be multifaceted and address a variety of factors. In keeping with methodological pragmatism, we are agnostic as to the ideological premises of any given remedy, provided that the remedy works in practice.

Here, one oft-cited advantage of our decentralized system of governance is the ability of different jurisdictions to experiment with different policy solutions for social and economic problems.[31] It is expected that conservative states and localities will try conservative solutions premised on agent-relative explanations, focused on personal responsibility, and implemented through the private sector. Conversely, we might expect liberal or progressive states to try progressive solutions that focus on combating discrimination, countering implicit biases, and removing systemic barriers.

This process makes it possible to identify programs and approaches that work, build coalitions to support them, and encourage their adoption in other jurisdictions. Finding postracial remedies will not be easy. Neither ideological nor racial disagreements will magically disappear, and postracial remedies cannot eliminate racial inequality overnight. Nonetheless, the pursuit of postracial remedies can provide an effective means for addressing racial inequalities and can provide tangible benefits in the near term for those who bear the brunt of racial inequality.

While postracial remedies are not race specific, they do not require society to ignore race or racial inequalities. Thus, postracial remedies include remedies that focus on ways to combat intentional discrimination, ameliorate implicit biases, and dismantle systemic barriers. The critical factor is to address these problems in ways that do not treat people differently based on race and that are cognizant of the philosophical and psychological roots of racial polarization.

Insofar as implicit biases are deeply ingrained and, by definition, unknown to those who hold them, it is unclear whether and to what extent they can be eliminated.[32] Nonetheless, research has shown that some strategies may be effective at reducing implicit bias, such as increasing awareness, self-checking, and the adoption of more concrete standards.[33] These approaches might be extended to various areas in which discretionary decisions may be affected by implicit bias, such as employment decisions or disciplinary actions in public education.

A related strategy is to reform traditional policies and structures that operate as systemic barriers to black progress. This approach requires that we identify those policies and structures and offer alternative means to accomplish the objectives nominally served by those policies and structures. Thus, for example, if the standardized tests relied on for admission to elite universities and law schools tend to be racially biased, the focus might be on alternative measures that provide a more accurate and racially neutral measure of merit.[34]

To a certain extent, implicit biases and systemic barriers are interrelated, in the sense that decisional structures that rely on individual discretion may increase the impact of implicit biases. Thus, for example, police and prosecutorial discretion plays a major role in the racial disparities within the criminal justice system. To the extent that this discretion is influenced by unconscious biases, the result is the disproportionate arrest, prosecution, and incarceration of black defendants, as well as the problem of violence against black suspects. Constraining discretion through the adoption of clear (and non-race-specific) policies may be one way to combat this problem.

Nonetheless, the psychology of race means that how these issues are framed is critically important.[35] Thus, for example, if the problem is police violence against blacks, rather than accusing police of racism, which produces a defensive reaction, postracial remedies might ask, "how can we avoid being the next Ferguson?" This is not to suggest that blacks or the Left should remain silent about racism or cease to advocate for other kinds of remedies. But—given the psychology of race and the Supreme Court's postracial equal protection jurisprudence—those who seek to reduce racial inequalities cannot afford to ignore opportunities to build coalitions for postracial remedies. The specific coalition partners would vary depending on context. In some cases, they might include economically disadvantaged blacks and whites along with progressive whites and blacks concerned about economic inequality. In other cases, strategies might produce unexpected coalition partners. For example, people in crime-ridden neighborhoods and police departments might have a mutual interest in improving relationships and cooperation, and so they may form productive coalitions. Thus, we do not have a preconceived and inflexible view about what prospective coalitions for postracial remedies might look like. Indeed, we are as pragmatic about these as we are about the remedies. We support coalitions that work to address the underlying problems.

By "political" remedies, we mean measures voluntarily adopted by policymakers at any level, whether federal or state legislatures, administrative agencies, or private actors. Political remedies may take the form of laws, programs, or practices that address problems such as poverty, mass incarceration, poor educational achievement, or failing neighborhoods. Political remedies require that proponents convince responsible policymakers, which in turn requires them to build political support so as to influence outcomes. The pursuit of postracial political remedies has two principal advantages—broader appeal and lower risk of constitutional invalidity.

To be sure, in our ideologically polarized society, the causes of and solutions for problems like poverty, mass incarceration, underperforming schools, or blighted neighborhoods are likely to be contested. Nonetheless, those divisions are exacerbated by arguments that focus on race and solutions that incorporate racial preferences, because such an approach brings additional psychological factors into play. In view of the problem of "in-group" and "out-group" thinking, focusing on race may encourage members of the in-group (whites) to place the responsibility for these problems on the out-group. Equally important, focusing on race is more likely to produce a defensive reaction from well-intentioned whites.

This is not to say that all postracial political remedies will be acceptable across the range of the ideological spectrum, or even that a large majority will embrace them. Nonetheless, postracial political remedies are more likely to appeal to the broad middle—citizens who may be amenable to practical solutions for real problems. On this point we believe that most Americans see persistent poverty, mass incarceration, failing schools, and disadvantaged neighborhoods as real problems that warrant constructive solutions. A key point here is that people may support efforts to ameliorate these problems without regard to whether they see the problems as the product of racial discrimination or are motivated by a desire to reduce racial inequalities. Addressing the underlying problem will benefit blacks who are disproportionately burdened by it. To the extent that whites perceive a problem as a "black" issue, they might be less motivated to address it. Ultimately, the pursuit of postracial political remedies must be incremental, focusing on what is achievable and initially targeting receptive audiences and communities to build a record of success. These successes, in turn, can be used to make the case for solutions that work, taking them to a broader audience based on solid evidence that the solutions are practical and workable.

Pursuit of remedies that break down implicit biases and systemic barriers may be a particularly sensitive and difficult undertaking. Programs designed to alleviate implicit biases, for example, require that political actors and the target audience accept the existence of such biases and the need to address them. Without such a recognition, implicit bias training may produce a backlash and be counterproductive.[36] Likewise, tackling systemic barriers may be problematic because doing so requires recognition that long-standing and familiar practices operate as a barrier, and a willingness to seek alternatives that are less exclusionary. Accordingly, advocating for solutions to implicit biases and systemic barriers cannot be undertaken in a wholly race-blind fashion, which implicates the psychological factors that lead to resistance. Nonetheless, such efforts have already made some headway (as in the case of police departments that have undertaken implicit bias training or the development of more neutral forms of standardized testing). Strategically, it makes sense to focus on receptive communities and policymakers first, so as to build a track record of success that can, over time, help to convince skeptics.

A critical difference between postracial and race-specific political remedies is that postracial political remedies would be less constitutionally vulnerable under the Court's equal protection jurisprudence. So long as the solutions are not race specific (i.e., do not treat or intend to treat people differently based on race), the postracial remedies would be subject to rational basis scrutiny. The purposes of ameliorating poverty, improving the criminal justice system, improving educational outcomes, revitalizing neighborhoods, and increasing political participation are clearly legitimate. Likewise, political remedies based on what works are easily defended as rational means to achieve these ends, especially insofar as they are evidence based. To the extent that the problems identified are disproportionately concentrated in the black community, solving those problems will tend to benefit blacks disproportionately and thus ameliorate racial disparities. Under the Court's postracial equal protection jurisprudence, this sort of disproportionate impact would not trigger strict scrutiny in the absence of proof of racially discriminatory intent. Thus, the primary vulnerability would arise only if there is evidence that the non-race-specific approach is a mere pretext for racial preferences or if they are implemented in a race-based manner. In this regard, it is important to distinguish between the permissible and legitimate purpose of redressing racial inequality and the constitutionally suspect purpose of establishing race-based preferences.

Consider the problem of admissions in higher education. The Court recently reaffirmed the consideration of race as a factor in higher education admissions (by a slim 4-3 majority) in *Fisher v. Texas*,[37] but satisfying strict scrutiny remains a difficult task. As an alternative, institutions of higher education might consider poverty, the applicant's family's level of education, and other socioeconomic burdens the applicant has overcome as positive factors in deciding on admission.[38] To the extent that a higher proportion of the black community bears such burdens, these preferences would disproportionately benefit black applicants. Nonetheless, because these factors are race neutral on their face, they would only have to survive the rational basis test—unless the record shows that these considerations were merely a pretext for racial preferences.[39]

Postracial remedies may be vulnerable to this sort of challenge if they simply substitute class for race in an effort to get around limits on affirmative action, especially if their implementation in practice effectively confines the program to racial minorities. On the other hand, solutions like improved early childhood education, technical job training programs, or other problem-oriented solutions are not invalid simply because one argument to support them is that they will help redress racial disparities. Likewise, a jurisdiction's decision to use implicit bias training or to alter its hiring structures to prevent unconscious discrimination is not constitutionally invalid just because it is intended to benefit blacks by combating racial inequality. If that were true, then the civil rights laws prohibiting racial discrimination would be invalid because they were intended to help blacks and other racial minorities.

Applying Postracial Remedies

In this section we consider how postracial political and judicial remedies might be brought to bear on persistent racial inequalities in the areas of economics, criminal justice, education, and neighborhoods. These examples are meant to be illustrative rather than exhaustive and are at this point provisional. We have also attempted to give examples from both conservative and liberal perspectives. Conservative perspectives tend to focus on self-help, personal responsibility, and the private sector, while liberal or progressive programs emphasize government benefits and other interventions to ameliorate inequality. From a pragmatic perspective, the critical question is whether these approaches work to solve the underlying problems, and if not, what other options might work better. Our premise is that tackling the underlying social and economic problems that disproportionately burden blacks will ameliorate racial inequality. Here the focus is on whether the remedy addresses the underlying social problem.

There are a variety of postracial approaches that might improve racial disparities in income and wealth by addressing the plight of the poor. In general terms, we might address high rates of unemployment and underemployment by expanding job training programs or initiating comprehensive national service requirements.[40] Both approaches would tend to improve the employability of those with limited credentials and experience, and a national service program would also increase demand for workers and reduce the supply of workers competing for available jobs.

Some of these programs appear to enjoy support among conservatives.[41] For example, conservatives have advocated in support of New York City's WeCARE program, which addresses barriers to employment by providing assistance and services to help clients achieve their highest levels of self-sufficiency,[42] as a potential model for reform of the Supplemental Nutrition Assistance Program (SNAP).[43] This approach has garnered attention in the House Committee on Agriculture, where the Republican Committee Chair, J. Michael Conaway, touted it.[44] Another approach that might enjoy some conservative support would be to promote entrepreneurship through programs that provide "microloans" and other encouragement for small businesses.[45]

From a more progressive perspective, it might be possible to change the terms and conditions of employment in ways that protect all vulnerable workers.[46] For example, Katie Eyer has suggested that a just cause requirement for termination of employees (i.e., elimination of at-will employment) would tend to protect black workers against hidden or unconscious racism in disciplinary actions.[47] It might also be possible to reform hiring practices in ways that reduce the effects of systemic barriers and implicit biases, perhaps by promoting tests that have been adjusted for racial bias,[48] adopting policies that constrain individual discretion, or promoting interventions to combat implicit bias among those who make employment decisions.[49]

Reforming the criminal justice system represents one of the most important and difficult tasks for the amelioration of racial disparities. As a threshold matter, the de-escalation of the war on drugs is an important starting point. Notwithstanding the popularity of the war on drugs in some circles, we think it is an area where libertarian conservatives and progressives may find common ground, as reflected in the legalization of marijuana in some states. Insofar as the war on drugs is disproportionately harming blacks, de-escalation would disproportionately benefit them. More broadly, needless violence against black suspects might be reduced if police methods were reformed to reduce confrontational and militaristic approaches.

Of course, the criminal justice system necessarily entails many discretionary judgments by police, prosecutors, judges, and juries. Given the prevalence of negative images and stereotypes of blacks—especially young black men—as dangerous, violent lawbreakers, implicit biases in the criminal justice system will be especially difficult to overcome. Training may help to reduce implicit biases, but the effectiveness of interventions is unclear. Another approach would be to limit the role of discretionary judgments. Here, for example, articulating clearer policies that limit discretion in police stops or reducing the number and use of peremptory challenges might be useful illustrations. One reform that has received the support of the conservative CATO Institute is the use of body cameras by police.[50] It is interesting to note that this report concludes that "[r]educing incidents of police misconduct will require reforms of use-of-force policy and training, and changes to how police misconduct is investigated, in addition to the increased use of body cameras."[51] This conclusion suggests that there may be room for a broader coalition between conservatives and progressives on a variety of police reforms.

Educational achievement gaps are among the most critical problems to address. Education is not only a critical factor in employment and economic success, but also an essential means of empowerment that enables us to participate in civil society and defend our interests. *Brown* assumed that eliminating de jure segregation would produce integrated schools and that integrated schools would equalize educational outcomes, but the problem is more complex. For example, integration is difficult to achieve in light of housing segregation. Put simply, the achievement gap is a complex problem that cannot be alleviated by the educational system alone.[52]

Liberals and conservatives have different ideas about what steps to take to improve educational achievement. Conservatives often propose school choice—in the form of charter schools and voucher programs—as a means of improving education. From a pragmatic perspective, such programs would be desirable if they work, but the evidence to this point suggests that they do not improve student performance.[53] Liberals, by way of contrast, focus on solutions such as early childhood education, investments in quality schools, and the use of complementary efforts (e.g., before- and after-school programs) to promote student success.[54]

Education is also an area in which implicit biases and systemic barriers may be important factors. Teachers may unwittingly perpetuate underachievement as a result of implicit biases that attach low expectations to black schoolchildren and often result in more aggressive disciplinary actions when black children act out.[55] Equally important, to the extent that black children come from families that lack education, are unstable, and lack resources, they must overcome a variety of barriers to succeed. In view of the complexity of the problem, it is especially important to determine what works in the area of education.

Residential segregation has also proven to be an especially difficult problem to overcome because there is a natural tendency to want to live around those who are "like" you. Thus, in many large cities there are distinctive ethnic communities that are concentrated in particular parts of the city. Eliminating these ethnic neighborhoods is not necessarily a good thing, but even if it is, it is likely impossible. The more important problem is ensuring that the particular neighborhood in which people live does not unduly limit their opportunities, and some postracial approaches might help in this regard.

As an initial matter, the traditional model for low-income housing, which often involves large complexes, proved to be disastrous on multiple fronts. Low-income housing projects, whose occupants were disproportionately minorities, tended to attract crime and violence and contributed to the deterioration of surrounding neighborhoods. Accordingly, they reinforced negative racial stereotypes and provoked a NIMBY ("not-in-my-backyard") reaction, especially in white suburban communities. Alternative approaches that disperse low-income housing across communities and into more prosperous neighborhoods are a possible response, although the impact and effectiveness of such programs has also been criticized.

More broadly, just as investment in our schools will be needed to promote high levels of educational achievement among all children, investment in neighborhoods and neighborhood development is a key to reducing segregation and, equally important, ensuring that all neighborhoods have the necessary resources for their residents, regardless of race. One especially complex aspect of this problem is that revitalizing neighborhoods may tend to drive out the people who live there by increasing housing costs.[56] Thus, neighborhood revitalization efforts must incorporate measures to protect the interests of current residents.

Vindicating Postracial Remedies

The search for postracial remedies draws on methodological and substantive pragmatism because it seeks to build consensus around workable solutions to common problems. In this sense, our approach fits comfortably within an emerging body of scholarship emphasizing what Reva Siegel has termed the "antibalkanization" principle, under which remedies should "ameliorate racial wrongs without unduly aggravating racial resentments."[57] When postracial premises prevail, race-specific remedies invite racial resentments and thus violate the antibalkanization principle. However, postracial remedies that are not race specific will not have this shortcoming, precisely because they do not turn on racial classifications. Thus, whether race-specific remedies would, in a perfect world, be the most desirable or direct approach to overcoming racial inequality—an issue some critics will certainly raise—is somewhat beside the point. Such remedies are constitutionally suspect and often politically infeasible in the real world.

Other scholars have also responded to the postracial ethos entrenched in the Supreme Court's jurisprudence by focusing on remedies that are not race specific. As noted earlier, some have suggested that we should replace race with class or "place" as a means of accomplishing the goals of affirmative action or race-based measures to desegregate schools or neighborhoods. Another approach is to promote what Samuel Bagenstos calls "universalistic" remedies that do not "seek to protect any particular group against discrimination, [but rather] provide uniform protections to everyone (at least as a formal matter)."[58]

Although both of these approaches are examples of postracial remedies, the approach outlined in this chapter is distinctive in two ways. First, it is sensitive to race, both in terms of the problem of racial inequality and the psychology of race. Targeting implicit racial bias and systemic barriers need not run afoul of postracial doctrinal and factual premises, provided that we do so in ways that are not race specific and are sensitive to the psychology of race. Second, this approach is not confined to a particular kind of remedy but, rather, embraces a broad array of possible remedies—so long as they work. In this regard, it is important to note that we do not argue that postracial remedies should be the exclusive means of combating racial disparities. Our argument is not that postracial remedies are sufficient for mitigating racial inequality. Rather, it is that they are necessary, in view of the influence of the postracial narrative on our political discourse and the Court's equal protection jurisprudence. Many on the Left have been exclusively preoccupied with arguing that race-specific remedies for racial inequality are still necessary in today's post-civil-rights era. We do not argue against such efforts but, rather, suggest that non-race-specific remedies are also necessary to mitigate racial inequality.

Postracial remedies share certain strengths with universalistic approaches. Because they are not race specific, they stand a better chance of gaining political support and surviving judicial scrutiny. They allow us to focus on systemic barriers to equality that impact the life prospects of citizens regardless of racial membership. They do not invoke worries about identity fatigue that have troubled race-specific remedies. And they hold promise to minimize racial resentment and backlash and to promote greater social cohesion, which is vital for securing the social cooperation necessary to address racial disparities.

Postracial remedies can be embraced for different reasons. One can be motivated by the belief that all racial classifications are invidious and thus should be prohibited or viewed with the highest suspicion (anticlassification). One can also be fully invested in the normative ideal of color blindness and so believe that the way to realize postracialism in practice is simply to stop treating people differently based on race (color blindness). Or, lastly, one can be motivated to avoid or minimize divisions that undermine the social cohesion needed to achieve democracy in a society with a legacy of historical injustice (antibalkanization). This last motivation, striving for social cohesion, best captures why we pursue postracial remedies and also connects it with antibalkanization approaches, which similarly embody not just a methodological but also a substantive or principled commitment to pragmatism. We cannot claim the strengths of this family of equal protection approaches without also taking on board similar objections.

Insofar as postracial remedies proceed from the standpoint of the race moderate, objections are expected from both ends of the political spectrum. These objections might take various forms and focus on various aspects of our approach. For convenience, these potential objections are divided into three categories: pragmatic, principle, and purity.

Pragmatic

Part of the case for postracial remedies turns on the premise that they have practical value—that is, they allow us to achieve consensus for programs that work. Critics may object that this premise is overly optimistic, both in terms of the prospects of building coalitions for postracial remedies and in terms of those remedies' ability to deliver real progress. The first pragmatic objection is that it will not be possible in practice to build coalitions or consensus to support postracial remedies. This objection could take various forms. Given the polarized state of our society, it may be unrealistic to think of a "big middle" or to suppose that the Left and the Right or blacks and whites can agree on anything. Thus, for example, there is little evidence that our currently dysfunctional Congress could ever reach consensus on anything, much less postracial remedies. Although polarized voices seem to dominate our political processes, especially political primaries, the public opinion research cited earlier indicates that a substantial proportion of the population accepts mixed explanations for racial inequalities and so are potentially amenable to compromise solutions.

Critically, postracial remedies avoid pitting blacks and whites against each other in a zero-sum game in which remedies for racial inequality require redistribution from whites to blacks. Of course, postracial remedies would have redistributional consequences (as do all social programs), insofar as they devote resources to ameliorating poverty, improving schools, or revitalizing neighborhoods, but such redistribution would tend to be from the wealthy (including wealthy blacks) to the less wealthy (including less-wealthy whites). Because this sort of redistribution is class based rather than race based, it provides an opportunity for alliances between poor or lower-class blacks and whites. To be sure, this sort of class-based redistribution is likely to meet opposition and may be ideologically contested, but postracial remedies take race out of the equation and so are less divisive than race-specific remedies. More broadly, ideological divisions and upper-class resistance can be minimized if the remedies actually work.

A somewhat different objection is to suggest that the big middle is unwilling or unlikely to support such proposals. Bagenstos, for one, doubts the premise that people are generally willing to back civil rights causes, expressing concern that casting too broad a net for civil rights protections and extending them beyond concrete and urgent cases of need may undermine rather than enhance political support (perhaps due to "compassion fatigue").[59] From this perspective, postracial remedies may undermine rather than build support for efforts to ameliorate racial inequality.

Using voting rights as an example, Bagenstos argues that focusing on removal of restrictions that burden all citizens will trivialize, and take support away from, efforts to eradicate laws that discriminate against and have a disproportionate impact on blacks in particular. A similar objection might be made against remedies that aim to remove barriers to the educational achievement of all students at risk, which may diminish the importance of removing ones that target or have disparate impact on black students in particular. Bagenstos also suggests that race-specific remedies capitalize on the powerful cachet of "civil rights" discourse in American politics, while universalistic approaches will "lose the support that comes with the civil rights label."[60] Given current polarization on matters of race, however, we doubt that the "civil rights" label continues to carry the powerful cachet that Bagenstos attributes to it. Nowadays, under conditions of deep polarization, when civil rights are invoked in ways that highlight black inequality and disadvantage, they are more likely to invoke the sentiment that we are dealing with another case of black grievance or special pleading. In view of the psychology of race, many will respond that these claims are best addressed not by government policies, handouts of more "free stuff," or penalizing the conduct of private businesses, but by blacks taking greater personal responsibility for their successes and failures.[61]

Conversely, others might object that postracial remedies are simply a pretext for benefiting racial minorities. This point has both a political and a judicial dimension. Politically, it suggests that postracial remedies may come to be seen as "code" for racial preferences, thus undermining support for them.[62] The extent to which this sort of result is a cause for concern is unclear. In practice, for example, programs to promote "diversity" are often perceived as "code" for affirmative action. Notwithstanding this phenomenon, employment programs to promote diversity have proven to be more effective in practice than affirmative action programs. The judicial dimension of this objection is based on the concern that judges may conclude that although these remedies are not race specific "on their face," facial neutrality is merely a pretext for programs adopted with the intent to favor blacks.[63]

Insofar as postracial remedies are race sensitive and seek to ameliorate racial inequalities, this is a real concern that highlights the need to be careful about advocacy, design, and implementation so that remedies really are not race specific. Simply recasting affirmative action programs in terms of class, rather than race, for example, and implementing them in ways that correlate strongly with race, is unlikely to persuade policymakers who do not already support affirmative action or to withstand a legal challenge based on pretext. But programs that focus on addressing underlying problems like poverty, mass incarceration, failing schools, and disadvantaged neighborhoods, based on evidence that they actually work, are less likely to be viewed as a pretext—even if they are promoted in part as a response to the problems that plague the black community.

In this regard, there is an important difference between programs to ameliorate racial inequalities that are a result of ongoing effects of past discrimination, implicit bias, and systemic barriers, and adopting policies with the intent to discriminate against whites and in favor of blacks. If the remedies actually work—that is, if the rising tide does lift all marginalized boats—then the worry about coding or pretext is less likely to be problem. These responses highlight the virtues of methodological pragmatism in the design and implementation of remedies, and the importance of showing that there is no tension between being race sensitive and not being race specific.

A second type of pragmatic objection to postracial remedies is that, even if it is possible to generate political support for their adoption, they will not achieve the real-world benefits that we claim for them. Critics from the Left might argue, for example, that a rising tide will not lift all boats. Given the problems of ongoing intentional discrimination, implicit biases, and systemic barriers, this argument posits that postracial remedies are likely to help whites while leaving blacks behind.

This sort of objection challenges the basic premise that solving the underlying problems that disproportionately affect blacks will ameliorate racial inequalities. As an initial matter, this strategy is incremental and involves tackling social and economic issues from a variety of angles, including measures to address implicit biases and structural barriers. In addition, even if gaps between blacks and whites remain, ensuring that blacks have some minimal level of opportunity is an essential step toward promoting more equal outcomes. For example, if minority schools are failing, then black students have no chance at success. Raising the quality of education for all may mean that white schools are still better than minority schools, but improving minority schools will at least provide the opportunity for black children to succeed and possibly gain ground, as a whole, on whites. Put differently, the marginal impact of relative inequality decreases as the overall level of opportunity and prosperity rises. Postracial remedies will not magically resolve racial inequalities, but improving outcomes for some substantial number of people in the near term is no small accomplishment.

A related objection is that it is inefficient to try to lift all boats to deal with problems that disproportionately harm blacks—this is simply too expensive, and society is better off targeting blacks alone.[64] But postracial remedies need not be expensive, especially if viewed in the longer term, because they are investments that will pay off later on. Thus, for example, investments in early childhood education, public schools, and wraparound programs may seem expensive, now, but those costs may be offset down the road through declining demands for welfare benefits, reduced law enforcement costs, and increased productivity. Of course, this sort of long-term thinking is not always influential in our current political discourse. More fundamentally, one reason that race-specific remedies are so divisive is precisely because resources are limited and providing remedies for blacks means that those resources are not available for other disadvantaged groups.

Ultimately, it is not clear that race-specific remedies are more effective when targeted at racial inequality than are postracial ones. From a pragmatic perspective, solutions that target the manifestations of racial inequality are at least as likely to solve them as solutions that target race.[65] Likewise, the postracial approach does not foreclose efforts to address ongoing barriers to black success and may even provide more effective means to address ongoing problems of intentional discrimination, implicit biases, and structural barriers. At bottom, it is important to bear in mind the limits of the argument. Postracial remedies will not eliminate racial and ideological polarization or completely solve the problem of racial inequality. Moreover, given the current political climate, seeking major legislation or new initiatives at a national level may be unrealistic. Postracial remedies are most likely to succeed incrementally through local efforts aimed at particular policies and practices. Such incremental efforts can produce immediate gains for some people and help to build momentum for expansion of programs that have a proven record of success.

Principle

A second objection that might be raised to the postracial approach is that it is unprincipled. From this perspective, by targeting the race moderate, postracial remedies try to be all things to all people and so lack any normative foundation in either conservative or progressive thought. In other words, this approach is merely a strategic approach to racial inequality, focusing exclusively on what will work more effectively to mitigate it and not on a substantive normative commitment.

Objections based on the lack of principle emphasize the tension between promoting remedies that are race sensitive and asserting that such remedies should not be race specific. From the perspective of the Left, if we believe that intentional discrimination, implicit biases, and structural barriers cause racial disparities, it follows as a matter of principle that race-specific remedies are essential to achieve racial justice. Conversely, from the perspective of the Right, if society wants to claim race neutrality, it follows that decisions about what problems to address must be color-blind and cannot be race sensitive.

Accordingly, this criticism would continue, our approach lacks a substantive commitment to any normative principle. For example, describing such opportunism as "postracial pragmatism," Kimberlé Williams Crenshaw writes,

> In the new post-racial moment, the pragmatist may be agnostic about the conservative erasure of race as a contemporary phenomenon but may still march under the same premise that significant progress can be made without race consciousness. This realignment brings liberals and some civil rights advocates on board so that a variety of individuals and groups who may have been staunch opponents of colorblindness can be loosely allied in post-racialism.[66]

Crenshaw's point is an important one. It compels pragmatists to explain why they are motivated not *merely* by what works at moving a polarized society forward but also by substantive normative principles.

This objection, however, ignores the principled normative foundations of pragmatism—a commitment to the democratic ideal of social cooperation to achieve common ends. We reject this objection because we reject the premise that pragmatism is unprincipled. As expressed by pragmatic idealists such as Cornel West, the link between methodological and substantive pragmatism expresses hopefulness in the power of strategic thinking for social transformation:

> American pragmatism is a diverse and heterogeneous tradition. But its common denominator consists of a future-oriented instrumentalism that tries to deploy thought as a weapon to enable more effective action. Its basic impulse is a plebeian radicalism that fuels an antipatrician rebelliousness for the moral aim of enriching individuals and expanding democracy.[67]

Thus, postracial remedies are grounded in principled pragmatism because they are rooted in a normative concern to make us better individually as well as collectively by realizing our common aims as a community. The normative underpinnings of a pragmatic strategic instrumentalism might be further developed—though we will not pursue this here—by tethering this democratic impulse to a concern with affirming the dignity of persons.[68]

So, pragmatism is not unprincipled simply because it contemplates strategic action in pursuit of what works, whether viewed from the philosophical perspective or as a means of appealing to the equal protection jurisprudence of race-moderate justices. In this regard, our approach builds on Reva Siegel's argument that racial conflict and division must be taken seriously given the composition of the Court.[69] She argues that swing justices on issues of race-conscious civil rights policies embrace an antibalkanization perspective that aims for social cohesion. Siegel argues, and we agree, that the pragmatism reflected in race moderates is a principled normative commitment to social cohesion, not merely a strategic one of negotiating a middle path between conservatives and progressives. This is also a key ingredient in the pragmatic democratic impulse, figuring out how, given that we must live and die together, we can work together to solve problems with which we all live. Postracial remedies take up the standpoint of the race moderates, who are willing to set polarizing commitments about race to one side in the interests of realizing the common good in a democratic society. If social cohesion is a mediating principle, it is best viewed as a democratic one. Similarly, postracial remedies can cultivate social bonds such that all members of a democratic society relate to each other as equals.

An essential common ground for social cohesion is the pursuit of equal opportunity for all—a principle uniting the libertarian and egalitarian themes that underlie our political and constitutional discourse. To be sure this commitment cannot be a one-way proposition, attending to white resentment without equal regard to black claims for justice. Indeed, insofar as racial discrimination occupies an infamously privileged place in American history, race-sensitive remedies for intentional discrimination, implicit biases, and structural barriers are essential parts of the solution. Indeed, as Justice Kennedy rightly observes, "The enduring hope is that race should not matter; the reality is that too often it does."[70] But focusing only on equality for blacks (or other racial groups) will most certainly divide us.[71] Thus, as Siegel argues, race-sensitive policies should work from what binds, rather than what divides, us.[72] Our approach should be situated alongside other forms of pragmatism that are motivated by a deep commitment to democracy and that seek to build the social cohesion necessary to sustain it in a highly polarized America where race still matters.

Race matters not only when we consider evidence of overt and implicit anti-black discrimination, systemic barriers to success, and gross racial disparities, but also when we consider how it shapes our psychological responses to inequality and injustice. It is this basic reality, and the obstacles it poses to addressing racial inequality through race-specific means, that motivates our support for postracial remedies.

Purity

A further criticism takes the question of principle to another level, arguing that postracial remedies are a form of appeasement that concedes too much to the other side. Although this objection might be made from either end of the political spectrum, it would likely be raised most forcefully and consistently from the Left.[73] As with the pragmatism and principle objection, the purity objection may come in various forms.

At its core, the purity objection criticism argues that we, in effect, "reify" the postracial narrative and thereby undermine efforts to advocate for true racial justice. Crenshaw makes this point forcefully:

> [T]he bargain that post-racial pragmatists strike is silence about the racial barriers that continue to shape the life chances of many people of color. This failure to engage racial power jeopardizes racial justice agendas by giving license to those who seek to stigmatize all discourse pertaining to ongoing inequalities.[74]

Accordingly, postracial remedies proceed from a weak negotiating position by ceding the issue of race-specific remedies and radical change and asking only for incremental changes that will produce modest gains at best. In political science terms, our approach allows the "Overton window" of the politically feasible to be pushed toward the postracial narrative without a countervailing demand for racial justice.[75] The purity objection does not allege that race moderates actually endorse the postracial narrative. Rather, it contends that by cashing in on "the opportunity to realign this conservative discourse [postracialism] to more progressive visions of the future,"[76] postracialists relegate race consciousness to the back of the postracial bus and stigmatize advocates of race-specific remedies.[77] While the hearts of race moderates might be in the right place, the politics of appeasement is wrongheaded.

We are not unmoved by these considerations, insofar as we reject the premises of the postracial narrative and have no desire to silence or undermine demands for racial justice. Indeed, it is critical that demands for racial justice be taken seriously if we are to bring people to the table to address ongoing racial inequalities. In this regard, several aspects of the postracial remedies approach must be underscored.

First, as we have repeatedly emphasized, we do not view the pursuit of racial justice as one that forces us to choose between the two approaches and do not argue that postracial remedies should be the exclusive approach to the problem of racial inequality. Postracial remedies are a necessary supplement to, not a replacement for, race-specific approaches. Both are vital for rooting out racial inequality.

Second, this approach to postracial remedies takes the realities of race and racism seriously. We do not ignore or discount ongoing discrimination, implicit bias, or systemic barriers. Whatever other forms of postracial pragmatism may have to say about these problems, advocates of racial justice should not be silent about them. However, there may be practical advantages to addressing them without race-specific remedies, which are both politically and legally unrealistic at the moment.

Finally, given what is known about human psychology, we must not be overconfident in this postracial moment that race consciousness alone can take us to the promised land. Indeed, whatever else "taking race and racism seriously" means, it most certainly involves taking the reality of resistance to race-specific remedies seriously. Having made the case for the kinds of big-tent remedies that postracial remedies represent, the next chapter argues for taking up collective responsibility to pursue them.

6
Collective Responsibility

> Every generation, by virtue of being born into a historical continuum, is burdened by the sins of the fathers as it is blessed by the deeds of the ancestors.[1]
> —Hannah Arendt

> When we speak of reducing social inequality, we often lose sight of or fail to capture the impact of organizational and collective processes that embody the social structure of inequality and have varied influences on different racial and ethnic groups.[2]
> —William Julius Wilson

In the United States it is not uncommon to find black Americans perceiving white people as morally responsible for slavery and contemporary black/white inequality.[3] Although doing this and inducing whites to feel collective guilt for the sins of their fathers can produce useful outcomes such as lowered racism and increased willingness to make various forms of reparations to blacks, this backward-looking strategy for assigning moral responsibility is not without problems. Some philosophers may object that only individuals, not collectives, can bear moral responsibility. And whenever individuals are held "collectively" responsible, this only makes sense if their personal deeds qualify them for membership in the group. While other philosophers are skeptical about collective guilt as such, they allow that a community of persons can indeed take political responsibility for the sins of their fathers, even though their own deeds do not causally connect them directly to the past wrongdoing.[4] Other proponents of political responsibility argue that a nonmysterious account requires an indirect, albeit quite complicated and diffuse, connection between persons and past wrongdoing and present unjust outcomes.[5] We shall take it for granted that this notion of political responsibility is useful for thinking about our duty to do something about inequality. However, we shall argue for grounding it in a forward-looking manner given the limits of a backward-looking approach brought to light by social psychological data.

Black Americans might remain hopeful that whites en masse will come to feel collective guilt and eventually take up political responsibility for historical injustice and its lingering effects. However, there are also nonphilosophical reasons for doubting that they will do so. Because dominant group members' identities are at stake and it is generally painful to see one's group as having acted immorally in the past and to feel guilt for having done so, people have a variety of defenses to avoid taking political responsibility for injustice or inequality. In previous work we consider the implications for philosophical theorizing about egalitarian justice of "shifting standards of injustice," namely, the amount and nature of evidence that persons—depending on their class, race, or gender—rely upon to reach their conclusions about the fairness of inequality.[6] In keeping with our general view that normative political philosophy should consider how people actually think and behave as members of social groups, this sequel considers some of these responsibility-deflecting defenses and examines their ramifications for how we ought to ground political responsibility for unjust racial inequality.

In this chapter we argue that a forward-looking basis for grounding our shared political responsibility to address unjust racial inequality is attractive given what we know from empirical research in social psychology about the limits of playing the blame game[7] about how majority in-group members frame inequality as a problem of minority disadvantage rather than majority privilege to avoid blame and collective guilt[8] and about how placing blame on the majority can be an obstacle to majority members forging the political solidarity with the minority that is necessary for collectively changing unjust social institutions.[9] We develop our argument by drawing upon the role that basic societal institutions—on which we all depend and have a stake in sustaining—play in shaping the distributive outcomes that stem from a unified system of social cooperation.

The Psychology of White Collective Guilt

When people categorize themselves as members of a social group that is associated with inequitable treatment or doing harm toward others, they can experience *collective guilt* even though they had no personal role in causing the harm. To the extent that they see their group (which is a part of the social self) as responsible for actions that they deem to be illegitimate, collective guilt for the group's past immoral actions can be felt.[10] Guilt for wrongdoing—whether it be personal or collective—is a highly aversive emotion and is therefore one that people have powerful defenses they can deploy to help them avoid it. However, when the experience cannot be avoided, and the individual is forced to conclude that their group is responsible for injustice that has not been repaired, numerous positive social benefits can emerge.

First of all, people can be motivated to restore justice and repair the harm done. A variety of empirical studies have linked the experience of collective guilt (e.g., "I feel guilty about white Americans' harmful actions toward black Americans"; "I feel guilty about the negative things my ancestors did to black Americans") with a willingness to make compensation in the form of monetary allocations, support for an official apology for the in-group's actions, and support for affirmative action to improve the outcomes of the previously harmed group.[11] By perceiving one's group as illegitimately privileged at the expense of another group, which can induce collective guilt, racist attitudes can be reduced.[12] This is consistent with Martin Luther King Jr.'s claim that "remorse can raise the moral threshold of a society." Collective guilt, which encompasses such remorse, can indeed promote the desire to correct unjust wrongs of the past.

When it can be induced, collective guilt clearly has benefits. But inducing it requires that we call attention to a group's negative history, and this is not without risks. In contrast to collectivist cultures where people define themselves in terms of their group memberships, in a highly individualistic culture such as the United States, where people often define themselves separate from the groups they belong to, it is especially easy for white individuals to deny collective responsibility and guilt for slavery.[13] There are other defenses apart from denial they can employ to lessen their group's responsibility and hence the extent to which collective guilt for slavery is experienced. People can minimize the harm done. They can perceive the harm as impossible to correct. They can derogate the victims, which, as Albert Bandura[14] (1990) has pointed out, allows perpetrator groups to be "less burdened by distress" when faced with their wrongdoing. And they can also legitimize the harm done as consistent with the times, with what other groups have done so not uniquely bad, or as having served some greater moral good.[15] Such defensive strategies can also affect attributions of collective responsibility by whites for why they are better off than blacks today on many measures of social inequality.[16]

When people's valued social identities are at stake, they may be strongly tempted to defend that identity and do so by legitimizing their group's "questionable" actions as a means of restoring the moral value of their group. To the extent that the differential outcomes of the groups can be seen as legitimate, collective guilt is undermined.[17] Likewise, perceiving the costs of correcting the past as very difficult or impossible can reduce collective guilt and the motivation to do so.[18] Thus, it is clear that perceiving the in-group as responsible for past wrongdoing will not inevitably evoke collective guilt, precisely because people can creatively legitimize those past actions and separate the current in-group from members in the past who did the harm.

Moreover, it is not certain that people will perceive existing racial inequality as directly stemming from that past, and to the extent that they do not there will be little motivation to correct existing inequality. For instance, it has been noted that reparations for past wrongs are more likely to be supported when past harms experienced can be linked to present circumstances.[19] But who we are (i.e., our political ideology, group membership) affects willingness to see links between unfair past victimization and the group's present situation. For white Americans, political conservatism predicts unwillingness to view historical injustice effects as persisting into the present and, therefore, low support for reparations. However, this is not the case for members of the group suffering the historical injustice. Political ideology in this case did not predict support for reparations; rather, African Americans support reparations for both their own group and Native Americans, regardless of their own political orientation.[20]

A further problem is that triggering these defenses is counterproductive to generating the multiracial collective societal effort necessary to reduce unjust racial inequality. William Julius Wilson[21] (1999) argues against allowing racial ideology to undermine building the multiracial political coalitions necessary for structural change and reducing social inequality. In the same vein, we call for moving from a politics of individual blame to a politics of forward-looking shared political responsibility for racial inequality. The benefits of backward-looking shared responsibility and collective guilt notwithstanding, in view of other empirical evidence from social psychology, we think that playing the blame game poses a serious obstacle to building the diverse political coalitions necessary to combat racial inequality *when taking people as they are rather than as we wish or imagine them to be.* The foregoing evidence invites us to retool the philosophical case for why we must share responsibility for racial inequality.

The Limits of Backward-Looking Responsibility

The inducement of collective guilt encourages us to ground responsibility by looking backward. Because collective guilt is an emotional experience that people are typically motivated to avoid, and because we assume that normative arguments should be rooted in realistic assumptions about persons, we defend a less-threatening means of motivating people to take political responsibility for doing something about unjust racial inequality. We do this by advocating a forward-looking approach to grounding political responsibility; however, we refrain from assuming that this approach is trouble free, though we will not address its problems here. In this section we distinguish these approaches and discuss shortcomings of the backward-looking one.

Atrocities such as slavery, genocide, rape, sex trafficking, and apartheid provide an occasion for thinking about moral responsibility. These and other evils compel us to raise questions such as: Who is to blame? Who should be liable for harm? Is the passage of time, or the psychological state of the perpetrators, relevant to how and whether we attribute responsibility? Can collective agents as well as individuals be held responsible for atrocities? Should we distinguish between those who are directly responsible for bringing them about due to their actions and those who are indirectly responsible due to their omissions, and is there a morally significant difference between the two? While these are among the important philosophical questions raised by atrocities, there is a further issue that gets to the nub of the matter we examine in this chapter.

For those who embrace the idea of collective moral responsibility, attributions of this sort can be backward looking or forward looking.[22] The former involve making a causal connection between agents' actions or inactions and the outcome for which they are being held morally responsible. "Sex traffickers are morally responsible for the physical and psychological harms done to victims of the sex trade" is an example of the former. If the trafficking was run by an oppressive government, which forced some of its citizens to participate, say, upon threat of death to a loved one, this would be a case where the traffickers were causally connected to the harm, though we might refrain from holding them morally responsible for it. Although a causal connection is necessary for assignment of backward-looking moral responsibility, it is not always sufficient since we must also rule out mitigating factors such as coercion. "Society is responsible for bearing the costs of treating victims of the sex trade" is an example of the latter. In cases of forward-looking responsibility, such as this one, a causal connection is not necessary to establish moral responsibility for doing something about the sex trade, anything from stopping it, alleviating current and future suffering of victims, or bearing the costs of enforcement or deterrence measures. A causal connection, in this case, is inessential for recognizing a collective moral duty to address the problem. This type of moral responsibility is more like holding one another collectively responsible for ameliorating the effects of Hurricane Katrina despite the fact that we are not causally responsible for the storm, the broken levees, or the inability of its victims to escape the devastation.

Moral atrocities like slavery, genocide, and sex trafficking, which we shall describe as instances of manifest evil, encourage us to adopt a backward-looking approach to shared moral responsibility. They invite us to look back to the past to determine guilt, to place blame, and to assign responsibility, sanctions, or remedies. Successful assignments of responsibility are predicated on identifying victims and perpetrators and establishing a plausible causal connection between harm done to the victims and the acts or omissions of perpetrators. But this can be difficult to establish, particularly when dealing with manifest evil that occurred further back in time, such as black chattel slavery. For example, some critics will make the obvious point that there are no longer living slaves or slaveholders. So even if we grant that slaves are owed reparations, those who rightfully stand to benefit and those who are obliged to pay are long gone.

We certainly do not deny the importance of holding persons—either individually or collectively—responsible for manifest evil, nor do we reject the value of seeking some form of reparations for historical injustice. Yet it is important to realize that manifest evil does not provide the only occasion for taking up questions of responsibility. As recent arguments in favor of racial reparations for Jim Crow and its effects appreciate, social inequalities in the distribution of goods, resources, capabilities, and opportunities also provide such an occasion.[23] For instance, disproportionate sentencing of blacks and whites for similar drug offenses and for receiving the death penalty; inequality in who gets stopped and frisked, in the quality and safety of neighborhoods where they live, in their home values, in their educational achievement and attainment, in their levels of income and wealth; inequality in their health outcomes such as infant mortality, obesity, and heart disease; and inequality in the resilience of their communities to recover from natural disasters also prompt us to think about responsibility. But these matters do not necessarily require us to look back to the past with the aim of locating blame and assigning guilt, though this has often been the case in practice. Indeed, this can even be counterproductive, particularly when the argument for shared political responsibility turns on what are bound to be controversial accounts of the causes of racial inequality, which are frequently complex, multiple, and difficult to disentangle.[24]

Critics of efforts to assign shared political responsibility for inequality may also question whether racial disparities are necessarily a problem from the standpoint of justice, while acknowledging that there may be other normative objections to them, for example, consequentialist ones.[25] It may be objected that such inequalities do not immediately raise cause for concern, especially if one thinks that they stem from the voluntary choices of persons rather than from what Ronald Dworkin calls bad brute luck or from circumstances beyond a person's control.[26] And, unfortunately, at least when it comes to racial inequality, this thought is fairly common in so-called postracial America.[27] An abiding feature of postracial thought is that black disadvantage and racial inequality—by whatever socioeconomic indicator of well-being one is considering—are largely due to the choices or lack of effort of blacks rather than past or ongoing formal or informal racial discrimination.[28]

Recent survey data on racial attitudes concerning racial inequality and black disadvantage shows that this perspective is not anomalous.[29] If one holds some such view, as do many critics of government-sponsored efforts to ameliorate racial disparities, then the search for responsibility will be deemed warranted only if it stays focused on those persons (blacks) who have allegedly failed to make the right choices or to put in the right amount of effort to avoid disadvantage. And this will have consequences for whether or not white majority members are prepared to take political responsibility for doing something about racial inequality, whether it be supporting affirmative action, social welfare, or school desegregation, or endorsing other strategies for enabling blacks to take full advantage of formal equality of opportunity.[30]

Of course, we can dismiss such explanations as mere ideology (in a pejorative sense), as race baiting, or as claims not supported by credible empirical evidence. Although we find it incredulous to think that group-based racial inequalities can simply be chalked up to poor choices and lack of effort given empirical evidence to the contrary,[31] at the same time, because of what we do know about group psychology, we think it is advisable to avoid tethering forward-looking political responsibility for doing something about inequality to backward-looking blameworthy responsibility for causing inequality.

Therefore, when considering social problems such as inequality and poverty, if we raise the same sorts of questions that we raise when considering manifest evil (e.g., Who is to blame? Who should pay?), and if we adopt the same backward-looking model for analyzing responsibility that we use in those cases, we will run into serious problems. Given what we know from empirical research on the psychology of groups, we will face substantial obstacles to persuading persons to take political responsibility for these inequalities and other social problems when they deny having responsibility for having "caused" them in the first place. Moreover, some data suggests that by following this model we also undermine efforts to get white majority group members to act in solidarity with blacks and other social reformers and to take political action to mitigate unjust racial inequalities.[32]

As we noted earlier in the case of responsibility for slavery, in view of various objections, including concerns about the passage of time and establishing links between past wrongs and present circumstances, the best way of responding has been to consider the relationship between present (inequality) and less ancient evils (Jim Crow). But this strategy will have limited effect on those who place great significance on *Brown v. Board of Education*, the civil rights movement, and Lyndon B. Johnson's Great Society programs and view them as having driven the nail in the coffin of the dark legacy of racial injustice in America, wiping the slate clean, and finally realizing the ideal of equality of opportunity.[33] In response, we can certainly argue that we still have formal and informal racial discrimination in America and that we are still living with the effects of past wrongs.[34] Yet we must acknowledge that these responses will have limited effect if the goal of recalling the past and linking it to the present is primarily to assign blame. At most, we can recall the past to understand where we are and how we got here, and to think from the standpoint of public policy about what to do moving forward. Nelson Mandela's politics of reconciliation in post-apartheid South Africa is arguably the most familiar example of this strategy.[35] And, along with Desmond Tutu's (1999) approach,[36] it requires a forward-looking emphasis, without ignoring or forgetting the past.

Admittedly, this will be a much less radical argument than some progressives might hope for, but it may be the most we can do given the limits of playing the blame game. Ironically, as current research shows, some whites have themselves played this game to their benefit, which further complicates the blaming strategy. For example, black Americans are underrepresented in US universities compared with whites,[37] which historically can be traced to past discrimination. Yet, when white Americans are focused on their group's responsibility for the disparity in college admissions, they respond in a "competitive victimhood" fashion.[38] That is, whites uniquely claimed that it was their racial group that was discriminated against in the college admissions process. In contrast, when another group was considered responsible for the racial disparity, no such claims of "white victimization by racial discrimination" were made. This same process of defending one's group by claiming to be the "true victims" when it is accused of having committed harm against another group has been observed in other powerful groups, such as men when accusations of harm to women are made. Thus, the threat that can be raised by implied in-group responsibility for harmful actions toward another group encourages majority groups to defend their group's moral identity (over and above any concerns with material benefits that might be gained).

Grounding our obligation to change unjust social institutions, or to do something about unjust racial inequality, in forward-looking political responsibility is advisable in view of these empirical findings. However, as those who fought against racial apartheid in South Africa appreciated, ignoring or forgetting about the past and its connection to the present is not an attractive option—even if our best hope for fostering shared political responsibility may ultimately require that we refrain from assigning each other blame for the past sins of our fathers. Such knowledge of the past, and its present effects, is clearly vital for determining the content of public policy to mitigate unjust inequality and for addressing absolute disadvantage. Moreover, minority in-group members will balk at forgetting the past and view this as an instance of disrespect, which will undoubtedly undermine their willingness to cooperate in a multiracial, ethnic, and class coalition to mitigate unjust inequality and address absolute disadvantage.[39]

Consider, for instance, that American ethnic/racial minority group members who perceive that white Americans do not respect their history and experiences of discrimination have less positive attitudes toward America and display less trust in the existing justice system. Such "forgetting of the past" is perceived as disrespectful. Although playing the blame game has serious drawbacks, we cannot confront our shared political responsibility without addressing the host of injustices (e.g., inequality, poverty, joblessness, and the "New Jim Crow") that flow from the basic structure of society, which is comprised of the interrelated practices and processes that we all have a hand in sustaining in our capacity as citizens actively pursuing our individual good and rational plan of life in cooperation with others within shared social institutions. This idea, which will be familiar to readers of Rawls, is crucial to our argument for forward-looking responsibility for racial inequality.

Inequality and the Basic Structure

A backward-looking model for grounding political responsibility for racial inequality is limited under nonideal circumstances when we consider evidence concerning the various problems, risks, and defenses involved when we make such attributions. Attending to empirical data regarding the relationship between attributions of responsibility and our social identities, and to how identity-driven attributions can derail backward-looking attributions of political responsibility for racial inequality insofar as this entails playing the blame game, suggests the need for an alternative strategy for grounding shared political responsibility that is compatible with these findings. But before arguing that citizens have a forward-looking shared political responsibility for racial inequality, which satisfies this constraint, we must first elucidate the nature of what Rawls calls the basic structure of society and its relationship to social inequality more generally and racial inequality in particular.

Social practices, which are comprised of a set of formal or informal rules that assign roles to participants, generally specify how participants may or may not act in pursuit of certain goals. And these practices often provide incentives or sanctions to encourage participants to act in the proscribed ways. Competitive games such as soccer or basketball are instances of social practices with these features, but so too are organized political societies. Political philosophers and theorists have staked out various explanations of why we choose to form and maintain this particular social practice. For example, social contract theorists have long argued that we collectively participate in organized societies (whether democratic or nondemocratic) to achieve mutually beneficial goals such as pleasure, welfare, security, or, as Hobbes might say, to attain the things we desire for a commodious living. Others, especially thinkers within the liberal philosophical tradition, have argued that we form political societies to pursue our individual good or rational plans of life in cooperation with others. However the purpose of organized political societies is understood, if we focus on our participation as citizens within society, we need rules to specify the terms of our social cooperation within this distinctive social practice.

Following Rawls,[40] we can use the term "social institutions" to describe the rules that constitute the basic structure of society, which "distribute fundamental rights and duties and determine the division of advantages from social cooperation." These institutions have the formal features generally described earlier: they assign roles, they specify the permitted range of action within the roles, and they provide persons with motivation for acting accordingly since they are generally backed up by various kinds of formal and informal sanctions. These major societal institutions, which collectively form a unified system of social cooperation, profoundly shape the life prospects of everyone participating in the practice. As Rawls puts it, the institutions that make up the basic structure determine a person's "life prospects, what they can expect to be and how well they can hope to do."[41]

Rawls identifies the political constitution, the economic system, which regulates markets and property, and the monogamous family as examples of major social institutions that, when considered together, comprise the basic structure of society. Political theorist Iris Young criticizes Rawls, somewhat unfairly, for seeking to identify some small subset of institutions within society that are more essential than others for determining our life prospects. She proposes instead that the injustice-generating features of society are not comprised of static institutions taken individually or collectively but, rather, are constituted by what she calls "social-structural processes," in which "the actions of masses of people within a large number of institutions converge in their efforts to produce [certain] patterns and positioning" in the distribution of goods, resources, and opportunities.[42]

Young's qualification has the virtue of emphasizing the interrelationship between individual agency and social institutions. It also disabuses us of the idea that there is some evil rational planner pulling the strings of the basic structure to intentionally advantage some and disadvantage others. Yet we see no harm in acknowledging, as Rawls does, that some institutions play especially important roles in this process. Rawls concedes that "the concept of the basic structure is somewhat vague" and allows that it may be filled out in different ways. Indeed, we might add more precision to the concept, and in ways that highlight the processes Young has in mind, by attending to observations made by Wilson:

> Among these processes are the institutional influences on mobility and opportunity, including activities of employers' associations and labor unions; the operation and organization of schools, the mechanisms of residential racial segregation and social isolation in poor neighborhoods; categorical forms of discrimination in hiring, promotion, and other work-related matters; ideologies of group differences shared by members of society and institutionalized in organizational practices and norms that affect social outcomes; and differential racial and ethnic group access to information concerning the labor market, financial markets, education and training, schools, and so on.[43]

However we render the concept more precise, one thing is clear: the basic structure and processes have a profound and comprehensive impact on our life prospects from cradle to grave. As Young observes, they have broad consequences for people's basic well-being, for the range of options available to them, and for their vulnerability to certain forms of oppression, domination, and deprivation.[44] Moreover, as Wilson notes, these "organizational and collective processes that embody the social structure of inequality have varied influences on different racial and ethnic groups."[45]

This last point is particularly significant for our argument. Although the basic structure determines life prospects, it does so in well-ordered societies by interacting with contingencies such as a person's social class background, their natural talents and abilities, their opportunities for education to develop these endowments, and their good or bad luck over their life course. In societies that are not well ordered, such as ones where all citizens do not enjoy equal rights and basic liberties or a fair chance to secure opportunities and offices open to others, additional contingencies such as race, ethnicity, gender, and sexual orientation may also contribute to the shaping of life prospects within the basic structure. They can do so either formally via exclusion based on group membership (e.g., racial segregation) or informally (e.g., subtle discrimination) or by affecting the abilities of the minority itself (e.g., stereotype threat). Therefore, given the ways in which these contingencies interact with the basic structure and the sorts of processes Wilson describes, some measure of social inequality in goods, resources, and opportunities appears to be an inevitable consequence of these background social practices that govern the terms of our cooperation. In well-ordered societies we would expect these inequalities to be solely class based, but in other societies such as the United States they will also be based on race and ethnicity.

For the argument we present in the next section, it would suffice simply to show that social inequality is a *consequence* of the basic structure. But Rawls goes one step further in claiming that social inequality is also highly advantageous for maintaining effective social cooperation in well designed and effectively organized societies for various reasons, including the need for incentives.[46] If Rawls is right both about this and about the inevitability of inequality, then social inequalities are both a consequence and a virtue of the basic structure. Of course, there are limits to how much inequality egalitarians are prepared to accept, which explains why they have distinguished permissible from impermissible ones. Many egalitarians have followed Rawls in holding that within a well-ordered society only inequalities that work to the benefit of the least advantaged persons are permissible. Now that we have elaborated on the nature of the basic structure and its relationship to social inequality more generally and racial inequality in particular, and with the claim that racial inequality is a consequence of the basic structure in hand, we have all that we need to complete our argument for why citizens have forward-looking, shared political responsibility for racial inequality.

Forward-Looking Responsibility for Inequality

One can adopt a backward-looking or forward-looking approach to grounding shared political responsibility for racial inequality: one that looks back to establish some normatively relevant causal connection between agents and particular outcomes, or one that looks forward to ground individual or collective obligations to bring about a state of affairs. The former is attractive because it takes personal responsibility seriously and squares with the intuition that persons should be responsible for what they *do*. The latter conception is sometimes disparaged for seemingly removing individual agency from consideration in grounding responsibility. Something to dislike about the backward-looking conception is that it too easily absolves us of responsibility where causation cannot be readily established. And something to like about the forward-looking conception is that it does not do this. A philosophically attractive account of shared political responsibility for racial inequality would be forward looking but without entirely setting aside the significance of individual agency in assigning responsibility.

Young rejects Hannah Arendt's account of political responsibility but applauds her for distinguishing it from collective guilt.[47] Young finds Arendt's account of responsibility deficient in two respects: it makes persons politically responsible for what they have not done, and it grounds political responsibility in merely being a member of some group, such as a nation, family, race, or class, and inheriting responsibility for the evils, wrongs, or injustice done by the group. Young proposes an alternative account of political responsibility rooted in an obligation to share responsibility for unjust social structures and processes and taking political responsibility for changing them. This obligation is rooted not merely in our *being citizens* but in our *participation as citizens* in a political system of social cooperation that facilitates the existence of structural injustices.

According to Young's conception of political responsibility, individual agency plays an essential role in accounting for our forward-looking, shared moral responsibility for injustice. This is attractive because it preserves the moral intuition that persons should only be held responsible for what they *do*, whether construed narrowly as actions or more broadly as omissions. What is commendable about Young's conception is that political responsibility can play this role without being conflated with the backward-looking moral responsibility typically associated with finding individual persons guilty of—and blaming them for—causing social injustice. The social psychological data we have considered gives us compelling reasons for insisting upon a distinction between forward- and backward-looking conceptions of political responsibility and for preferring the former under nonideal circumstances.

Young develops her forward-looking account of shared political responsibility for injustice using the case of vulnerability to homelessness. She observes that persons can end up in this position due to *social-structural injustice*, which "occurs as a consequence of many individuals and institutions acting to pursue their particular goals and interests, for the most part within the limits of accepted rules and norms."[48] And she argues that our active participation in social processes (of the sort that Wilson identifies), which facilitate these countless interactions, gives us political responsibility for this injustice. This argument can be adapted and developed to make a similar case for responsibility for inequality.

All citizens pursue their life plans and exercise and develop the capacities essential for citizenship within the basic structure of society. And this interrelated system of rules and processes, which regulate our political constitution and our markets and system of exchange, as well as the production, development, and education of future citizens within the institution of family are essential for facilitating our social cooperation in pursuit of these aims over the course of a complete life. There is great variety in the life plans that people choose. These choices impact our individual share of primary social goods such as income and wealth, and they often figure in moral assessments of our individual conduct and character. Yet they are made within the opportunity set afforded to us within the basic structure of society, which allows some to amass advantage and others disadvantage based on their social position.

So, for example, our choices about raising a family, work, schooling, and housing are all constrained by rules and processes, such as taxation, inheritance, property, zoning, and school finance, which impact the opportunities available to us given our class background, our talents, our luck, and our race—in societies such as the United States that are not well ordered. Young observes that this feature of the basic structure need not be coercive.[49] As she says, "Social structures do not constrain in the form of the direct coercion of some individuals over others; they constrain more indirectly and cumulatively as blocking possibilities." We should add, pace Rawls, that the basic structure also facilitates possibilities insofar as it is also an institutional scheme "for satisfying existing desires and aspirations" and "fashioning desires and aspirations in the future."[50] It thus provides the structural context for determining who we are and who we want to be.

Given the profound, comprehensive, and inescapable impact of these institutions on our lives, and assuming that our life prospects within the cooperative practice of organized society are exceedingly better than fending for ourselves in the state of nature, we all have a fundamental interest in *sustaining* the institutions that make up the basic structure of society. The creation and continued existence of the major institutions and social structural processes that determine our life prospects and facilitate our actions in pursuit of various ends all require our social cooperation.

In the course of such cooperation, we must make, accept, and abide by, and moreover, enforce conventions, which we do in different ways depending on our system of government. We do these things through voting within a democratic society, which is why political liberties are counted among the primary goods by Rawls. But even if we do not vote or find ways to evade active participation in democratic governance, we clearly still have an interest in sustaining these institutions and processes. Were it the case that many fewer people or no one voted or participated in democratic governance, then the social practice of organized society would wither away, and we would be stuck with our least preferable outcome of fending for ourselves in a state of nature. So, clearly, we all have an interest in the basic structure remaining intact and ensuring that our social cooperation takes place on fair terms. Therefore, on this forward-looking model of responsibility, our agency is absolutely essential for preserving the major institutions that set the terms of our social cooperation, and we all share a political responsibility for bearing the costs of its unjust consequences.

Within the social contract tradition considerable attention has been placed on the *creation* of society and the establishment of institutions and rules that constitute its basic structure. This focus on origins may partly explain why philosophical accounts of political responsibility are backward looking. For instance, if we focus exclusively on the extent to which parties helped to create the life prospect-shaping basic structure, we may be inclined to attribute whatever negative consequences flow from this to all who had a hand in creating the basic structure, and this encourages us to look back to make such determinations. The shift to a forward-looking account of political responsibility requires placing greater emphasis on the interests we all share in sustaining the major social institutions that so profoundly shape our life prospects—a point that Young does not fully appreciate in focusing on the complex way we contribute to injustices that flow from them. So even though we may not have created the basic structure—having inherited it from our ancestors—we nonetheless have a vital interest its endurance. Therefore, assuming with Rawls, Wilson, and Young that social inequality is an inevitable outcome of the basic structure, and further assuming that we share responsibility for its outcomes, we should also take political responsibility for inequality given our vital interest in sustaining the system of cooperation and institutions that give rise to both permissible and impermissible inequalities.

Unfair racial inequalities in the distribution of goods, resources, or opportunities, or in the various benefits and burdens of our social cooperation are a paramount concern of social justice. Such inequalities can certainly stem from intentional efforts on the part of specific parties. Within the social sciences there is ongoing debate over the extent to which persisting racial inequalities in wealth, political power, education, and other measures are due to such efforts. Where these efforts are motivated by social group animus or racial bias they are described as instances of discrimination. Although they can arise and be perpetuated without conscious intention,[51] in postracial America many believe that racial inequalities can only be judged unjust if they can be traceable to discrimination with racist intent.

Although formal and informal discrimination continues to account for racial inequalities, a point that is far from uncontroversial, they need not stem from such discrimination. In other words, we need not presume that bias is operative, or that some parties are not playing by the rules, or that government is out to get those most disadvantaged by racial inequalities to declare them unjust. The basic structure provides us with an alternative perspective from which to evaluate racial inequality normatively. And provided that we remain focused on our individual and shared interest in sustaining this structure, it affords us a forward-looking justification as to why we should take political responsibility for doing something about it, which aims to circumvent blame-switching and other defenses by which those who are not disadvantaged aim to absolve themselves of responsibility. This is a virtue because, as Young notes, when focused on structural injustice (or racial inequality), "it is difficult to make blame 'stick' to anyone in particular, because almost everyone is involved."[52]

Thus, on this model, we have shared political responsibility for inequality even if we have not acted unfairly in our dealings with others, have treated others with equal respect and concern, have minded our business, and have not caused their plight in the sense of being morally blameworthy for it. The basic structure and processes can produce inequality even when individuals are acting justly. Inequality can result, as Young puts it, "from a complex combination of actions and policies by individual, corporate, and government agents—actions and policies that most people consider normal and acceptable, or even necessary and good."[53] As we noted earlier, Wilson offers a useful account of some of the policies and processes that produce racial inequalities in the United States.[54]

This forward-looking model of responsibility can be fruitfully elaborated upon using Margaret Gilbert's notion of being jointly committed.[55] We might say that citizens have a "joint commitment" to sustain the institutions and processes that make it possible to pursue their aims cooperatively. How and why they form, uphold, or breach this commitment are not germane to our present purposes. All that matters is that this commitment be viewed as unifying citizens to work toward a common project, namely, sustaining the basic structure and processes that vitally shape the terms of their social cooperation, which all have an interest in contributing to. Some accounts of collective responsibility are interested in examining the relationship between the blameworthiness of the collective and the blameworthiness of particular members; however, this would be unattractive for our purposes. Indeed, the reason to advance a forward-looking model of responsibility is precisely to avoid analyzing responsibility for inequality in personal terms. But to eschew analyzing this in personal terms is not to reject the importance of agency in establishing responsibility altogether. Hence, the attractiveness of rooting political responsibility in joint commitment is that it locates agency in undertaking such a commitment. It is important to emphasize that this commitment only serves to locate a person within the relevant group, which shares responsibility, and not to hold them morally blameworthy for its action, or even for their membership in this group.

We must be careful, however, about how we specify the content of this joint commitment. For example, consider our premise that racial inequality is an inevitable consequence of the basic structure, which means that some will be disadvantaged in the distribution of income and wealth based upon their social position. To say that citizens have a joint commitment to sustain the basic structure will not, then, be tantamount to saying that they have a joint commitment to a common project of wronging certain members of society, say by subjugating them or treating them unequally.[56] This would negate the point that participants within organized society might be acting in accordance with the prescribed norms and that there still will be unfair racial inequalities. Moreover, this way of understanding the content of citizen's being jointly committed amounts to an indirect way of interpreting shared political responsibility as a special case of blameworthy personal responsibility. Instead, the content of this joint commitment is, more generally, sustaining the institutions and processes needed to pursue our individual aims. Because these have consequences such as creating inequalities when persons act in accordance with the rules, we must share the burden of these outcomes even in the absence of moral blame.

So, the joint commitment, as we envision it, is not to be bound by the decisions of the authorities or the social contract (either past or present), but, rather, it is to sustain the basic structure, which makes the common pursuit of ends in organized political society possible. The former envisions responsibility as backward looking to repair or to make amends for unjust acts and decisions. The latter conceives of it in a forward-looking manner to sustain the structures that make our collective life possible. Therefore, the notion of joint commitment for inequality allows us to treat citizens as being jointly committed to bearing the burden of sharing responsibility for doing something about racial inequality without also accepting personal responsibility for it. This is not ideal; but neither is the world we live in. And in our less-than-perfect world, this strategy is attractive given the evidence of the real problems associated with waiting for collective guilt to induce whites to take political responsibility for doing something about the pressing social problem of unjust racial inequality.

In this chapter we have argued for a forward-looking approach to grounding political responsibility for racial inequality. This enables us to avoid the pitfalls of a backward-looking approach, which empirical research in social psychology brings to light. Some critics will worry that our argument lets off the hook those who might be guilty of racial inequality–generating discrimination. They may also complain that it does not squarely confront the ideological assumptions that blame the victims of racial inequality for their disadvantage. These are serious concerns. However, if we attend to evidence concerning how people actually think and behave given their respective social identities, thereby taking persons as they are rather than as we wish or imagine them to be, it is clear that playing the blame game—regardless of where the blame is taken to rest—will not be a winning strategy in this day and age.

Assuming that addressing unfair racial inequalities will require multiracial collective action or shared burdens on the part of citizens who are differently motivated based on their social identities, the evidence we have considered justifies grounding political responsibility for racial inequality in a forward-looking manner. We have done this by rooting it in a joint civic commitment to do what we must to sustain the basic structure that makes organized society possible and productive. Forward-looking political responsibility for inequality may not give us all that we want, but it gives us all that we can reasonably hope to get in our nonideal world.

To take up collective responsibility in pursuit of postracial remedies requires pressing and undertaking the demand to make American democracy more inclusive. Part III turns to this final matter.

PART III
THE DEMAND FOR DEMOCRACY

7
Power to the People

> The beginnings of the present failure of democracy in America was the repudiation of the democratic process in the case of black American citizens in the South.
> —W. E. B. Du Bois, "Democracy Fails in America"[1]

> The question which you and I have to settle is this: can we envision and do we want a democracy where the rights of all citizens are equal? It is not necessary to meet this clear statement by the trite remark that all people are not and probably never will be equal and similar in their abilities, their gifts and their accomplishments. The problem which is now proposed is a problem of legal rights to recognized political, civil and social equality for every citizen.
> —W. E. B. Du Bois, "No Second-Class Citizens"[2]

The chapter presents a neglected yet potent argument by W. E. B. Du Bois for affording all people, especially black and other marginalized populations, a hand in democratic rule.[3] This is vital for achieving a realistic blacktopia. Du Bois maintains that not doing this puts America at risk of democratic failure.

Democracy can fail in different ways. It can do so when its fundamental foundations—the right to vote, freedom of the press, the rule of law—crumble. Since these are basic institutions, we can call this *institutional failure*. It can also fail when self-proclaimed democratic nations do not realize certain normative ideals such as freedom and justice for all. Since these are basic aspirations, we can call this *aspirational failure*. Both kinds of failure, which are obviously related, can stem from the action or inaction of political elites, including elected officials and administrative appointees. But one can also link democratic failure to the action or inaction of citizens whose decision to vote or to refrain from voting for a certain candidate can create the opportunity for elected elites to engineer institutional and aspirational failure. The great mass of citizens—women, blacks, the poor, working-class whites, and other historically marginalized groups—will worry that the system is not working for them. Du Bois addresses this threat to democracy from below, that is, from the submerged masses who may use what little political power they have to propel us toward democratic failure. His solution speaks to how we can address the masses' legitimate complaint that democracy is not working for them but for the elites, the wealthy, and the powerful. The hope is that by doing this we can decrease the odds that the masses will give political elites an opportunity to engineer institutional and aspirational failure.

If we are committed to achieving a more perfect democracy—one that moves us closer to securing the broadest measure of justice for all—we have a political duty to address the circumstances that contribute to the masses potentially doing us harm by securing for them certain legal rights. Rights to education, economic opportunity, and protection from discrimination are normative safeguards against democratic failure. Unfettered access to the ballot is essential because the right to vote helps the masses secure these other rights. Du Bois proposes that the way to avert democratic failure is to guarantee civil and political rights, social equality, and economic justice for every citizen. Of course, this is no guarantee that democracy will endure. Other factors can contribute to democratic failure. Nevertheless, offering a solution that makes it less likely that the masses will use their votes to hand aspiring autocrats and political elites an opportunity to engineer democratic failure is an important safeguard worth pursuing.

Why Democracy

W. E. B. Du Bois's philosophical engagement with democracy extends over five decades in books, essays, articles, speeches, and correspondence. Although he touches on the topic of democracy earlier, it gets his undivided attention for the first time in chapter 6 of *Darkwater*, published in 1920. But here he does not advance an ideal theory of democracy—dwelling on the meaning, implications, and justification of its basic principles, which may prompt some to dismiss mistakenly what he has to say as irrelevant to political philosophers and political theorists. Instead, he draws on a way of understanding the normative function of democracy and develops his thoughts on why America falls short. Due to this deficiency one can say that the nation is not a genuine democracy or, as I will say, that it is an imperfect one.[4]

I use "Of the Ruling of Men," which is essentially an essay about democratic failure, as the primary text for my reconstruction of Du Bois's defense of democracy, incorporating other works only to elucidate and expand upon what he says there. For Du Bois, the widest possible distribution of political rule is the democratic default position: *As many citizens as possible should have the right to vote*. Yet history shows that exclusion, which always benefits the interests of a select few, has been supported on different grounds, including by claiming that the excluded are too ignorant to rule. On my reading of this insightful chapter, Du Bois defends democracy by rebutting this and other justifications for less inclusive political rule.[5] But here, and elsewhere, he says things that acknowledge there are other ways to proceed with a defense grounded in taking democracy to have both instrumental and non-instrumental value. Let us briefly consider some of what Du Bois has to say about the nature and value of democracy, more generally, before considering his rebuttal of the ignorance justification in the next section.

In an ideal democracy, political rule should benefit everyone—the high and low classes, the powerful and powerless, the rich and poor, men and women, white and black alike. But being far from ideal, for much of its history political rule in America has only aimed at the good of a select few. One hypothesis for this is that many people have historically been excluded from political rule or, if not excluded entirely, have been afforded diminished and unequal political power. Because of this, those in power have used it largely for their own benefit rather than for the benefit of all. And under these nonideal conditions all people have not been beneficiaries of political rule.

To be clear, to say that *all* people should be beneficiaries of political rule is not to say that all the people should rule. The work of politics, which includes enacting policy, can be assigned to public officials. The point is that everyone should have a say in who occupies these roles, and this can be the result of affording all people an equal opportunity to select their government representatives through voting.[6] In this popular sovereignty model of democracy the people—all the people—should have real political power over their rulers and government. This is something that Du Bois espoused in some of his earlier and later reflections on democracy.

In a 1907 speech delivered at Carnegie Hall in New York City, for example, Du Bois says, "We believe not that every man should rule, but that every man—black and white, high and low—should have power over the rulers and that every man's personal desires, personal ideals, personal powers, should be counted in the great workings of the nation."[7] Affording every citizen such power is, on his view, essential for establishing democratic authority and sovereignty. Failure to do this can have grave consequences, and avoiding them supplies an instrumental justification for democratic rule: it allows us to avoid certain bad results.

Forty-three years later, Du Bois lamented that the great mass of American people did not have such sovereignty and that political rule in the nation was effectively controlled by a small class of plutocrats. In a 1950 radio broadcast, after defining democracy as "the form of government in which each citizen has a voice in all decisions of policy and action," Du Bois observes, "We entered the 20th century, not as a democracy ruled by the votes of the people but as a plutocracy ruled by wealth and for wealth. The slave power was replaced by the money power and under neither can democracy flourish."[8] Unfortunately, this still rings true today. The super wealthy have a disproportionate share of political power, and as historian Nancy MacLean has powerfully argued, they are using it to put democracy in chains.[9]

With this more modest conception of democratic political rule in hand, where each citizen has a voice that counts and exercises real political power over rulers and the nation, we can say that rule of all the people for the greatest good of all is the ideal of *perfect democracy*. Rule of the few for the benefit of some is the nonideal reality of an *imperfect democracy*. Struggles for ideal democracy, usually led by the lower, less powerful, and more impoverished classes, aim to change things by expanding the beneficiaries of political rule to include all the people. They aim to move a society from an imperfect state of democratic rule to a more perfect one by securing a share of political rule for the downtrodden, dispossessed, and despised. They seek to afford all citizens, not merely the wealthy, a voice in determining government policy and action. In sum, democratic movements seek to give real political power to the people. Du Bois's earliest and most sustained reflections on the nature and value of democracy begin with these thoughts.

"Of the Ruling of Men" starts with the claim that the greatest good of all should be the aim of the ruling of people. Du Bois calls this the *universal good*. Democracy, when perfectly realized, is a form of political rule that organizes the actions of all persons who are subject to political rule to realize this end. A form of rule seeking the good of fewer persons or that organizes the actions of few persons to achieve this aim is imperfect. So from this vantage point, were we to ask, "Why Democracy?," the answer would be that it is instrumental for realizing the universal good. This normative ideal admits of different interpretations, and two are at work here.

On the one hand, Du Bois adopts an instrumentalist interpretation of democracy that is essentially utilitarian, where utility maximization is about aggregating the political preferences or interests of the greatest number of citizens in setting government policy and directing government action. When more people participate in democracy, he tells us, "the appearance of new interests and complaints means disarrangement and confusion to the older equilibrium. It is, of course, the inevitable preliminary step to that larger equilibrium in which the interests of no human soul will be neglected."[10] And then he concludes, "The problem of government thereafter would be to reduce the necessary conflict of human interests to the minimum."[11]

However, as the argument unfolds, he introduces another description of the normative aim of democracy, which invites a deontological interpretation of the universal good. Du Bois writes, "Democracy is a method of realizing the broadest measure of justice to all human beings."[12] And we accomplish this, he says, by affording the ballot to excluded groups such as women, not as a privilege, but as something they need "to right the balance of a world sadly awry because of its brutal neglect of the rights of women and children."[13] These thoughts suggest that democracy seeks the universal good by recognizing the rights of all citizens so that they can advance their interests.

In "Of the Ruling of Men" there are, therefore, at least two readings of Du Bois's instrumentalist justification of democracy—one that puts a utilitarian spin on what realizing the universal good amounts to, and another that gives this a deontological twist. I will not attempt to reconcile these two interpretations. But I will adopt the latter one in my reconstruction of his defense of democracy, and in thinking through what needs to happen for American democracy to survive.

One might suppose, as Du Bois does, that the more people involved in political rule, where this means having a voice that counts, and having real political power over government policy and action, the more likely the case that the broadest measure of justice for all will be secured. He also supposes that "the right to vote is the only effective weapon of democracy" and that "disfranchisement deprives any individual or group of its opportunity to realize and guide democracy."[14] Thus, if voting constitutes a way to give people a hand in political rule, then we have a straightforward instrumental justification for affording as many people as possible access to the ballot. Du Bois sums this up as follows: "if All ruled they would rule for All and thus Universal Good was sought through Universal Suffrage."[15]

It might be objected that this instrumental justification puts the case for democracy on too weak a footing. What if we could achieve the universal good without inclusive or maximally inclusive political rule? If popular sovereignty is only valuable because it helps us secure this good, and we can secure it with something less than rule of all, and there are compelling reasons for wanting to do so, then we should opt for imperfect democracy or no democracy at all. Du Bois entertains this possibility but flatly rejects it. For one, he thinks human history shows that this is not a realistic possibility; that is, no nation that excludes citizens from political rule has secured the broadest measure of justice for all.

But even if this were possible, we have additional reasons for embracing a popular sovereignty model of democracy to achieve this aim. Democracy helps us secure valuable collective goods such as the progress of culture and civilization. It also secures the individual goods of self-development and self-knowledge. Du Bois makes and connects these points quite elegantly. He writes,

> The vast and wonderful knowledge of this marvelous universe is locked in the bosoms of its individual souls. To tap this mighty reservoir of experience, knowledge, beauty, love, and deed we must appeal not to the few, not to some souls, but to all. The narrower the appeal, the poorer the culture; the wider the appeal the more magnificent are the possibilities.[16]

Insofar as some of these goods might be said to have non-instrumental value, Du Bois can say that popular sovereignty, apart from being instrumental for securing the broadest measure of justice for all, is also good for us even if it does not lead to this outcome.[17] So, if we could secure the justice benefit with less inclusive political rule, the non-instrumental benefits of inclusive democracy would be lost. And these are good for us regardless of whether they lead to justice. Thus, we see that Du Bois values democracy both instrumentally and non-instrumentally.

However, as valuable as it is, democracy does not require specific policy outcomes. As he puts it,

The theory of democracy does not call for equality of gift, universal college education or absolute individual integrity; but it does depend upon the widest possible consultation with the mass of citizens on the theory that only this way can you consult ultimate authority and ultimate sovereignty.[18]

History has shown that failure to do this can have dire consequences for democracy, which include chaos and even revolution. In addition, undemocratic rule denies all citizens—both those excluded and included—the benefits that are non-instrumentally good for each and every one of us.

Du Bois's conception of the nature and value of democracy is rich with insights. It offers us various ways of defending democracy. We can argue that it helps us secure benefits that are valuable instrumentally and non-instrumentally, and that we should avoid burdens that are bad because of their effects and regardless of them. But the main burden of his *Darkwater* essay on democratic failure is not to unpack these philosophical claims about democracy's nature and value. Rather, it is to offer a defense of democracy that turns on rebutting justifications for excluding some citizens from democratic rule. And conceding that citizens are not omniscient is central to this task.

Ignorant Citizens

The general thrust of Du Bois's pre- and post-*Darkwater* writings on democracy is to contrast perfect and imperfect democracy, to document how and why Western democracies and American democracy in particular have been so imperfect, and to offer guidance on how to move from our grossly imperfect democracy to a more perfect one. His primary purpose in "Of the Ruling of Men," as I read it, is to identify, interrogate, and invalidate familiar justifications for not giving power to all of the people—so that they may pursue the broadest measure of justice for all.

Because of his lifelong focus on America's problem of the color line, Du Bois keenly appreciated how the presumption that excluded citizens were ignorant was a significant obstacle to moving from an imperfect to a more perfect democracy. His writings dwell upon this and other acute challenges, including poverty and prejudice, that subvert our democratic aspirations. However, the problem of ignorance looms large in his 1920 assessment of democratic failure, though this problem was on his radar long before then.[19]

For example, as early as 1898, in laying out a general plan for the study of social problems affecting American blacks, Du Bois notes that this group was largely ignorant due to the legacy of slavery and its aftermath. Of all the groups in the nation at the time, he writes, "the Negro is by far the most ignorant; nearly half of the race are absolutely illiterate, only a minority of the other half have thorough common school training, and but a remnant are liberally educated."[20]

Du Bois cautioned his readers against thinking that the social problems raised by the color line were new. At the dawn of the nineteenth century, America was struggling with the question of what to do with a class of persons—American Negroes[21]—who were subordinated, exploited, and rendered second-class citizens. But a century before, the nation was fixated on how to deal with "the great mass of its ignorant and poor [white] laboring classes." Hence, the problem of this earlier age was the political rights of the masses, which raised some of the same social questions as the race issue.

One such question was whether the so-called ignorant classes (of white laborers) should be afforded a voice in democratic rule. The Enlightenment ideal that the rule of the people, and the legitimacy of government authority, is based on the consent of the governed has long been considered a feature of all "civilized" societies. Yet there have been people who have always sought to make exceptions, as Du Bois observes,

> There were men—and wise men, too—who believed that democratic government was simply impossible with human nature in its present condition. "Shall the tail wag the dog?" said they; shall a brutish mob sway the destinies of the intelligent and well-born of the nation? It was all very well for Rousseau to sing the Rights of Man, but this civic idealism must make way for calm criticism.[22]

In many self-proclaimed democratic societies, it is likely that some class of persons will be declared too ignorant to share in democratic rule. Of course, these people will be expected (unreasonably in my view) to pay taxes, to obey the laws, and to pledge allegiance to the flag. But when it comes to political governance, they will be expected to hold their tongues. Therefore, if we take a broader historical view of democracy, as Du Bois urges, we will find that a pretext for excluding persons of different class, race, or gender from political rule has been to declare them too ignorant to rule.

Today, when we hear that some Americans are entertaining the thought that the ignorant masses—who are willing to entrust our democratic future to leaders with bad intentions—should be excluded, we should know that the epistocracy solution is not new. We have been down this road before, and Du Bois thought we should resist epistocracy. But he did not do so, in the first instance, by denying the premise that the masses are ignorant. Rather, he partly conceded, contextualized, and co-opted it to defend democracy, and to supply a normative understanding of the duties of democratic rule.

According to Du Bois the great majority of people—with and without smarts—are ignorant of many things that must be known for ruling to serve the good of all. Obviously, the masses lack knowledge about other individuals as well as groups of individuals. For example, we live in close proximity to our neighbors, yet many of us know little about their interests, fears, and pains. Similarly, we encounter individuals in our daily lives who share certain faiths and class status, and who are marked differently by race and ethnicity, but we know little, if anything, about what interests they share in common by virtue of these group-based identities.

But, even more important, as Du Bois intimates, reflecting on the predicament of late nineteenth- and early twentieth-century America, the masses did not know enough about the complex set of issues and problems such as poverty, inequality, and discrimination associated with a growing industrial society, or, most important, about how the titans of industry—plutocrats and their political stooges—used the industrial age to serve their narrow interests.

He argues that the rapid growth of industry in America at the time created "an invincible kingdom of trade, business, and commerce," which placed the fate of democracy in the hands of "the Captains of Industry and their created Millionaires," which proved difficult for the masses to understand.[23] This lack of understanding, and corresponding lack of control over their well-being, created discontent among those who labored the hardest but reaped the least during the Industrial Revolution.

During the first reconstruction, America had a chance to secure a more inclusive democracy, and it took some steps with amendments, education, and setting up federal oversight to make sure that the newly acquired legal rights of black Americans were respected. But the former slave-owning class conspired with captains of industry to establish white rule and block the formation of a unified class of black and white laborers to challenge the industrial order. And this was done largely through voter disfranchisement and unequal schooling, and by using racial hatred to gain broad support for sustaining a democracy ruled by whites to benefit whites.

But working-class whites saw the handwriting on the wall and sought to use what little political power they had to secure their rights from being trampled by the captains of industry. However, as Du Bois astutely observes, their battle was doomed to fail because they tried to secure a share of rule for themselves while leaving black laborers on the outskirts of democracy, which would allow industrialists to undercut their efforts by threatening to use cheaper black labor. Thus, many whites were willing to stifle the pursuit of a more perfect democracy, including making industry democratic, to maintain their privileged place in an imperfect racial democracy where whiteness was the currency of the realm.

So, to be sure, the masses are ignorant of many things. And this was certainly true of blacks, who at the start of 1900 were less than four decades removed from having suffered through a brutal slave system that criminalized literacy.[24] Thus, it was no surprise, as Du Bois noted, that when it came to society's understanding of the Negro problem, and the thinking of some that blacks were unfit for democratic rule, it was widely taken to be a problem of ignorance. And the point was not merely the obvious one, namely, that most blacks were indeed illiterate (having suffered through a brutal slave system that prevented them from learning); it was said that they suffered from "a deeper ignorance of the world and its ways, of the thought and experience of men; an ignorance of self and the possibilities of human souls."[25] Let us suppose, for the moment, that this too is true.

Ignorance was not only a Negro problem. And their lack of knowledge was not the only challenge to satisfying the Enlightenment ideal of popular sovereignty. A more general obstacle to achieving rule by all through universal suffrage was the widespread ignorance of the people in general, including those who fancied themselves as smart. "The mass of men, even of the more intelligent men," writes Du Bois, "not only knew little about each other but less about the action of men in groups and the technique of industry in general."[26] This ignorance did not render them helpless, but it meant that they could only apply the political power they had with their ballot to the things that they knew or only knew partially. And this is precisely what we would expect of any group of persons who had to rule with limited knowledge.

So, if ignorance is put forward as a reason for limiting political rule to exclude blacks, then white ignorance—both of the white masses and the white elite—was also a serious challenge to democracy. Yet this had not stopped the nation from forming and running a democratic society with white citizens who were far from omniscient. Indeed, as Du Bois claims, America taught the world that the "most unlikely classes and races" could govern themselves provided that they had education, economic opportunity, and protection of their basic civil, political, and social rights.[27]

Du Bois develops his thoughts in the chapter by showing how the shift from agricultural and small-scale economies to a larger industrial one not only compounded the problem of ignorance, as there was much that the great mass of people did not understand about commerce and trade under these new circumstances; it also allowed captains of industry to mock democracy and claim that they were best suited to rule (since they at least had the requisite knowledge of industry) and could be counted on to use their surplus wealth to help the unfortunate ignorant masses with philanthropy.

A widely used justification for excluding blacks from democratic rule—by denying them the ballot or making their exercise of it more burdensome—was the assumption, as Du Bois put it, "that only the intelligent should vote, or those who know how to rule men, or those who are not under benevolent guardianship, or those who ardently desire the right."[28] But this was merely a pretext for advancing the narrow self-interest of de facto industrial rulers, and—when used by white laborers and their unions—it was a pretext for advancing their white racial group interest in general. Thus, to paraphrase Du Bois, the pretextual argument for black disfranchisement went like this: Civilized democratic societies did not allow the ignorant to rule. America is a civilized democracy. American blacks are ignorant. Therefore, they should not be allowed to rule.

But this argument is, of course, too strong, as working-class whites quickly came to realize. Attributions of ignorance by those with industrial power, white power, or male power do not respect caste, race, or gender divisions. Just as blacks, Asians, or women could be denigrated with this label, so could whites considered to be of lower descent relative to whites of high birth. Indeed, as Du Bois points out, early twentieth-century America was being ruled by whites who a century earlier had been deemed unable to become a genuinely self-ruling people. They had proven the skeptics wrong, showing that ignorance and inexperience were not impediments to democratic rule. The American experiment with democracy, which extended political rule beyond a privileged few, who were believed to be better fitted to rule by "blood" or "divine right," turned out to be good for the development of civilization.

Rebutting the appeal to ignorance as a justification for less inclusive political rule suggests that Du Bois was a rationalist about political change. From this point of view, if we overcome ignorance (particularly white ignorance), we can then appeal to people's sense of reason to persuade them to extend the benefits of democracy to all. Du Bois understood, however, that this appeal to rational moral suasion would be ineffective against those moved by racial animus and who acted politically based on a narrow tribalism.

For instance, he knew that in the early-twentieth-century South some people "must vote always and simply to keep Negroes down."[29] And as he says, "such a denial of the fundamental principles of democracy is dangerous to the Nation." Part of the danger is that wherever such a steadfast commitment to racial prejudice prevails, this renders reason helpless. "It means," as he observes, "that there are certain parts of the country where reason cannot be applied to the settlement of great political questions."

Elsewhere in his work Du Bois illustrates with great effect the irony that tribalism, or what he calls the "mob mind, the herd instinct," stands to do the greatest damage not to black folks, but to whites. When they, particularly working-class whites, allow themselves to be co-opted in supporting the political disfranchisement of blacks (and other groups), they unwittingly undermine their own authority to raise grievances about their own plight and to advance political reforms. He writes,

> Again and again we see the individual tragedy: a young white man, Southern by birth, tradition and belief, sees one matter he would reform, one point of disagreement. He is tolerated a while and then the herd turns and tramples him in fury. It is worse than lynching. The South lynches the bodies of black men, but the souls of white.[30]

I think that Du Bois overstates this point. However, the basic idea, which is that political tribalism serves as much to control and harm whites as it does to maintain the status of blacks as second-class citizens, is clear and compelling enough.

The United States is arguably seeing this play out in real time today, as working-class whites who signed up for Trump's plan to make America great again—helping to vault him into power despite his veiled and not so veiled appeals to a divisive white racial tribalism—are now feeling the pain from many of his policies, from gutting the Affordable Care Act, to supporting anti-union legal rulings, to starting a trade war with tariffs, and to cutting taxes on corporations and the wealthy.

If Du Bois was a rationalist about political change, then, he was certainly not a naive one who underestimated the power of racial tribalism and the racial prejudice that accompanied it to prevent clear thinking about political matters. By the same token, he knew that lack of knowledge is not the only thing that matters for political rule aiming for the universal good.[31] Selfishness, rooted either in concern for one's narrow self-interest or for one's narrow group-based interest, can also be an obstacle to realizing the universal good. When this takes the latter form, the tribalism that results becomes a significant tool in the arsenal of antidemocratic forces that use racial politics to keep the working classes divided.[32]

At the same time, we must not overemphasize the role of race in Du Bois's account of democratic failure. In some of his earliest thinking about the repudiation of the democratic process in the South, in which blacks were denied the right to vote, Du Bois viewed this as primarily an economic problem that was strategically used by powerful factions to serve their selfish economic interests.

As blacks became more educated, especially due to industrial training in black schools, they competed increasingly with white laborers for jobs, creating an opportunity for some to stir up racial divisions to keep black and white laborers from joining forces to assert a claim to be equal partners in democracy with the de facto ruling class—the captains of industry. Southern politicians, who had their own fears about the formation of an industrial democracy, blamed the ills of the white working class on their black competitors and implored whites to use their ballots to keep blacks from power, which would only make matters worse. And "exploiting capitalists," as Du Bois describes them, threatened to replace white workers with black ones if they did not stop complaining about unfair treatment, low wages, and poor working conditions. Thus, according to Du Bois, attention to race prejudice, though a serious problem in its own right, was basically a way to put the spotlight on "a great labor problem."[33]

So, establishing what Du Bois calls an "industrial democracy," in which the black and white working classes recognize their common oppression by plutocrats and politicians on their payroll seeking to save capitalism from democracy, and move to close ranks to demand a political voice in determining the rules of business and the distribution of its outputs, is vital for realizing a more inclusive ideal of democracy. More controversially, as I read him, achieving industrial democracy also means reassessing, and, alas, de-emphasizing, the prominent preoccupation with white supremacy in understanding how we move twenty-first-century America toward a more ideal expression of genuine democracy.

Largely because of ignorance about class exploitation and the workings of tribalism, Du Bois thought that the education of blacks as well as whites was crucial to counter divisive uses of race politics to prevent coalition building. Some sort of radical education would help develop a class consciousness to oppose the counterproductive use of racial politics by antidemocratic forces. If fearing loss of economic and physical well-being made the masses willing to entertain autocrats and others who supported the rule of the few, a radical education was necessary to help the masses resist and to see the wisdom of joining forces to combat a common oppression. Of course, if people were moved to do this not merely by reason or even by the perception of common interests but also by emotional appeals, then building the needed coalition would have to account for this.

However, with respect to reason, Du Bois argued that the labor movement had a vital role to play in imparting the knowledge needed to encourage the white and black working classes to close ranks, especially because schools and the press could not be counted on to do this. An educative labor movement, with a radical agenda, could dispel certain myths about workers, capitalists, and property to unmask the injustice of wealth inequality. One of these myths is that the poor envy the rich and want to deprive the rich of the just fruit of their efforts by law or force. Other myths are that property is gained solely by individual effort and is thus something that capitalists have the right to use as they see fit, and that industry is owned by one group—the capitalists—and that gives them the sole authority to set wages and working conditions, and that public interference with any of this is always unjust.[34]

So, in addition to tribalism and the selfishness that it breeds, as Du Bois appreciated, one problem among others for democratic rule based in universal suffrage certainly consists in "widespread ignorance." But this was not only about the masses lacking certain kinds of knowledge needed for political rule, e.g., policy knowledge or technocratic knowledge of social problems; it was also about the so-called smarter ruling elites lacking the knowledge necessary for democratic political rule built on a normative foundation of justice for all. Securing this knowledge required consulting directly with the masses about their pains, sufferings, and circumstances. According to Du Bois, the masses had first-person knowledge of their own souls and could be counted on to use this knowledge to pursue their self-defense. So, as far as Du Bois was concerned, both rule of the masses and rule of the few posed dangers in the absence of the right sort of knowledge.

Sage Souls

Earlier I said that Du Bois did not resist epistocracy, *in the first instance*, by denying that the masses lacked certain knowledge. Thus far I have established that his first move was to show that ignorance was widespread, yet this was no obstacle to the white men who founded the United States—after being denigrated as too ignorant to rule—from launching their grand experiment in democratic government. Du Bois's second move was to argue that the masses did indeed possess certain knowledge. As is the case with all individuals, he claimed, the masses know their own "souls," and this knowledge is vital for securing democracy's normative aim to secure the broadest measure of justice for all. Du Bois's third and final move in "Of the Ruling of Men" is a response to a sound objection. If we suppose that the masses do indeed have knowledge needed for securing justice in society, one may object that they need not be given the ballot to secure it. Perhaps we only need to consult with them, say by conducting surveys of what they think, and then others can use this knowledge to secure justice. Du Bois answers this objection by arguing that the ballot is also necessary for self-defense: women need to vote because they can be counted on, more than men, to secure the neglected rights of women and children, and blacks can be counted on, more than whites, to secure protection from lynching and discrimination, and other basic rights.

There are places in his writings where Du Bois shows that his defense of democracy is rooted not in blind, uncritical, devotion to it but in a pragmatic realism (democracy's not perfect but it's the best game in town) and an abiding faith in the masses to better their own conditions when give a real opportunity.[35] For example, in a conference paper published by the *American Historical Review* in 1910, he states, "The theory of democratic government is not that the will of the people is always right, but rather that normal human beings of average intelligence will, if given a chance, learn the right and best course by bitter experience."[36] Du Bois would be the first to admit, then, that democracy can make the wrong calls. Yet the answer was not to pursue less democracy. It was to have more. This was not only because he thought it was the best game in town, and he had faith in the masses. There was also an epistemic reason for this, which speaks to Du Bois's second move in the case against epistocracy. Here it is important to distinguish between a more exclusive form of epistocracy and a more inclusive one. If Du Bois could be described as an epistocrat, his ruminations on democracy support viewing him as the latter type. He thought that the masses had important knowledge that was needed to achieve justice for all—the normative goal of popular sovereignty.

Du Bois envisions a perfect democracy as one that is truly ruled by the people to secure justice for all. In such a society, "there shall be no man or woman so poor, ignorant or black as not to count."[37] We can fuss over whether to call this social democracy or something else, but whatever we call it, the point is that rule of all, including those labeled ignorant, can put us in a better position to realize justice or the universal good. Yet epistocrats ask: But what if this turns out to be false? What if preventing some people from wielding political power, say, by disenfranchising them, discounting their votes, or double-counting the votes of the wise, proved to be a more reliable way to secure the universal good? Should we act accordingly? For Du Bois, the answer to this question is a resounding "no." And, ironically, the reason is that the challenge reflects a profound ignorance connected with overrating the knowledge of the "wise," and underrating the knowledge of the masses.

For Du Bois and some of his contemporaries, most notably Walter Lippmann and John Dewey, who grappled with American democracy's promises and perils during the second decade of the twentieth century, this question of whether to withhold political power from certain citizens did not arise on the heels of a fanciful philosophical thought experiment involving runaway trolleys. Rather, it was rooted in real doubts about whether the great masses of voters knew enough to deliver, collectively, benefits to secure the universal good. Du Bois did not deny that ignorance was a problem for democracy. However, he denied that black ignorance was its only epistemic problem. White ignorance—including ignorance of the ruling white (male) plutocracy about blacks, the white working class, and women—was also a serious epistemic barrier to attaining the universal good. The core of Du Bois's defense of democracy, in "Of the Ruling of Men," is to expose and eradicate this barrier.

The crucial premise of this defense is clearly stated in a speech entitled "Diuturni Silenti," which Du Bois gave at Fisk University—his alma mater—two years after *Darkwater*'s publication. He went to campus to address concerns raised by students (including his daughter) and alumni that the university president was lording over the campus like a dictator. His speech succinctly sums up the pivotal insight we find carefully developed in "Of the Ruling of Men." Du Bois says, "The theory of democracy is not that the people have all wisdom or all ability, but it is that the mass of people form a great reservoir of knowledge and information which the state will ignore at its peril."[38]

In *Darkwater*, Du Bois exposes how those who have wanted to hoard political power for themselves—making the franchise a special privilege for the few—have always found it convenient to justify excluding others by appealing to factors such as lack of ability, experience, or knowledge. They wrongly presume, however, that democracy requires participants to have complete knowledge. Thus, the excluders assume that they know what is best for those excluded and know this better than the excluded know it. They also assume that they can be trusted to secure what is best for those excluded. But these assumptions must be flatly rejected.

History disproves the latter as well as the presumption that participants must be all-knowing. And as for the excluder-knows-best thesis, Du Bois accords persons epistemic deference regarding knowledge of one's own soul—particularly knowledge of one's hurts and suffering. As he puts it, while each person may not fully understand his unfortunate condition or how to fix it, "he knows when something hurts and he alone knows how the hurt feels."[39] And in response to men who presume to know what is best for women, Du Bois writes, "With the best will and knowledge, no man can know women's wants as well as women themselves."[40] Societies that do not consider this knowledge, whether they are effective aristocracies, benevolent dictatorships, or imperfect democracies, are bound to fail.

From here Du Bois's argument unfolds by attending to how imperfect democracies ignore the excluded wisdom of women and blacks, and in the case of industry, the wisdom of labor.[41] He sums up the case as follows:

> The real argument for democracy is, then, that in the people we have the source of that endless life and unbounded wisdom which the rulers of men must have. . . . Democracy alone is the method of showing the whole experience of the race for the benefit of the future and if democracy tries to exclude women or Negroes or the poor or any class because of innate characteristics which do not interfere with intelligence, then that democracy cripples itself and belies its name.[42]

So, according to Du Bois, all persons, even the so-called ignorant masses, are what I call sage souls. His multifaceted argument for democracy, which highlights this fact and the necessity of including them in political rule to achieve democracy's possibilities, is an epistemic argument. The reason why all must rule, and not only those thought to have certain experience, ability, or knowledge that the masses lack, is because democracy is a way for society to secure the broadest measure of justice, and this can only be done if all souls have a hand in democratic rule. While the historically excluded souls are not omniscient because no mortals are, each person knows things that others do not, and this excluded wisdom is indispensable for our collective striving toward perfect democracy.[43]

Hence, a society steadfastly and sincerely pursuing this ideal has a dual imperative: (a) to make the class of ignorant persons as small as possible, and (b) to make the class of mature, voting-age persons as large as possible. Because when sage souls can speak for themselves politically, which they can do with the ballot, they can take steps to secure the full schedule of legal rights needed to undo the circumstances of democratic failure. And this is how they can contribute to democracy's survival.

How Democracy Survives

Democratic failure was a prominent theme in Du Bois's speeches and writings in the mid- to late-1950s. After recounting his long history of voting for the lesser of two evils in US presidential elections—taking account of the prospective candidates' positions on Negroes to determine the lesser evil—Du Bois resolved not to vote in 1956 because, as he put it, "democracy has so far disappeared in the United States that no 'two evils' exist. There is but one evil party with two names, and it will be elected despite all I can do or say. There is no third party."[44]

Many people in America today, especially those who have been disproportionately harmed by democratic failure, e.g., black and brown people as well as working-class whites, undoubtedly share a similar view. Some of these folks hold out hope for a third-party movement, which is driven by the people rather than corporate power. Others are less hopeful about this prospect, maybe holding out hope that an existing party could be made a better champion of the pursuit of perfect democracy. Du Bois had his doubts about creating a viable third party in the United States.[45] He noted that efforts to create a viable third party, with a progressive social agenda calling for limits on corporate influence on the law, greater worker protections, nationalized healthcare, greater federal investment in education, and an expansion of social welfare, would be labeled "communist" or "socialist" to stifle the movement. And here, as in many other matters, Du Bois was prophetic.

After her stunning victory in June 2018 over longtime Democratic Party boss, Rep. Joseph Crowley of New York, Alexandria Ocasio-Cortez began making her media rounds to explain what it means to be a "democratic socialist," which television host Stephen Colbert said was "not an easy term for a lot of Americans." In what could be the stirrings of a viable movement toward a third party with a socialist bent (though for now it's being billed as a progressive reworking of the Democratic party), echoing Du Bois, Ocasio-Cortez explained to Colbert that in a society as wealthy and as moral as America professes to be, no one should be too poor to live. A democratic socialist believes this, and she also believes that healthcare, higher education, having a place to live, and having food are human rights necessary for living a dignified life in the United States.[46]

Du Bois would add to this that guaranteeing such rights is also essential for the preservation of democracy in America. The problems that Ocasio-Cortez raises—poverty, illness, and ignorance—are among the *circumstances of democratic failure*. Thus, the right to economic security, healthcare, and education are the normative safeguards of democracy. When these rights are secured for the masses and their needs are met, Du Bois presumes, plausibly in my view, that they will be less vulnerable to antidemocratic leaders promising to address their woes while working to undo the fundamentals of democracy and to advance their autocratic ambitions.[47]

To address any of the circumstances of democratic failure, and to gain the rights needed to undo them, the masses require the power of the ballot. And they must have it on the same terms as other citizens.

The right to vote is not merely a privilege. It is, more important, a means of self-protection. Indeed, as Du Bois states it, "We believe that the right to vote is not for purposes of power primarily, but for the purpose of individual defense."[48]

Reinhold Niebuhr tells us that "Man's capacity for justice makes democracy possible; but man's inclination to injustice makes democracy necessary."[49] Echoing this thought, one can say that our inclination to create and sustain injustice—by contributing to the circumstances of democratic failure—makes the right to vote a necessity for those who are most disadvantaged by ignorance, illness, poverty, and the like. Du Bois would agree. Having voting rights does more than simply allow particular groups to meet needs or satisfy individual wants and desires. It provides them with a means of self-defense. Furthermore, the right to vote allows them to help a democratic society secure the broadest measure of justice for all citizens.

Du Bois did not claim that democracy must guarantee certain rights and freedoms. Nor did he claim that its continued existence was necessary. The United States is certainly free to reject popular sovereignty and to opt for an alternative arrangement, which limits rule "by education, occupation, ability, birth, wealth, race, or some combination of these factors."[50] But if it does this, Du Bois says, "we must face the change frankly and adopt it logically."[51] To put it bluntly, his point was that if we are going to strip "ignorant" people of their voting rights, and ignorant people of all colors can be found in all classes—high and low—then let's make sure that all are equally excluded. Moreover, if state representation in Congress is constitutionally based on the proportion of voting citizens, then let us ensure that those states that choose to disfranchise voters see their representation reduced accordingly. These states should not be able to have it both ways.

In "Of the Ruling of Men," Du Bois limits his focus to just one circumstance of democratic failure—the problem of widespread ignorance and the need for a right to vote to remedy this situation. But in addition to ignorance, he identified poverty and crime as the three principal problems blacks face.[52] Although his argument applies to the other circumstances of democratic failure, I have limited my attention to the problem of ignorance.

Du Bois is well known for establishing the black contribution to these problems, and for outlining their duties to eradicate them. However, he devoted considerable attention to showing how these problems were largely the product of historical black subordination and oppression under slavery, then under Jim Crow segregation, which meant that white America had duties to address them as well.[53] One such obligation was to empower blacks politically to fix these problems by making them equal partners in the democracy. Thus, "a sincere desire among the American people to help the Negroes undertake their own social regeneration means," Du Bois says, "first, that the Negro be given the ballot on the same terms as other men, to protect him against injustice and to safeguard his interests in the administration of law."[54] And one of the most consequential things African Americans could do with the ballot was to advance their interests in black education, black colleges, and industrial schools so that ignorance could be overcome with knowledge. This would go a long way toward undoing this circumstance of democratic failure.

But Du Bois's argument was not only about establishing a moral responsibility to support black rights. It was also about taking proactive measures to reduce the risk of democratic failure by addressing a circumstance that was contributing to it in both the South and the North. If America truly considered itself a democracy and wanted the nation to flourish and survive as such, then Americans had a duty to use their political power to remedy the circumstances of the masses that threatened this. White America was certainly free to believe that blacks were primarily responsible for their own misfortunes and should therefore bear the greatest burden in fixing them. However, to do this, they needed the ballot—and not just on paper but in practice.

Thus, supporting more inclusive political rule by supporting blacks and women was, according to Du Bois, also about mitigating the risk of total democratic failure. This bad outcome would give plutocrats free reign to tyrannize not just blacks but also working-class white laborers and the great mass of Americans who were not wealthy and powerful. Some said that whites could be counted on to secure black interests, just as some said that men could be counted on to secure the interests of women. But Du Bois rejects this, contending that those who suffer most from the circumstances of democratic failure will have the most steadfast commitment to undoing these circumstances.

Yet this does not mean that one must have the same experiences as the sufferers to be inclined to help. And Du Bois certainly did not believe this. When women's suffrage was coming up for a vote in states across the United States in 1914, some blacks were rightly concerned that white women would use their ballots to support the continued exclusion of and domination of blacks. Du Bois's response was frank:

> [T]here is not the slightest reason for supposing that white American women under ordinary circumstances are going to be any more intelligent, liberal or humane toward the black, the poor and unfortunate than white men are. On the contrary, considering what the subjection of a race, a class or a sex must mean, there will undoubtedly manifest itself among women voters at first more prejudice and petty measures toward Negroes than we have now. It is the awful penalty of injustice and oppression to breed in the oppressed the desire to oppress others. The southern white women who form one of the most repressed and enslaved groups of modern civilized women will undoubtedly, at first, help willingly and zealously to disfranchize [sic] Negroes, cripple their schools and publicly insult them.[55]

Despite all of this, Du Bois insisted that white women should have the ballot and that blacks should support their efforts to attain it. Although white women did not share the same experience of anti-black animus and discrimination, or the unique experience of racial and gender oppression known to black women, white women had their own experience of oppression and injustice and thus could be counted on in the long run, or so Du Bois hoped, to use their voting rights to make democracy more inclusive, which was necessary for "the universal appeal for justice to win ultimate hearing and sympathy."[56]

Du Bois's case for how to save democracy from failure comes to this. There are circumstances such as widespread ignorance as well as illness and poverty that can lead to democratic failure. In addition to bearing responsibility for the existence of these circumstances, Americans who profess to enjoy a democratic society are obliged to use their political power to undo the circumstances that put democracy at risk of failure. They can do this by making democracy more inclusive, extending the right to vote even to those said to be ignorant, not only so that the disadvantaged can contribute to undoing these circumstances for their own self-defense but also so that they can help realize the normative aim of a more perfect democracy, which is to secure the broadest measure of justice for all citizens. Others can certainly contribute to this, and those who are intimately familiar with other kinds of domination are likely to do so. However, because persons who suffer most directly can be most reliably counted on to secure justice for themselves, they must be empowered as equal partners in political rule. So, all citizens—including those deemed ignorant—must vote. And with the vote they can work to secure the other rights they need to undo the circumstances of democratic failure.

Thus, Du Bois believed that extending political power to the excluded classes through the franchise was a path toward perfect democracy. He acknowledged the possibility that harm could come to the state and its citizens by putting the power to rule in the hands of persons suffering from ignorance, poverty, and disease. And he also conceded that this would be resisted and resented, especially by those who had the greatest investment in the status quo.[57]

Instead of depriving suffering citizens of the ballot, which renders democracy imperfect, we must remove the conditions that could result in harm. So, for instance, Du Bois reasoned that the enfranchisement of blacks should be accompanied by "education, a minimum of land and capital and a guardian Freedman's Bureau."[58] Education would guard against harms resulting from ignorance. Economic resources would guard against harms resulting from poverty.

Empowering an administrative agency to protect newly acquired civil and political rights would guard against harms resulting from discrimination.

Du Bois certainly did not think that the right to vote was the magic silver bullet that would vanquish all of the social troubles associated with antidemocratic rule. For instance, he did not believe that popular sovereignty would "immediately abolish color caste."[59] Nor did he think it would make "ignorant men intelligent or bad men good." After all, blacks were able to vote in the North, yet there was still color caste and discrimination, and there was some social progress in parts of the South despite blacks not having unfettered access to the ballot. Nevertheless, he thought that the only way to make real and sustainable progress toward perfect democracy would be to guarantee a right to vote—giving blacks and other excluded classes a permanent voice in shaping government policy and action. "[N]o permanent improvement in the economic and social condition of Negroes," Du Bois concluded, "is going to be made, so long as they are deprived of political power to support and defend it."

Moreover, as I have indicated, the right to vote was not merely an effective weapon of self-defense for the excluded classes, it was also necessary for securing the broadest measure of justice for all, or what Du Bois also calls the "real good of the world."[60] And to realize this good we must, he says, ultimately be guided by principles, not parties. He was not neutral regarding what these principles should be. They constituted a list of demands, which those fighting for a more perfect democracy should deliver to persons or parties seeking to represent them. Here are the demands:

1. Down with force and lawlessness.
2. Democracy unlimited by race, sex, religion, or color.
3. The abolition of poverty.
4. Health for all.
5. Education for all according to ability and regardless of wealth or birth.
6. Limitation of private wealth by public welfare.
7. Work for all at a decent wage.

8. Social equality of all human beings in accord with wish and without compulsion.
9. The right to all men to life, liberty and happiness, so far as this is possible under the Golden Rule.[61]

It is noteworthy that this list contains big-tent issues that we find today's most progressive political candidates running on. Du Bois maintains that the masses should use the weapon of voting to select representatives committed to seeking justice for all. He proposes these and other demands to add substance regarding what this entails. It is also worth noting that these are non-race-specific remedies, and that Du Bois anticipates the pragmatic importance of seeking such remedies to address the profound inequalities that stem from imperfect democracy.[62] To achieve a more perfect democracy, in a country where our many differences have been used to divide us and distract us from all the ways in which the plutocrats have fleeced us, we must use political power to undo the circumstances that affect everyone excluded. We must also make voting easier.

8
Making Voting Easier

> In decision after decision, this Court has made clear that a citizen has a constitutionally protected right to participate in elections on an equal basis with other citizens in the jurisdiction.
>
> —US Supreme Court, *Dunn v. Blumstein*

> Equal political liberty when assured its fair value is bound to have a profound effect on the moral quality of civic life. Citizens' relations to one another are given a secure basis in the manifest constitution of society.
>
> —John Rawls, *A Theory of Justice*

This chapter presents an argument for making voting easier for the masses that does not turn on flying the race-first flag. The Supreme Court removed an obstacle to making voting more burdensome in *Shelby County v. Holder*.[1] It invalidated a key provision of the 1965 Voting Rights Act (VRA) that imposed a requirement on certain states to secure federal permission before changing their voting laws.[2] In the aftermath of losing the White House in the 2020 presidential election, Georgia's Republicans, who watched their state turn from red to blue, exploited this opportunity to pass restrictive voting rules that would have most certainly needed federal preclearance prior to *Shelby County*.

At the center of partisan disagreement over this controversial decision, which settles the issue of whether to afford states with particularly shameful racist histories more or less autonomy in regulating current elections, we find sharply different views about racial progress in the United States since the civil rights era. Conservatives argue that racial progress has been considerable and so the restrictions on state autonomy should be removed to reflect current conditions. Liberals reject this argument, noting that there is work yet to be done and further argue for upholding the VRA fully intact to guard against rolling back the gains for black voting rights.[3] Post–2020 state election law restrictions are grist for the mill.

Empirical evidence from political sociology and political psychology gives us reason to believe that agreement on the racial progress issue is not forthcoming.[4] How, then, should progressive liberals defend unencumbered access to the ballot where there is intractable disagreement over the status of racial progress in America?[5] Should they rely upon a race-first justification or should they embrace a broader one? I believe that unencumbered access to the ballot can and should be justified without getting mired in questions about whether and how much progress has made in addressing invidious racial discrimination and racial prejudice.[6] This is not because I deny that there is still much work to be done. Rather, it is because the racial realist in me (committed to taking a hard-eyed view of racism) does not have much hope of convincing diehard partisans or even many "reasonable" people who disagree.

In this chapter I offer a *race-neutral* justification for unencumbered access to the ballot by drawing on a central idea in philosopher John Rawls's theory of justice as fairness, namely, the idea that basic political liberties should be afforded fair value in a just liberal, democratic society.[7] I argue that an important guideline for guaranteeing the fair value of voting rights, that is, the usefulness to citizens of their right to vote, is to make it easier, not harder, to exercise this basic political liberty. This entails that just societies with a constitutional commitment to equal protection, and the value of equality more broadly, have a prima facie duty to secure unencumbered access to the ballot absent narrowly tailored compelling state interests for restricting it (hereafter Unencumbered Access). And where there are such interests, the burden imposed on voting must accord with the basic priority of voting rights. One implication of this argument is to shift the burden of justification from liberals to present sufficient evidence of voter suppression to conservatives, who are currently pushing restrictive voter ID and other laws, to produce compelling evidence supporting their reasons for doing so (chief of which is fraud prevention and deterrence) and demonstrating that these laws are carefully crafted to remedy the alleged problem. The evidence shows that they have yet to meet this burden.[8]

Equal Political Liberty

John Rawls affirms the importance of political liberties as a normative ideal in the abstract by including them on the list of equal basic liberties along with the liberties of thought, conscience, association, and those associated with the rule of law in his liberal egalitarian conception of justice as fairness. However, less abstractly, the principle of equal political liberty is also identified with the principle of equal participation within the constitutionally defined political process of a just democratic society.

Rawls has been criticized for not being entirely clear about why political liberties are included on this list,[9] and for failing to offer a detailed argument for their special status and a proposal for how it can be captured institutionally.[10] Yet there is no question that the liberty to participate politically on equal terms is meant to carry the abstract normative commitment to equality modeled in the original position—where parties are selecting common principles from a position of equality—to the constitutional stage where they collectively participate in "the highest-order system of social rules for making rules" by participating in the vital political process of lawmaking.[11]

Taking the Constitution to be foundational, as the highest-order system of rules regulating and controlling all other institutions of society's basic structure, Rawls concludes that satisfying the principle of equal participation in practice affords all persons with access to the political process "common status of equal citizens."[12]

Having affirmed the importance of equality within an institutional context, Rawls further contends that a just constitutional democracy should endeavor to "enhance the value of the equal rights of participation for all members of society."[13] Such participation can take different forms: serving as an elected representative of the people, making financial contributions to political campaigns, participating in public debate about the issues and the candidates for office, and casting a vote for government representatives and for ballot measures. These are all ways of determining the results of the constitutionally proscribed means of making the laws that bind us and shape our lives from cradle to grave.

The appeal to equal participation to ground a normative defense of voting rights trades, in part, on the intrinsic or non-instrumental value of equal political liberties, which are, in many ways, a good for citizens. As Rawls puts it, "These freedoms strengthen men's sense of their own worth, enlarge their intellectual and moral sensibilities, and lay the basis for a sense of duty and obligation upon which the stability of just institutions depends."[14] But in addition to this, Rawls offers an instrumental justification of equal political liberties that is also germane.[15]

It proceeds as follows. Other basic liberties, e.g., speech, association, and thought (which some may take to be more fundamental), are protected by the principle of equal participation and lose their value when citizens do not have meaningful opportunity to determine outcomes of the political process in an appropriate fashion.[16] The haves, that is, citizens with more income, wealth, and other resources, can leverage these resource inequalities to be better informed about issues, to assess more accurately policy proposals and how they bear on their interests, and to add ones more effectively to the political agenda that advance these interests and their conception of public welfare. All of this will result in the resource-rich having disproportionate influence over lawmaking and settling social issues.[17] It is patently unfair for the equal basic liberty to political participation to be of greater usefulness to the resource-rich than to the resource-challenged.

While resource disparities in income and wealth may be justified and tolerated on grounds that they maximize the primary goods enjoyed by the least advantaged, if indeed they do, we reject the prospect that such disparities should affect the usefulness of citizens' political liberties, which explains why Rawls rightly insists upon securing their fair value. This normative imperative requires that their worth be sufficiently equal to allow *all* citizens a fair opportunity to influence outcomes of the political process. Specifying how exactly a just constitutional democracy might enhance the fair value of political participation is, as Rawls admits, a complex matter that goes beyond the scope of philosophy. And this is true whether we are focused on free speech or on voting—both ways of influencing political outcomes. Settling upon the necessary arrangements and regulations requires, among other things, the requisite historical experience and knowledge. But philosophy is not altogether useless for this pursuit. It can offer, endorse, and defend possibilities that seem compatible with the normative principle of equal participation.[18]

Rawls, as we know, was particularly interested in the adverse effects of private money and wealth disparities on equal political participation in a private-property democracy.[19] So, he proposed as a guideline for guaranteeing the fair value of political liberties, and as compensating steps to offset resource disparities that make them less useful to the resource-challenged, that political parties in a constitutional democracy operate as independently as possible of large concentrations of private economic interests. He also called for adequate government funding of public elections to prevent candidates from having to rely on private money and thereby risk being beholden to their private benefactors when making laws.[20] Failure to take such steps will, Rawls argues, not only diminish the worth of political liberty for the have-nots, thus depriving them of fair opportunity for political influence, but it will also risk alienating them and facilitating their complete withdrawal from the political process due to apathy and resentment.

And though he does not make this point, it can be added that a withdrawal of the resource-challenged from the political process would also diminish the character of American democracy. To be sure, this proposal seems quite impractical now in view of how expensive running for office has become. Still, these are plausible suggestions for the kind of reforms needed to bring the United States more in line with the principle of equal participation given a certain form that it might take.[21]

Unencumbered Access to Voting

What about the right to vote? This is arguably the most recognizable and coveted form of democratic participation. What concrete guideline might ensure its fair value to citizens?[22] Separating big money from politics and campaign finance reform does not directly speak to what might be done to enhance the usefulness of equal participation made possible by the exercise of this basic political liberty. One general prescription for realizing the fair value of the political liberty to vote, namely, Unencumbered Access, is to ensure that social arrangements and legal regulations governing voting should as much as possible and subject to certain constraints aim for maximal citizen participation in determining political process outcomes. Hence, a constitutional democracy committed to the principle of equal participation and to ensuring its worth to citizens should make access to the ballot easier, not harder, in the absence of compelling reasons for doing otherwise.

For the United States, which is a paradigm exemplar of a constitutional democracy on paper, if not always in practice,[23] Unencumbered Access imposes a prima facie duty upon the government to take meaningful steps to ensure that all citizens irrespective of their allotment of income and wealth and other basic goods, e.g., education, are able to participate on equal terms in the democratic project of voting. This normative principle of participation imposes on society a duty to make sure that the political liberty to vote is thus substantively and not merely formally guaranteed.[24]

Of course, this principle does not require that citizens vote, nor does it entitle them to equal results at the ballot box. They may vote and their preferred candidate may not win. What is at stake, however, is the fair opportunity to have a shot at influencing political outcomes rather than having particular voting outcomes secured. Hence, fair equality of opportunity to determine the political outcomes at the ballot box necessitates that income, wealth, and education among other basic goods unevenly distributed across the population of citizens are neither obstacles nor facilitators to the meaningful exercise of the right to vote.

In a well-ordered society where there is compliance with the principles of justice, we might be justified in restricting our philosophical attention only to the ways in which disparities in income and wealth might interact with the exercise of voting rights to generate injustice. But under less favorable conditions, of the sort that have endured throughout US history, we must also attend to the ways in which other basic goods like education as well as features of persons such as their race and gender might also bear on their fair opportunity to participate on equal terms in affecting the political process.[25]

The fair-value guarantee is a normative benchmark for directly assessing the former obstacles and indirectly assessing the latter ones. For as I noted earlier, we can argue that making the usefulness of voting rights a function of resource endowments can have a disparate impact on blacks insofar as they have significantly fewer of them relative to whites. But this would be using the fair-value guarantee to assess racial impact indirectly rather than directly to assess resource disparities. The racial prejudice standard can, of course, directly assess racial impact, but because it is *race conscious* it will lack strategic value.

Calling for the separation of money from politics, as Rawls does, and proposing restrictions on corporate speech in public elections and for campaign finance reform presume that political mischief will result in their absence. Likewise, calling for unencumbered access to the ballot, as I do here, presumes that political mischief is at work when access is made more difficult. This is not a matter of idle and uninformed philosophical speculation. We can consider the infamous history of black voting rights in America. Historically, as Rawls notes, "one of the main defects of constitutional government has been the failure to insure the fair value of political liberty."[26] This has unquestionably been a profound failure in America.

The United States has not been well ordered: race has long played a role, directly and indirectly, in determining participation in the political process through voting. Some states have historically made it excessively burdensome for black Americans to vote.[27] For example, after the Civil War many more blacks than whites were illiterate, and some Southern states exploited this to negate the fair value of black voting rights. For example, in 1882, the South Carolina General Assembly adopted an "eight-box" ballot law. Voters were required to put the correct ballot in each of eight boxes, one for each office up for election. The boxes were then continuously shuffled so that election officials could not assist illiterate voters. This indirect literacy test—which exploited racial disparities in education to diminish the worth of blacks' right to vote—was a precursor to more direct ones like requiring citizens to read or recite a section of the Constitution before they could register to vote. Such tests were among the many cunning ways some states curtailed the fair value of black citizens to influence the political process and to influence democratic governance on equal terms with whites. Other methods included poll taxes, moral character standards, and property requirements.[28] At the time, some critics complained that each method had the shortcoming of targeting poor and illiterate whites, and not just blacks. So, in response, states such as Oklahoma, Louisiana, Virginia, and Georgia addressed this complication with grandfather clauses that deemed citizens qualified to vote only if they, their father, or grandfather was eligible to vote before 1866.[29]

It is no surprise that during these times, and long after them, substantial racial disparities in political influence prevailed and that the basic political liberty to vote was of little or no worth to black citizens. They had a constitutionally recognized right to vote (thus, their right was formally guaranteed), but their enjoyment of it was seriously constrained by social institutions and practices (thus, it was not substantively guaranteed). From the post-Reconstruction period well into the twentieth century, Southern states—sometimes without but mostly with the support of the courts—found crafty ways to diminish the worth of the black vote in local, state, and federal elections.[30]

Hence, it is uncontroversial that states have used all kinds of devices with the intent and effect of imposing barriers to voting to deprive black citizens of their formal liberty to vote along with a fair opportunity to influence the outcome of the political process. The richness of our historical experience in the United States, and our knowledge of nonideal circumstances where voting rights have *not* been guaranteed to be useful for blacks, places philosophical speculation about what it would take to guarantee the fair value of voting rights on firmer footing. Given the historical record of mischief, and the intrinsic and instrumental importance of the right to vote, Unencumbered Access is an attractive default position.

So far, I have argued that the concern with securing for all citizens equal participation in the political process on fair terms is what makes my proposed defense of voting rights normatively appealing. Exactly how the imperative to provide voting rights with their fair value by affording citizens unencumbered access to the ballot supports a race-neutral defense that circumvents the contentious racial progress debate remains to be shown.

Race Neutrality

A way to defend voting rights—when appeals to racial progress and racial prejudice will do nothing but expose how highly polarized we are about race matters—is to advance a race-neutral normative justification, one that does not turn on resolving or even taking a stand on such divisive matters. The imperative that we secure the fair value of voting rights fits this bill.

Although allowing for maximal citizen participation in the political process is the goal of Unencumbered Access, there are important constitutional and practical considerations that justify qualifying the right to vote. Fundamental rights have a special status in US constitutional law. Regulations that impose burdens on them generally trigger strict judicial scrutiny. To withstand this exacting scrutiny a law must serve a compelling state interest and must be narrowly tailored, or required, to advance this purpose.[31] It should come as no surprise that Supreme Court justices often disagree over the relative historical importance of liberty interests in the United States and thus over which liberties constitute fundamental rights. Perhaps no area of law makes this clearer than the Court's voting rights jurisprudence.

Here the most telling case is *Crawford v. Marion County Election Board*,[32] in which the Supreme Court (in a plurality decision) affirmed a Seventh Circuit Court decision not to apply heightened scrutiny to an Indiana law requiring voters to present government-issued photo identification at the polls. Three Justices in the plurality (Stevens, Roberts, and Kennedy) called for a sliding-scale balance approach in which burdens on the right to vote are balanced against state interests so that the stronger the burden, the stronger the interests must be, and the weaker the burden, the less compelling the interests must be. Three justices (Scalia, Thomas, and Alito) defended a threshold analysis in which only severe burdens on the right to vote warrant strict scrutiny, that is, ones that "go beyond the merely inconvenient." And in their dissenting opinion, Justices Souter and Ginsburg recognized the right to vote as fundamental but denied that the burden imposed had to be severe in arguing that the onus was on Indiana to show that its voter ID statute could survive heightened scrutiny. Hence, the Court has yet to speak with a unanimous—or even a majority—voice on whether and when laws burdening the right to vote merit strict scrutiny.[33]

Given the Court's widely divergent opinions on whether and when government burdens on the right to vote require strict scrutiny, its status as a constitutionally protected fundamental right remains ambiguous.[34] Still, even if it is fundamental, it is certainly not an absolute right.[35] According to the US Constitution, certain state interests can warrant imposing burdens on it. The Tenth Amendment reserves certain powers regarding political participation to the states. In addition to setting the conditions under which the right to vote may be exercised, the qualifications of political representatives and how they are chosen, individual states also have primary responsibility for determining congressional districts. To be sure, guaranteeing the fair value of equal political participation rights is not meant to contravene these broad powers. Indeed, as Rawls puts it, "there may be qualifications of age, residency, and so on," which states impose on serving as an elected representative as well as on voting for one.[36] But the ways in which states exercise this power must not impose burdens on political participation that unfairly single out citizens and that are not shared evenly by all in the normal course of life.

In addition to retaining its Tenth Amendment powers, states seeking to make access to the ballot harder have claimed further interests, including wanting to modernize elections, prevent noncitizen voting, improve election integrity and fairness, restore and sustain voter confidence, and increase voter turnout. However, a concern with preventing voter impersonation fraud has been the most popular justification for doing so, and voter ID laws have been the tools for realizing this goal. These laws allow resource disparities to affect the fair value of political liberty for black Americans and for many other citizens. Requiring certain forms of photo ID to vote implicates resources such as time and money, which allows the haves to leverage resource inequalities to gain easier access to the polls than the have-nots. The monetary and nonmonetary burdens such laws imposed on potential voters have been well documented. Estimates have been made of the numerous costs involved in procuring valid voter identification, including the cost of purchasing necessary certificates, e.g., birth and marriage certificates, travel costs to relevant agencies to procure documents, potential time away from work or additional childcare costs, as well as possible legal and notary fees to get documents.[37]

While some state statutes have incorporated provisions to mitigate resource disparities, and so may be relatively more just in how they handle elections than other states, obvious measures to offset them have not been universally incorporated into law, e.g., free photo ID necessary for voting, being able to acquire the ID in places that the resource-challenged must go to on a regular basis, and requiring forms of ID that they are more likely to possess.

Obviously, failure to mitigate resource disparities that impact fair opportunity to influence political outcomes at the ballot box will have similar consequences to not doing so in the case of political speech. Thus, it is clear that the same justification for guaranteeing the fair value of political speech applies here, and that certain compensating steps are also required in this case. The net effect of these steps is to secure the fair value of voting rights by making voting easier, not harder, in accordance with Unencumbered Access, which is rooted in the principle of equal participation—a principle that has both intrinsic and instrumental value.[38]

Voter ID laws clearly run afoul of the normative requirement not to impose burdens on the right to vote that unfairly single out citizens who are resource challenged. And clearly, we do not need to make any appeal to race, racial progress, racial discrimination, or racial prejudice to make this point stick. It is a further and entirely independent consideration to note that such laws, and the burdens they impose, have a disproportionate impact on black voters. They clearly do and the evidence is undeniable.[39] While this is certainly a race-conscious reason for objecting to voter ID laws, one can set considerations of race entirely to the side to make the more general point that such laws are unfair to resource-challenged citizens whose right to vote is made less useful relative to the resource-rich. This suffices to explain why my fair value defense of voting rights is race neutral and offers us strategic value that race-first defenses lack in our postracial milieu.[40]

Shifting the Burden of Proof

My Rawlsian defense of voting rights is certainly not a capitulation to racial injustice, or a license to look the other way and ignore persistent first-and-second-generation voter discrimination against black Americans, as some on the left may fear. Rather, it is a normative path toward vindicating voting rights that makes sense in our present circumstances where racial appeals increasingly fall on deaf and doubtful ears. But more than this, I believe that it better captures the essential injustice involved in making access to the ballot more burdensome—an injustice rooted not in what we owe one another as members of this or that racial or ethnic group, this or that gender, or even this or that class status, but rooted in what we owe one another as citizens of a liberal constitutional democracy that purports to value liberty and equality. In this regard, my defense aims to be grounded in normative reasons for ensuring unencumbered access to the ballot we all can share.

An important consequence of this shift to securing the fair value of voting rights is that this places the burden entirely on states to justify making voting harder. While preventing fraud has been the main justification for imposing this burden on the right to vote, and making access to the ballot harder, the evidence of in-person fraud at the polls is woefully weak.[41] Indeed, it is much too weak to justify making access to the ballot more cumbersome.[42] Astonishingly, in the *Crawford* ruling, which upheld Indiana's restrictive voter ID law, the Court acknowledged that the state had produced "no evidence of any such fraud actually occurring in Indiana at any time in its history." However, it downplayed this by arguing that evidence of voter impersonation elsewhere in the country provided sufficient grounds for Indiana's fraud prevention law. So here the justification for burdening the right to vote expands from not only preventing fraud—of which there is hardly any—to also deterring fraud for the sake of the public good. But this too is a problem.

Like all other basic liberties, the right to vote and the guarantee of its fair value cannot be infringed merely because doing so might realize some broad social purpose. For example, suppose that the United States would be better off if there were less gridlock in Washington, as this would enable lawmakers to draft and pass legislation faster and more efficiently. And further suppose that this would be good for society as a whole, and this good could be realized by allowing one political party, say Republicans, a monopoly on political offices. Finally, suppose that this outcome could be realized if persons likely to vote for Democrats, including African Americans,

Latino/a Americans, college students, and the poor, systematically had their votes diluted (preventing them from actually getting the persons they support into office) or they faced insurmountable burdens to exercising it (dramatically decreasing their turnout on election day).

Affirming that the fair value of the right to vote has priority entails that it cannot be traded off for reasons having to do with achieving the public good or some larger welfare goal. Like other basic liberties, this right imposes a substantive normative constraint on the pursuit of socially beneficial outcomes.

That the usefulness of voting rights to citizens cannot be traded off for the public good does not mean, however, that the right to vote can never be justifiably restricted. As I mentioned earlier, it is not an absolute right. Like all other basic liberties, the right to vote and the guarantee of its fair value can be traded off for other basic liberties. Therefore, suppose that we sought to establish rules within the basic structure of society that incorporated within a coherent system of rights both the political liberty to vote and the liberty of thought and political expression—two other basic liberties. Further suppose that recognizing the liberty of some to engage in commercial speech smearing dispreferred political candidates just prior to an election limited the right of others—without access to commercial speech—to use their vote to get their preferred candidate in office.

This trade-off, which might bring to mind the Supreme Court ruling in *Citizens United*, would not be ruled out straightaway insofar as it constitutes a case of limiting a basic liberty for the sake of another basic liberty and not for the greater social good. Such trade-offs of rights for the sake of other rights, while possibly objectionable on other grounds, is consistent with assigning basic political liberties and their guarantee of fair-value, normative priority.[43]

One virtue of noting that the right to vote is not absolute is that it takes account of the contingent possibility that social conditions necessary to its exercise could change in ways that required limiting this right to fit within an adequate scheme with other basic liberties. If, for example, social conditions changed so that voter fraud had indeed become rampant or new technology made it possible to commit in-person voter fraud with ease, then regulation limiting the right to vote, say by making it harder to vote by imposing more checks—even moderately costly ones—against fraud, might be in order for the sake of upholding one or more competing basic liberties. Of course, we would have to be very clear about what these other liberties are, and the case for the dramatic change in social conditions would have to be compelling enough to justify such restrictions. But insofar as the right to vote and the guarantee of its fair value have priority, we could not justify limiting this right merely by citing a concern with maintaining public confidence in elections, deterring possible voter impersonation fraud, or any of the public-good-based reasons that have been advanced thus far.

Obviously, it would not count as an infringement of the right to vote and the guarantee of its fair value for a state to regulate the time, manner, and place of voting—powers reserved to it by the Tenth Amendment. Such rules are clearly necessary for ensuring the possibility of voting and the orderly exercise of the right to vote. Not everyone can vote at once or in the same place, so it is necessary to plan for and organize the voting process to bring about the aim of affording citizens the power and equal opportunity to influence the political process. It is important to be clear, however, that all such regulation must be in the service of realizing or recognizing the right to vote and its fair value, that is, taking it from an abstract ideal to a concrete way of acting.[44] We might call this *right-enabling* regulation.

Although such regulation does not amount to an infringement on the right to vote, to maintain the priority of this basic liberty, imposing burdens on voting that go beyond what is absolutely necessary for making the exercise of voting possible, or providing for its orderly exercise, can only be justified for the sake of one or more other basic liberties. So, while one may reasonably be asked to prove that one is authorized to vote at a particular polling place, as part of ensuring the orderly exercise of the right to vote, it is unreasonable for these purposes to demand that one produces proof of citizenship or produces a specific kind of state ID, say a firearms identification card, rather than a university ID card. Such a rule would be *right inhibiting*.

These fine-grained ID restrictions, which threaten to make the resource-challenged and resource-rich distinction consequential, could only be justified in a society where the priority of the right to vote and its fair value were affirmed if access to the ballot was being burdened for the sake of some other basic liberty. And there is no credible evidence that this has been the case in the United States.

My distinction between right-enabling and right-inhibiting rules may also help to address what lawyers refer to as the *baseline problem*. This is the problem of grounding a complaint about mundane decisions that a legislator might make, such as holding elections on days or hours when black citizens find it harder to make it to the polls. This has been posed as a general objection to my race-neutral defense of voting rights. One might think that race-conscious appeals are *necessary* to object to such rules, which may have a disparate negative impact on black citizens. However, I am doubtful. It seems that we can also assess them by asking whether these rules are right enabling and in line with *Unencumbered Access*. If they are not, then they would be objectionable on grounds of justice along the lines I have defended here. Obviously, as Rawls would agree, philosophers (or jurists for that matter) cannot offer us detailed guidance on how to realize *Unencumbered Access* in practice. And for legislators to do so they must draw on historical experience and knowledge. Nevertheless, norms of justice, just like constitutional norms, can certainly be invoked to assess particular rules and particular social arrangements.

Some critics of my race-neutral defense of voting rights will complain that it takes the focus off of where it needs to be, namely, on the persistent discrimination suffered by *black* Americans in the electoral process that deprives them of the equal opportunity for political influence. However, we do not need to ground our normative case for *Unencumbered Access* in race-conscious considerations to call attention to the peculiar plight of blacks in America. For this, it would suffice to show that the basic injustice involved in depriving citizens without resources such as money, time, or education the fair value of voting rights falls disproportionately on blacks, as a group, who generally have fewer of these resources than other racial and ethnic groups.

Even though this does not constitute the basic injustice, which can be articulated in entirely race-neutral terms, it nevertheless suffices as a way of calling special attention to the predicament of black Americans when access to the ballot is contingent on resource endowments. It is, however, only a derivative normative reason stemming from the basic injustice involved in unfairly tethering the usefulness of a citizens' right to vote to the possession of certain primary goods. And to say this is not to diminish its importance but only to distinguish it from the more fundamental injustice.

To be sure, where we can offer evidence that legislators make access to the ballot resource sensitive precisely *because* they intend to exploit the historically documented racial disparities in income, wealth, and education to make voting more difficult for blacks in particular (say, because they are dead set against being governed by persons they deem inferior, or perhaps because they want to defeat an opponent who will be supported by the black vote), we have strong grounds for complaint. But as compelling as this evidence may be to some of us, others will most certainly demur. Anticipating this possibility shows the wisdom of being able to articulate the basic injustice involved in making voting more cumbersome without getting pulled into a hopeless debate about intentions, prejudice, and discrimination. The "pragmatic" benefit of a fair-value-based normative defense of voting rights, as I understand it, is that it serves this purpose, which makes it very attractive in a nation so highly polarized about race matters.[45]

Although is important to mount a defense of voting rights with strategic value, political philosophers will rightly want more than this. They will demand that it be normatively grounded as well. Thus, a vindication of *Unencumbered Access* must do more than increase the likelihood of winning over conservatives, moderates, and all of those who are fatigued with and dismissive of arguments playing the race card, which constitutes a rather large bunch that even includes a growing number of blacks and Latinos. Even more importantly, it must be firmly grounded in reasons of justice and its demands in the political realm.

Identifying the essential unfairness involved in voting rights discrimination with racial prejudice, as some philosophers have done, fits this bill.[46] But, as I have argued elsewhere, this justification now lacks strategic value.[47] However normatively attractive the imperative to avoid the impact of racial prejudice on electoral outcomes might be, the argument joining it with empirical assumptions about the persistence of racial prejudice to justify equal opportunity for political influence is likely to fall flat in a nation where views about the latter are so highly polarized. The main flaw of this argument in our current nonideal circumstances is that it demands race consciousness where race neutrality is needed.

I have argued that recognizing the fair value of the right to vote constitutes a concrete way of affirming a commitment to the ideal of equality not merely in the abstract but within the context of our participation in the political constitution, which is among the major social institutions that shape our life prospects on fair terms.

Exercising the political liberty to vote is an avenue for participation in the political process. Society's commitment to equality is not diminished if citizens choose not to vote. Nor is it diminished if they vote but their candidate does not win (unless, of course, the voting process is rigged—either by gerrymandering or vote dilution—so that some voters have a much lower chance of getting their candidate in office). However, if it takes resources like money, education, or time to exercise this basic political liberty, and these are unevenly distributed across the pool of potential voters, then the commitment to equal participation in the political process is wanting. Under such circumstances the value of the right to vote is only meaningfully guaranteed for citizens who have the relevant resources.

To guard against making the right to vote resource dependent in ways that are deeply unfair to all citizens regardless of race, but especially deleterious for black citizens as a group, who are more resource challenged relative to others, we should recognize a prima facie duty of unencumbered access to the ballot. A moral commitment to the dignity of persons gives us grounds for guaranteeing all citizens the right to vote within a legal system of rights. Martin Luther King Jr. offers important insights on this matter that we must take up before concluding.

9
The Dignity of Voting

> Any democratic nation that cannot guarantee all of its citizens the elemental right to vote is suffering from a moral sickness that must be cured if it is to survive.
> —Martin Luther King Jr., *People in Action: Literacy Bill Dies*

A nation espouses fundamental values and decides how to realize them within a system of rights. Failing to guarantee rights that promote these values, such as the right to vote, can be costly. It can lead to societal instability and civil violence, putting at risk the basic institutions that order our lives. It can result in some citizens perceiving that their lives do not matter and that they are not full members of the polity. And as white resistance and ambivalence to black civil rights have taught us in the United States, it can also diminish a nation's moral authority at home and abroad. America's democratic experiment has, in many ways, been about working out our fundamental values of freedom, equality, and dignity within a coherent system of rights. At times we have moved closer to this aim—if not always with deliberate speed—and at others we have moved further away from making these values and rights a tangible reality for all citizens. This chapter vindicates a legal system of rights that guarantees all citizens the right to vote by drawing on philosophical insights about dignity found in the writings of Martin Luther King Jr.

An Expressive Commitment to Dignity

King presumes that respect for human dignity is part of America's founding tradition and is thus one of the fundamental values it espouses. This important point, which I shall take as a given, informs his dignity-based internal critique of the nation when it does not guarantee the right to vote; this "moral sickness," as he describes it, constitutes an assault on the dignity of persons in multiple senses. King does not offer us a uniform conception of dignity. But neither does Immanuel Kant. Indeed, as we shall see, King, like Kant, uses the concept in different ways. Sometimes King directs attention to the importance of dignified conduct, which calls for behavior in accordance with particular norms. At other times, dignity indicates that something, such as human nature, or someone, such as a creature with the capacity to make choices, has inherent worth. King combines these uses to argue that in their struggle against racial injustice black Americans have a moral obligation to comport themselves in a dignified manner, as they work to pressure society to treat them as creatures with inherent worth, and to vanquish injustices (such as vote denial) that prevent them from being regarded by others as persons of equally high social status or rank.

Kant, in addition to having much to say about the nature of persons, also makes explicit the connection between being a person and having rank and dignity. He writes, "The fact that the human being can have the 'I' in his representations raises him infinitely above all other living beings on earth. Because of this he is a *person*." Kant adds, "and by virtue of the unity of consciousness through all changes that happen to him, one and the same person—i.e., through rank and dignity an entirely different being from things, such as irrational animals, with which one can do as one likes."[1] Here Kant is distinguishing between humans and animals, but European colonialism and New World slavery contributed to introducing distinctions of rank and dignity within the class of human beings based on racial categories.[2]

Although this link between dignity and rank is not as explicit in his thought, King intimates that dignity is the equalization of an honorific social status that obtains when sources of hierarchy-sustaining social relations such as racial segregation are expunged from civic and social life by the force of law.[3] And here his thought about dignity resonates with a contemporary conception of dignity as rank.[4] One virtue of this conception, which links dignity to an honorific social status rather than the inherent worth of all persons, is that it allows us to register the historical reality of hierarchical social relations that diminish dignity (such as slavery, segregation, voter suppression) while also capturing the content of our normative aspiration to arrange our social world to undo these relations through the force of law. Another virtue is that it affords us yet another way to articulate and vindicate the distinctive normative importance of voting rights.

Voter suppression is among the injustices, according to King, that can undermine a citizen's capacity to make choices, thereby assailing their dignity. Within its system of rights, law can play a vital role in addressing the indignity of this and other hierarchy-sustaining injustices. King counts the right to vote among the rights essential to promoting dignity, understood both as the inherent worth of a citizen's capacity to make deliberative choices and as an honorific social status. Failing to make this right a reliable reality—one that every citizen can count on regardless of their race, gender, or how little time or money they have—is a distinctive moral failure according to King. But what exactly is the nature of this failure? Is it a failure to enact a right somehow grounded in dignity as inherent worth? Is it a failure to establish a right that expresses the kind of nation we profess and aspire to be, namely, one where dignity as equalization of social rank for persons deemed to have inherent worth is publicly affirmed?

The first alternative suggests that the connection between dignity and rights is what I shall call a *grounding relationship*. Simply put, the idea is this: that someone has dignity entails that they have, or should be recognized as having, certain rights within a system of rights. Failing to enact the appropriate legislation is a grounding failure. The second alternative suggests that the connection between dignity and rights is what I shall call an *expressive relationship*. Here the idea is this: the system of rights we enact expresses the content and scope of our commitment to dignity. Failing to enact the appropriate legislation within a system of rights is an expressive failure.[5] Discerning King's vindication of voting rights is a matter I shall resolve by attending to King as an astute political philosopher in addition to being a radical black Baptist preacher and civil rights activist whom we can no longer sanitize.[6]

My specific goals in this chapter are to develop King's account of the moral value of voting rights, and his vindication of a public system of rights that includes them, by drawing on the expressive relationship between dignity and rights. From reading his work it is clear that he also considers the grounding relationship. He takes dignity, when understood as "one's capacity to deliberate, decide and respond," to be a value from which the right to vote can be derived. Yet I will not resolve the question of whether one or the other is a better or truer interpretation of his understanding of the relationship between dignity and rights. Nor will I take up the vexing question of whether the two possibilities are exhaustive or incompatible with one another.

There are, however, at least two good reasons for featuring his less obvious expressive understanding of the relationship between dignity and voting rights: (1) the grounding relationship between dignity and rights has come under heavy attack,[7] and (2) the expressive relationship may afford us a better way to unify King's philosophical outlook on the morality of voting rights with his preaching and activism, all of which, in large part, involve getting America to make value choices—and own up to and publicly express the value choices it has made—about the kind of nation it professes and aspires to be. In his various roles, as preacher, political activist, and political philosopher, King holds America morally accountable for bringing its legal system of rights in line with its professed value of categorical respect for human dignity.

The Struggle against Racial Injustice

King was there when President Lyndon B. Johnson signed the Voting Rights Act into law in 1965. LBJ reportedly told King—in so many words—to go home, after he witnessed the signing of the Voting Rights Act. As the president handed King one of the more than fifty pens used to sign the bill into law, he told King that "his work was now done, that the time for protest was over."[8] Johnson was not happy with the disruptive voting rights movement. He was not happy with the bad press, with having to tame Alabama Governor George Wallace, or with having to divert attention from his other domestic and foreign policy agendas, most notably the war in Vietnam, to help blacks overcome. To his credit, the president signed the bill. However, as King appreciated, it would be naive to assume that this was because Johnson or any other member of government "had somehow been infused with such blessings of goodwill."[9] This was hardly the case.

King espoused *mature realism*, a methodological approach to achieving racial justice under nonideal conditions, animated by the plausible insight that agents, whether individuals or governments, must sometimes be moved to action by appealing to their base interests, notwithstanding the possibilities of love as a political emotion.[10] "We must develop, from strength," as King puts it, "a situation in which the government finds it wise and prudent to collaborate with us."[11] Johnson was undoubtedly moved to action by the overwhelming "situation" created by brutal and shameful white resistance to black civil and political rights, the peaceful nonviolent movement that responded to it, the bad press America was getting at home and abroad, and the looming threat of a potentially more explosive Black Power Movement waiting in the wings if the turn-the-other-cheek strategy failed.

Telling King to go home—with the hope that things could get back to normal—shows that Johnson clearly overestimated the significance of passing the civil rights and voting rights bills into law in the nation's exhausting struggle against racial injustice. To be sure, black Americans are not the only ones who have grown weary in this ongoing struggle, though they have historically been on the most brutal end of it, as was the case on Bloody Sunday in Selma, Alabama. White conservatives, moderates, and even white liberals sometimes show signs of fatigue when they ask, "When will things get back to normalcy?"[12] This question, which can stem from hopeful optimism or mean-spirited patronizing, usually arises following periods of racial progress. Indeed, as King observed, after civil and voting rights were secured—on paper if not in practice—many white Americans, including President Johnson, were eager for the marching to stop, for the protestors to return home, and for everyone to celebrate the new birth of democracy so that things could return to normalcy.[13] From their perspective, the comprehensive federal antidiscrimination legislation and statutory protection of voting rights during this historic era afforded blacks "tremendous gains in the struggle for dignity and decency."[14] What more could blacks demand as a matter of justice?

Well, as it turns out, they could demand much more. To appreciate King's answer to this question, and ultimately to understand why many people, including President Johnson, overestimated the significance of this historic legislation, and why King refused to go home, we must take up two closely related matters. First, we must ask: What is normalcy? Apparently, in the heat of the civil rights demonstrations, a Birmingham, Alabama, newspaper asked, "When are Negroes going to end these demonstrations and allow things to return to normalcy?"[15] Addressing this question, which undoubtedly comes up today whenever marchers gather to proclaim that black lives matter, was a recurrent concern for King. He consistently argues that there are two types of normalcy, one of which we should always reject outright and "never work to preserve." There is the kind that represents the racial status quo that has existed in America for most of its history, where blacks do not really enjoy the rights promised to them by laws on the books, such as ones that prohibit school segregation by race, neighborhood redlining and lending discrimination that restricts blacks to segregated dark ghettos, as well as ones that guarantee them equal protection, due process of law, and access to the ballot box. Status quo normalcy, or what King calls "negative normalcy," is also the kind in which black citizens and their children do not really enjoy fair equality of opportunity to participate in the full range of possibilities that America has to offer. And beyond these things, showing that his political morality was not limited to combating racial injustice, King also identifies class inequality, militarism, and environmental pollution with the kind of normalcy we must reject.[16]

Blacks, and indeed "every people who have ever struck for freedom," have rejected status quo normalcy in favor of the abnormal, or more emancipatory, "positive normalcy," says King.[17] But what exactly is this? Is it merely the absence of racial discrimination and the end of brutal violence against blacks marching for their rights? Surely it is not, though these are certainly components of it. To be sure, under more ideal conditions of positive normalcy we would not see acts of terrorist violence against blacks such as "the tragic and ungodly murder of four innocent girls" in Birmingham, Alabama, in 1963, or the brutal massacre of nine people, including the pastor, at the Emanuel African Methodist Episcopal Church in Charleston, South Carolina, in 2015. We would not see the kind of normalcy that prevented blacks from registering and voting in places like Mississippi, Louisiana, Georgia, and throughout Dixie before and after the Voting Rights Act became law. And we would not see the kind that now makes registering to vote and voting much too dependent on resources like time and money, which are so unevenly distributed across the population and which the black poor have a disproportionately lower share of. Yet these points only speak to what "positive normalcy" is not. They are compelling examples of what's wrong with the world we live in but say little, at least in the way of truly inspiring us, about the world we wish to achieve. We want to become a country where persons are not treated in certain ways based on arbitrary factors like racial membership. But surely there are loftier, more aspirational things we can say about how persons *ought* to be treated. Indeed, there are, and King—the political philosopher—obliges us.

He supplies substantive positive insights about what "positive normalcy" should look like, and more specifically about the broader normative ideals it aims to realize. There are the generic points he makes: it's about making the brotherhood of man a reality and bringing the nation closer in line with the truth of its creed, articulated by Thomas Jefferson, that all men are created equal; it is also about being a more just and righteous nation, and about creating a better world for our children. Fraternity, equality, and justice are familiar and much discussed ideals, often called upon to describe how persons ought to be treated in a more ideal society where positive normalcy prevails. However, for King positive normalcy is also and perhaps chiefly about recognizing the dignity of all citizens and publicly expressing respect for it within a legal system of rights. The value of dignity is where we find King's most fertile normative insight for assessing the problem with racial injustice generally and with the particular injustice of vote denial.

In an ideal world where there is positive normalcy, and racial and other types of justice, will indeed "roll down like waters." But in our nonideal—unjust and imperfect—world, what is the moral compass that can take us there, guiding our way, normatively? How do we move from negative to positive normalcy? What normative ideal can facilitate our journey from a racially unjust world to a racially just one? Here King tells us, "We will only reach out for that type of normalcy in which every man will respect the dignity and the worth of human personality."[18] And, he further adds, "We only reach out for that normalcy where *all* of God's children in this nation will be able to walk the earth with dignity and honor!"[19]

Dignity, for King, is the moral torch that lights the way to positive normalcy and racial justice in a nonideal world. And, as I shall discuss later, he takes it that a legal system of rights plays a vital role in facilitating this journey. Although some people may take issue with his interpretation of America's grand moral mission— following a tradition of black political thought that includes Frederick Douglass, Frances Ellen Watkins Harper, and others— King offers his own moral reading of America's famous founding declaration, highlighting its association with the value of dignity. "The Declaration of Independence," King tells us, "proclaimed to a world organized politically and spiritually around the concept of the inequality of man, that the liberty and dignity of human personality were inherent in man as a living being."[20] The American Civil War, Lincoln's Emancipation Proclamation, and eventually the Thirteenth, Fourteenth, and Fifteenth Reconstruction Amendments to the US Constitution were all key moments in bending the arc of the moral universe, and America's system of rights, toward extending the blessings of liberty to blacks and toward realizing an upward equalization of rank.

This illuminating and historically sensitive conception of human dignity, which philosopher Jeremy Waldron thoughtfully develops in his work, takes dignity to be a matter of having rank or high status, akin to what is reserved for nobility in some societies, a status that both morals and law can aim to protect and vindicate. If, as King says, "mankind through the ages has been in a ceaseless struggle to give dignity and meaning to human life," then America's experiment in representative democracy has been an ongoing struggle to realize an upward equalization of high rank for all persons under the authority of its laws.[21] I will say more about how King understands dignity and its demands in the next section, after tying up a second loose end.

Earlier I said there were two closely related matters we needed to understand to appreciate why many people, including President Johnson, overestimated the significance of the Civil Rights Act and the Voting Rights Act, and why King refused to go home after the latter was signed. The first had to do with settling for negative normalcy. Preferring to be maladjusted to this, King rejects the call—often from well-meaning liberals who want to end the war for racial justice—to return to normalcy unless this means marching forward with the goals and policies needed for the next, and high-priced, phase in the struggle against racial injustice and for dignity. Thus, the second matter pertains to King's more radical stance on what this phase of struggle required.

Dignity's demands are multifaceted in the pursuit of racial justice. The initial phase in America's epic struggle for dignity during the civil rights movement was to treat blacks with decency. Although doing this was no easy matter, many white Americans believed that eliminating the last vestiges of de jure discrimination from society, and the brutality with which racial caste had been enforced and nonviolent, peaceful protestors had been dishonored and debased, would—along with guaranteeing blacks the right to vote—suffice to restore balance to the scales of justice and realize the value of dignity.

So, for many whites the great victories in Montgomery, Birmingham, and Selma that paved the way for the Civil Rights and Voting Rights Acts were taken to be the end of war. With these transformative legislative accomplishments, it was believed that America's legal system of rights was finally aligned with affirming human dignity. King did not see it this way, however. For him they were but successful battles in the first phase of a larger struggle for racial justice, a larger struggle to express the moral ideal of dignity within positive law and the lived experiences of blacks in America. Phase two—the battle for equality—required taking on poverty, exploitation, and racial disparities.[22] And this meant reforms to create quality education, decent jobs that provided living wages, eradication of slums and substandard housing, and improved health outcomes, among other things. In addition, it required making sure that formally guaranteed rights such as the right to vote became more than nominal rights within America's system of rights.

Hence, the historic civil rights era antidiscrimination legislation did indeed afford blacks gains in the struggle for racial justice, important ones at that, but it did not suffice for working out the nation's normative commitment to upward equalization of rank or equal dignity for all. According to King, dealing with poverty and racial disparities were also necessary components of achieving this more lofty and demanding aim.

King was not naive about the serious challenges these second-phase battles would encounter. For one thing, as he keenly appreciated, because pursuing economic justice was much more expensive, the indispensable political alliances with liberal whites would be severely tested. "When Negroes looked for the second phase, the realization of equality," King observes, "they found that many of their white allies had quietly disappeared."[23] There are various reasons we can give for this. For instance, we might surmise that blacks and whites have rather different views about what the fulfillment of equality required, and about the extent to which winning phase one of the war against racial injustice was sufficient for this. King was charitable, preferring to give white Americans the benefit of the doubt, and loath to assume that they were acting in bad faith.

He presumed that the majority of them supported racial justice. However, he further surmised, "They believe that American society is essentially hospitable to fair play and to steady growth toward a middle-class Utopia embodying racial harmony."[24] And he thought they were just plain wrong about this.

King had much to say about white psychology to explain white apathy and stiffening white resistance in the second-phase battle for racial justice, though I will not take this up here. He was well aware of how costly the struggle against poverty and racial disparities would be for blacks and whites. As he put it, "Negroes have not yet paid the full price for freedom. And whites have not yet faced the full cost of justice."[25] So, when asked to go home by President Johnson after the signing of the Voting Rights Act in 1965, King could not heed this request. America still had much more work to do. From King's perspective, treating blacks with decency is not the same as treating them with equality, and both are necessary components of racial justice and organizing America's legal system of rights toward an upward equalization of rank, or dignity for all.

Dignified Conduct and Dignified Creatures

Selma, Alabama, was ground zero in the struggle for the right to vote in 1965. At the time, as King saw things, it was also the epicenter of a larger battle for dignity. As he put it, "This yearning for the franchise is another flash of the same quest for human dignity piercing the American sky."[26] Dignity is, to be sure, a philosophically contested concept. King does not offer us a theory of dignity, and I see no point in shaping his thoughts into a careful, comprehensive, and consistent package. There are, however, a few prominent features worth highlighting and connecting. Some of his many discussions of dignity can be situated within two broad categories—one about how we should act when pursuing justice (*dignified conduct*) and one about the kind of beings we are (*dignified creatures*). These categories, which will be familiar to readers of Kant, who also influenced King's thoughts about dignity, provide us with conceptual resources for understanding the normative demands of the struggle for voting rights in the overarching quest for an upward equalization of rank.

Amelia Boynton Robinson bled and nearly died on the Edmund Pettus Bridge on Bloody Sunday. She and other brave African Americans unsuccessfully attempted to march from Selma to Montgomery in 1965 to demand the right to vote. On that solemn day, they settled instead for giving blood offerings in their struggle against racial injustice. Unfortunately, the vicious beating Robinson suffered was not her first. In an earlier encounter with the notorious Sheriff Jim Clark, she was punched in the face, beaten, and dragged off to jail for trying to register people to vote. It is no small feat to maintain one's dignity under such gruesome circumstances, but Robinson managed to do so. King the pastor would have said "well done."

In sermons on "the evil system of segregation" King implored fellow Christians to be dignified in their righteous protest and struggle.[27] "As you press on for justice," King preaches, "be sure to move with dignity."[28] He would undoubtedly have said the same to those struggling against vote denial and could have identified Robinson as a model to emulate. But "move with dignity," "be dignified," and "comport oneself with dignity" are things we can implore or ask persons to do. And presumably they can be unsuccessful at it, in which case they would be without dignity and would warrant rebuke. Had Robinson armed herself not with the method of nonviolence and the Christian of weapon of love but with a firearm and the method of fighting brutal violence with the same kind of violence, and defended herself accordingly, King would have strongly disapproved. This would not have been an example of moving with dignity. This conception of dignity, which plays an essential role in King's normative understanding of what is required of persons struggling against racial injustice, is rooted in the idea that having dignity is about acting in accordance with standards of dignified conduct, particularly when confronting injustice or oppression. According to King, the imperatives of Gandhian nonviolent protest and unconditional Christian love supply the content of these normative standards.

We might agree with King that victims of racial injustice or racial oppression should not stand for these indignities, and that they should protest. They should act from a sense of dignity, as Rosa Parks did in not giving up her seat on the racially segregated bus in Montgomery, Alabama. As King saw it, "Mrs. Parks's refusal to move back ... was an individual expression of a timeless longing for human dignity and freedom. She was planted there by her personal sense of dignity and self-respect."[29] Yet there is a worry about the kind of nonviolent protest King takes to be sufficient for dignified conduct.

Acting with dignity is necessary to help persons regain a sense of self-respect, which is often lost or damaged under circumstances of injustice such as enforced racial segregation in public spaces or being denied the right to vote. These injustices contribute to a deeply felt sense of personal degradation as an inferior human being. Although engaging in nonviolent protest of these injustices may be sufficient to move with dignity in the face of injustice, it may not be enough to supply the needed evidence that one is *actually* moving with dignity. Refusing to comply with an order to give up one's seat to a white person on a racially segregated bus is one thing. Responding to the use of brutal physical violence to frustrate an attempt to exercise one's formally recognized rights without lifting a finger is another thing. In this case, turning the other cheek can also be read as servility, particularly if it becomes a consistent unbroken pattern of activity. So, at some point it may be necessary to fight back, in ways that cannot be mistaken as "fighting back," to supply evidence to the oppressor, and perhaps more importantly to oneself, that one really has the self-respect indicative of moving with dignity.

To be sure, a person taking the brutal blows of injustice without returning blows might only be pretending to be servile, ultimately to get the best of the oppressor or to help others see the oppressor's brutality and evil. But at some point his pretense must betray the protestor. "If only occasionally," as philosopher Bernard Boxill observes, "he must shed his mask. And this may not be easy. Not only does shedding the mask of servility take courage, but, if a person is powerless, it will not be easy for him to make others believe that he has been wearing a mask."[30] Nevertheless, he must be "driven to make the evidence of his self-respect unmistakable."[31] Annie Lee Cooper, the voting rights activist portrayed by Oprah Winfrey in the movie *Selma*, took about all that she could before punching Sheriff Clark in the eye. Although Cooper's protest here could not be mistaken for servility, King may have nevertheless reprimanded her for not moving with dignity. According to King, in a racially unjust society where negative, not positive, normalcy prevails, African Americans, who are on the receiving end of injustice, must do their part in bending the arc of the moral universe toward a more just society by engaging in dignified conduct as they struggle and protest.

Immanuel Kant believed that humanity has dignity and that this imposes both self-regarding and other-regarding duties. At the highest level of abstraction, his categorical imperative—the formula of humanity— famously tells us never to treat humanity, "insofar as it is capable of morality," as a mere means to an end. Doing so would be "assaulting its holiness."[32] According to Kant, we must take care to comport ourselves in ways that do not have this consequence. Although this imperative is not negotiable, we can go in different directions when bringing it down to earth to put respect for the dignity of humanity into practice within our everyday lives. This will depend on what standards, values, or virtues we, or the communities to which we belong, espouse. Our conduct and character are judged according to this measure. We promote it in our everyday practices. We find ways to sanction those who fail to measure up.[33]

From Kant's perspective, incurring debts that one cannot pay, begging, whining, and kneeling down (even to pray) are incompatible with paying proper respect for our dignity. In addition, Kant tells us, letting others violate our rights with impunity must not be tolerated.[34] Our status as dignified beings, in this sense, is clearly precarious. Were we to bow and scrape before others or in veneration of religious objects, to let others tread with impunity on our rights, or do anything that assaults our holiness, we would forfeit the respect we can demand as beings capable of morality. The same can be said of anyone who failed to heed King's call to move with dignity in the struggles against racial discrimination, segregation, and vote denial. Had Robinson and others not embraced nonviolence and love, they would have forfeited respect they were owed.

I am not sure if Kant and King would have seen eye to eye on how to respond to violence under circumstances of injustice. I suspect that Kant might have been critical of the turn-the-other-cheek approach, particularly insofar as it could be mistaken for allowing others to tread on one's rights with impunity. However, even if they disagree on this matter, it is clear that both associate dignity with acting in accordance with certain standards of dignified conduct. Moreover, they both believe that individuals have certain self-regarding duties to show proper regard for the holiness of their humanity, irrespective of whatever treachery or injustice befalls them. Moving with dignity in the struggle against racial justice is such a duty for King. But this is only one element of the equation. The other one, which construes dignity as something that cannot be compromised on account of failing to abide by certain standards of conduct, draws upon another sense of dignity also familiar to readers of Kant.

In an unambiguous, and especially strong, condemnation of denying blacks the right to vote, King remarks, "The denial of the vote not only deprives the Negro of his constitutional rights—but what is even worse—it degrades him as a human being."[35] Here King's debt to Kant is unmistakable. However, elsewhere in an argument on why racial segregation is immoral, he explicitly invokes Kant's formula of humanity. For King, both vote denial and segregation are injustices that reduce blacks "to things rather than persons," and they do so by cutting off "one's capacity to deliberate, decide and respond."[36]

Hence, there is another conception of dignity, bound up with the inherent value of our humanity, according to which dignity cannot be lost, no matter how one acts or fails to act. From this standpoint, to say of a person, such as Robinson, that she has dignity can also be understood as an ascription of inherent value or worth. Of course, this raises the question: What is the source or basis of this value? Here we can say any number of things. We can say that she has the capacity to move with dignity, in which case this sense of dignity and the foregoing one would be joined. Under the influence of the

Judeo-Christian tradition, as King was, we can say that the source of Robinson's inherent worth is her being created in the image of God. Or, as King puts it, "Every human being has etched in his personality the indelible stamp of the Creator."[37]

In addition, following King, we can adopt a secular formulation of the value of humanity rooted in our capacity to make deliberative choices. "When I cannot choose what I shall do or where I shall live," King tells us, "it means in fact that someone or some system has already made these decisions for me, and I am reduced to an animal."[38] Indeed, from early on in his thinking, King regarded man as a rational being, noting that it was one of the "supreme resources of man," distinguishing him from his animal ancestry.[39] This perspective resonates with the long-standing tradition of linking the worth or dignity of humanity to rational autonomy, which we find not only in philosophy but also in law, especially in judicial reasoning about privacy, abortion, and gay marriage.

So, in this sense, dignity—understood as worth—marks the sacredness of humans. This worth commands respect irrespective of how human beings act, what kinds of lives they live, and what they believe, and no matter their intellect, racial origin, or social position.[40] And this kind of dignity cannot be forfeited.[41] This conception, which is also essential to King's understanding of what the struggle against racial injustice demands, captures the familiar idea that dignity is rooted in the essential nature of certain beings.[42] Depending on how this nature is understood, some creatures have dignity and others do not.[43]

In step with Kant's view that human dignity imposes peculiar self-regarding duties on us, King's two conceptions of dignity can be joined to formulate such a duty. Individuals struggling against racial injustice have a self-regarding duty to comport themselves with dignity, as they work to move society to respect their inherent worth as creatures with the capacity for deliberative choice within its legal system of rights. In other words, they must move with dignity in struggling to be treated as required by their dignified natures. Understanding the distinction between dignified conduct and dignified creatures and how they are related disambiguates this statement.

Perhaps King would not have welcomed even these minimal efforts—falling far short of attributing to him a theory of dignity—to clarify his various uses of dignity and their relationship to one another. He certainly would have had little interest in this were it a mere philosophical exercise. But I suspect if it were done to illuminate what is morally required of us and of society in the war against racial injustice, as I aim to do in this chapter, he would have approved. Although King indulges our philosophical curiosity in having a loftier, indeed, more aspirational, perspective on how persons ought to be treated, he is mainly concerned with describing how dignity is assailed under nonideal circumstances of negative normalcy. Moreover, he aims to say what is required to right this wrong, moving us closer to positive normalcy and a fuller achievement of racial justice. That individuals engaged in the struggle move with dignity is one requirement; another requirement is that the law do its part in righting the indignity of racial injustice.

The Indignity of Racial Injustice

In a sermon on being a good neighbor, King describes segregation and discrimination as "evil monsters," calling attention to the nation's struggle to conquer these monsters that have "[stripped] millions of Negro people of their sense of dignity."[44] His list of evil monsters is long. Elsewhere in another sermon on the death of evil upon the seashore, King also counts oppression, colonialism, and imperialism as evil monsters that have reigned around the world. But, as he notes, these gradually gave way to the force of human dignity with independence movements in Africa and Asia that broke the yoke of colonial subjection, political domination, economic exploitation, and humiliation.[45]

If stripping Negro people, or any people, of their sense of dignity is a hallmark of an evil monster, then denying people the right to vote, a form of political domination about which I will say more later, is surely on the long list of monsters. In a reflection on successful independence movements in Africa, King laments that the struggle against political domination of blacks in America had not kept pace. "Voting as a badge of full citizenship has always had a special meaning to the Negro. But in 1965, in the context of worldwide developments," King tells us, "the denial of the right to vote cuts painfully and deeply into [the Negro's] new sense of personal dignity." When other blacks were gaining liberation around the world, he found it appalling that in the United States, African Americans could not exercise one of the most fundamental of all privileges of democracy—the right to vote.[46] Thus, for King, voting is a public badge of citizenship as well as dignity, which can be stripped away by the indignity of vote denial. Indeed, he went further: "There cannot be citizenship without the right to vote. A voteless citizen is no citizen. Men and women who can not vote are forcibly exiled from their national heritage."[47]

It is also clear that King considers substantive inequality and unequal protection of law to be evil monsters. He points out that blacks and whites have grossly unequal shares of income. In 1963 King observed that "the average income of Negroes is approximately $3,300 per family annually, against $5,800 for white citizens."[48] And he provided examples, such as bombings of black Christian churches, where law and government clearly do not afford blacks the same protection and justice under the law. "If a government building were bombed in Washington," King maintains, "the perpetrators would be shot down in the streets, but if violence... affects the life or property of a Negro, not all the agencies of government can find or convict the murderers."[49] Hip-hop artist J-Live, in his socially conscious rap single "I Am a Man (American Justice)"—which quotes Malcolm X and Huey P. Newton and also bears a title inspired by signs from the 1968 Memphis sanitation workers' strike that King addressed the day before he was assassinated—vividly captures the deeply felt assault on black dignity, today, when blacks are not afforded equal protection of law against police brutality and are instead made to fear the ones charged with protecting and serving them and their communities. He raps, "When you're treated less than human by a beast / It doesn't matter if it's the whole beast or nothing but the beast / If it's systemic, pandemic / and you don't even have the decency to condemn it? Goddamn it!"

All of these racial injustices, which sustain unequal social relations, have the effect of damaging the souls of black and white folk. They give blacks "a false sense of inferiority" as human beings, and they give whites "a false sense of superiority."[50] As King says in his famous Letter from Birmingham Jail, referencing Martin Buber, an injustice such as segregation substitutes "an 'I-it' relationship for an 'I-thou' relationship and ends up relegating persons to the status of things."[51] For black folk terrorized by these monsters, their social status is degraded to a lower rank, which corrodes their personality by instilling in them a sense of inferiority. The imposition of inferiority by these evil monsters, King explains, represents "the slave chains of today."[52] Insofar as blacks and whites are equally human beings, created in the image of God, as King assumes, with the capacity to make deliberative choices, that is, insofar as they have dignity in the sense of worth, King presumes that they should relate to one another, and be publicly regarded, as equals of the same high rank in civil society. But the reality of racial injustice in America, which has historically sustained unequal social relations and where positive normalcy has yet to come about, leaves the nation far short of achieving the normative ideal of upward equalization of rank.[53] In other words, America has yet to create circumstances were blacks have equal dignity with whites in the sense of social status.

Treating persons as equals with the same high rank does not preclude individual differences in income, wealth, and education, and differences along other substantive dimensions. I find no evidence that King thought that it did. Furthermore, his remarks on the need for, and worth of, the labor of low-wage nonprofessional workers suggest otherwise. He locates the dignity (worth) of their vital labor in the serving and building of humanity.[54] That said, the differences in these resources certainly should not be so great as to preclude persons from being able to relate to each other as equals, nor should they be such that persons identified by some visible marker of difference enjoy a disproportionately lower or higher share of either the good or the bad things that society has to offer. Both of these outcomes—too much inequality or a seemingly nonrandom distribution—could impact both personal and public perceptions of high rank.

The indignity of racial injustice has a personal and a public dimension. The capacity to deliberate, decide, and respond, or what I have been calling the capacity for deliberative choice, is what endows human beings with dignity as inherent worth according to King. It distinguishes them from other creatures. The personal dimension of segregation, discrimination, political domination based on race, and the other evil monsters is that they assail blacks' personal sense of worth. They impact how individual blacks perceive themselves. They impose upon the Negro "manacles of self-abnegation," says King, preventing them from saying and truly believing "I am somebody. I am a person. I am a man with dignity and honor."[55] How others perceive us, on the other hand, is the public dimension of these monsters. And it is significant that King mentions honor here.[56] The relationship of honor to dignity calls attention to another use of dignity as social status in King's thought, which is vital for elucidating the public dimension of the indignity of racial injustice.

The old saying "clothes make the man," Kant observes, "holds to a certain extent even for intelligent people." And as powerful as it can be, even our understanding "cannot prevent the impression that a well-dressed person makes of obscure representations of a certain importance."[57] In 1651, the colonial laws of Massachusetts regulated what apparel and adornments people could wear. These sumptuary laws aimed to maintain a rigid hierarchy of persons regarded as ladies and gentlemen, a high social rank, and persons of modest means and pedigree, a low social rank. They restricted the wearing of what we now call "bling"—gold, silver, silk, lace, and the like—to persons and their relations whose wealth exceeded a certain value (making exceptions for public officials, military personal, the well-educated, and persons whose estates had diminished in value) and imposed fines on violators of these laws. Ladies and gentlemen were deemed persons of honor, who retained a sense of dignity tied to this status. The bling laws gave dignity as honor public force by setting out specific rights to give it content. Persons without such standing were, of course, no different from those with it; they were likewise dignified creatures with the capacity for deliberative choice, which gives all who possess it dignity as worth. The amount of bling one has or lacks has no bearing on dignity in this sense. But clearly these sumptuary laws aimed to do more than "make the man." They aimed to bestow a socially recognized sense of dignity on certain men and women.

It is very much an open question, then, whether someone is a person of honor. If one's honor is tied to inherent worth, then one can claim to be a person of honor, even in the absence of bling laws that publicly mark this social status. But if it is tied to the public recognition of one's standing as a person of honor, then a legal system of rights is indeed a way of settling the matter. In a society where the distribution of honor is ranked, as it was in colonial and antebellum America—a stratified social hierarchy situating persons on a scale from low to high rank—we can have various reasons for wanting to undo this hierarchy and level up rank. We could, for example, maintain, as King most certainly did, that all human beings by virtue of being dignified creatures should be afforded the same high rank in civil society. We could also say, as King also did, that because all human beings are created in the image of God and are loved by God, they are of equal, high rank, and that positive law should mirror divine law, eradicating hierarchy and leveling up social rank. But whatever one's reasons, on this conception of dignity it is *not* constituted by the metaphysical nature of our beings. Instead, it is rooted in concrete social practices such as legal systems of rights that create legally supported ways of acting and being treated. An obvious consequence of this perspective is that because dignity must be granted, it can also be withheld or withdrawn. It can be won or lost. It can require sacrifice and struggle. Our inherent worth is something we have, even when we are not recognized as having it, as in a racist society that regards blacks as subpersons or subhuman. But our high social rank, on the other hand, and the public recognition that constitutes it, is something that we must struggle to achieve and retain.

King's extensive writings are full of references to the struggle for human dignity. In his famous speech on the steps of the Selma state capitol after the historic march, he includes public respect for dignity as one of the hallmarks of a yet-to-be-achieved great society, which he describes as "a society of justice where none would prey upon the weakness of others, a society of plenty where greed and poverty would be done away, a society of brotherhood where every man will respect the dignity and worth of human personality."[58] The conception of dignity tied to the social conferral of honorific status affords us a fruitful way to make sense of King's talk about the struggle and fight for dignity.

In colonial Massachusetts, bling laws regulated apparel and adornments to shape how some individuals were perceived by others. Because it was important in that society for ladies and gentlemen to be publicly regarded as such, there needed to be tangible ways of distinguishing their honorific status from the status of those with more modest means and pedigree. Their legal system of rights gave expression to this value of dignity as high rank. The evil monsters of racial segregation, discrimination, and vote denial essentially serve the same function as these bling laws. They publicly mark persons, within a socially stratified hierarchy, as having lower and higher ranks, with persons of high rank being conferred greater dignity. The public dimension of racial injustices, of the sort that King condemns, is that they diminish the social rank of blacks, denying them the same honorific status afforded to whites. Dignity as high social rank is thus denied to blacks under nonideal circumstances of negative normalcy.

My reading of King on dignity comes to this: black Americans, as dignified creatures, have a self-regarding obligation to move with dignity, engaging in dignified conduct, in their ongoing struggle to be socially recognized as having dignified status. This is necessary for moving America toward positive normalcy and a fuller achievement of racial justice in ways that are feasible and not counterproductive. However, the law must also do its part to bend the arc of the moral universe toward these ends. After all, laws are instrumental in why the nation falls short of these ends, and why blacks occupy a degraded rank. Law does its work within a system of rights. Through this system, law can level the social rank of persons up or down, and it should be judged accordingly. As King argued in 1963, "Any law that uplifts human personality is just. Any law that degrades human personality is unjust." Moreover, what was true then is arguably still true today: "Now is the time to lift our national policy from the quicksand of racial injustice to the solid rock of human dignity."[59] But apart from this judgment about the justness of laws, we can also ask whether the system of rights contains rights that express the values the nation professes to hold dear. If it does not, this would give us grounds to condemn the nation for the contradiction between its existing practices and its professed ideals. I shall take up this final matter by attending to King's case for the distinctive normative importance of a legal system of rights that guarantees all citizens the right to vote.

Vindicating the Right to Vote

This chapter began by identifying consequences that can befall a nation that does not guarantee its citizens the right to vote: damage to its stability, national solidarity, and moral authority. On this last point, King noted on more than one occasion that if the United States allows states like Mississippi to deny voting rights to blacks, it cannot argue against undemocratic practices elsewhere in Asia, Africa, and Latin America.[60] But there are also dire consequences for the individuals or groups who are denied the right to vote. In an annotated draft copy of an article on voting rights and jobs, King writes,

> When Negroes are denied a right to vote and have their voices heard in Southern politics, they are denied the equal protection of the law, for Southern [sheriffs] like all politicians protect the people who put them in office; they are denied education opportunities, adequate wages, the right to organize and bargain collectively; and they are left to the mercy of those in political control.[61]

Here King appreciates the connection between political representation through voting and one's interests being represented. I want to dwell, however, on this last observation, about being at the mercy of others. This is a prominent theme in King's normative argument for the right to vote. And it puts an ethical concern with dignity front and center.

Were we to set the foregoing grave costs of vote denial to one side, we would still have moral reasons for denouncing a government's failure to guarantee the right to vote. Moreover, we would also have reason to rebuke legislation that makes access to the ballot box conditional upon possessing resources like money and time, which are unequally distributed across the population of eligible voters—a serious consequence of today's voter ID requirements.[62] These moral reasons may focus on the harmful consequences for the happiness or well-being of persons whose right to vote is either denied or made more burdensome. But we may also take moral issue with them, following King, by highlighting how they result in a harmful form of interpersonal relations in the political sphere, making some persons vulnerable to domination by those who enjoy the full exercise of the right to vote. He makes this point in a speech at the Lincoln Memorial in 1957. "So long as I do not firmly and irrevocably possess the right to vote I do not possess myself," King declared.[63] "I cannot make up my mind—it is made up for me. I cannot live as a democratic citizen, observing the laws I have helped to enact—I can only submit to the edict of others."[64] Here we find King taking nondomination to be a political ideal and applying this ideal to defend the rights of African Americans to participate in the democratic political process on full and equal terms.[65]

This argument is, in part, about the adverse consequences of vote denial. However, this reading of the argument assumes that having to submit to the edict of others is detrimental to our happiness or well-being. But this may not be the case. If we suppose that those to whom we must submit not only have our best interests at heart but also succeed in making laws that best promote our happiness and well-being, then our consequentialist reasons for objecting to vote denial dissipate. Even if these fanciful assumptions were true, King would still take normative issue with leaving persons vulnerable to the political will of others by denying them the right to vote or making its exercise unduly burdensome. This is because his appeal to nondomination also has a deontological dimension. It is rooted in a prohibition against actions that violate a categorical moral imperative calling upon us to respect agents who have the capacity for "making up their mind" or the capacity for deliberative choice. With this argument the value of dignity—in two senses in which King uses it—looms large. And both senses—dignified creatures and dignified status—can be brought to bear in expounding the expressive relationship between the right to vote and dignity, which in turn illuminates the normative significance of a public practice of rights that includes the right to vote within a legal system of rights.

Here is the short form of the argument I shall unpack: The right to vote is one of the rights in a legal system of rights that promotes the exercise of deliberative capacity in the political sphere as well as the leveling up of social rank. Both senses of dignity, as the source of our inherent value and the source of honorific social status, are thus advanced by the right to vote. The first is advanced because this right gives one a say in making laws to which one is subject. The second is advanced because when we have a say, others do not subject us to political domination.[66] Both enable us to look others in the eye as political equals and to be socially recognized as having the same political rank. If protecting our interest in being so regarded is valuable, not just personally but as a professed national aspiration of an egalitarian democracy, then a nation whose commitment to the right to vote realizes these things has a robust commitment to dignity, whereas a nation that does not lacks such a commitment.[67]

So, according to King, having a capacity for deliberative choice or to make up one's mind is a metaphysical source of the worth of dignified creatures. A public commitment to valuing dignity aims to respect or promote the worth of persons within a legal system of rights. Mindful of the grounding problem, we may have real doubts about whether this notion of dignity affords adequate guidance in generating specific rights, and whether it is "sufficiently robust to deliver the full range of human rights recognized in contemporary international human rights doctrine."[68] But thinking about dignity as the ground of rights, such that we are aiming to infer particular rights from it, is not the only way to proceed. We can also consider the actual practice of rights we have before us, and ask whether, how, and to what extent it is dignity respecting or dignity promoting. If it is fully dignity respecting, then it conforms to the categorical imperative to respect the dignity (worth) of persons.

Dignity, for King, is also an honorific status we should confer upon those we deem to be dignified creatures with inherent worth. But in this case the dignity is not metaphysical, simply flowing from the nature of one's being; it is something social that is conferred by de jure and de facto social practices and institutions. A public commitment to valuing dignity aims to level up or universalize this honorific status to all dignified creatures. We do not have to go too far back in American history to find a time when many questioned whether blacks were dignified creatures with the metaphysical source of inherent worth. During this time, they allowed social practices and institutions that maintained a stratified social hierarchy where blacks occupied a low rank and whites a much higher one. Back then there were Americans such as Frederick Douglass who proclaimed and defended the inherent worth of blacks and argued for the abolishment of chattel slavery and racial segregation to facilitate a leveling up of their social rank.

Political domination via vote denial has long been an injustice perpetrated against blacks in America. Many people, blacks and whites alike, have worked tirelessly to win blacks the right to vote, from getting the Fifteenth Amendment passed to winning the Voting Rights Act.[69] In doing so they recognized the power of a legal system of rights in bending the arc of the moral universe to justice, and in making respect for dignity part of the lived experience of persons whose dignity had long been denied and diminished. They appreciated that a legal system of rights with the right to vote can address the evil monster of political domination and thus promote dignity as a capacity for deliberative choice, and as recognition of an honorific status for those we deem to be dignified creatures. A public practice of rights that includes the right to vote advances and promotes the value of dignity: it respects our deliberative capacity to make up our minds in matters that concern us, and it levels up our rank by freeing us from the indignity of having to submit to the edict of others by following laws we had no part in enacting. This practice observes Kant's categorical imperative, which King embraced, to respect humanity as an end in itself.

The right to vote gives people a public basis for making claims against others and empowers them to demand respect.[70] It gives people a "furious" sense of their rights, as Waldron puts it, and generates "a willingness to stand up for them as part of what it means to stand up for what is best and most important in oneself."[71] And, more broadly, it publicly expresses a governmental commitment to dignity, and to bringing our practices in line with our professed ideals, which in turn promotes stability, belonging, and the moral authority of the state. Making this expressive commitment is something that King—as a preacher, political activist, and political philosopher—was tirelessly devoted to getting the nation to do. Martin Luther King Jr. teaches us that we have much to gain by ensuring that everyone has the right to vote.

Epilogue

Democracy Born of Struggle

This book has argued for lowering the race-first flag and for fostering a united front of marginalized groups to advance the cause of racial progress in postracial America. Some scholars who accept the standard progressive story of racial progress appeal to thinkers within the black radical tradition to support the case for flying the race-first flag. While there is ongoing debate concerning how to understand this tradition, and over which black thinkers count as radical, there is a danger of ignoring lessons from this tradition that support the case for pursuing progress via a more united front among a broader cross section of marginalized groups. Thinking about the contributions of black thinkers to America's understanding of its democratic experiment, the nation's failure to realize its democratic values, and how to struggle productively in making it do better, is a place to extract these lessons.

After the bright light of Reconstruction faded over the ominous horizon in 1877, the American South was determined come hell or high water to "keep the Negro in his place" as a second-class citizen. In his first work of history, *The Negro* (1915), W. E. B. Du Bois reports that when the former defenders of slavery arrived at the moral crossroads of allowing blacks to pursue the American dream with the same obstacles faced by whites or to construct additional ones, they elected to institutionalize racially unequal citizenship. From then forward in the land where all people are declared free and equal, the promises of American democracy could only be achieved for those riding Jim Crow with blood, sweat, and tears.

The election of Donald J. Trump, who rode the high tide of populism and anti-immigration to the White House, has fueled increasing anxiety about the health of American democracy. Liberals have had considerable anxiety over the Trump victory. However, unlike many people I know, I did not shed any tears after the ballots were counted and Trump's vision for "making America great again" was victorious. That's because I do not believe that American democracy is only now under siege or is experiencing a threat unlike any it has endured before.

Those of us who have been riding Jim Crow longer—before marching against police violence and white vigilante terrorism, marching against expressions of anti-black hatred on college campuses, and marching for black lives mattering became the things to do—know better. Those of us who have been brought up on the wisdom of David Walker, Frederick Douglass, Anna Julia Cooper, Ida B. Wells, Langston Hughes, Zora Neale Hurston, Martin Luther King Jr., James Baldwin, Huey Newton, Angela Davis, and Audre Lorde know better. Those of us who have been students of past and present social movements that have placed the suffering and democratic aspirations of black folks at center stage know better.

The heightened state of alarm among anxious liberals suffers from a lamentable lack of historical perspective. Appreciating Du Bois's historical lesson, and the wisdom of black folks that came before and after him, accounts for why some of us did not think that the Trump presidency and the precarious state of American democracy today are anything more than business as usual. This is not to say that we should surrender to tyranny of the wicked without a good fight. Nor is it to deny that there are relative differences in value among government regimes such that we can prefer a lesser of two evils. And I agree with Richard Rorty and with Cornel West that we must certainly not let political nihilism tempt us to lose all hope for achieving our country—an America that is worthy of its democratic aspirations. The point is that we have no novel reasons to be alarmed today. To appreciate this insight, we must take up the politics of resistance that has been relegated to the back of the political theory bus.

Against this backdrop, three recent books, *The Making of Black Lives Matter* by Christopher J. Lebron,[1] *An Impossible Dream?* by

Sharon A. Stanley,[2] and *Struggle on Their Minds* by Alex Zamalin,[3] feature black voices and social movements from the past. Taken together, these books extract valuable lessons from the African American experience for understanding and advancing the resistance struggles of those still fighting to achieve democracy today with blood, sweat, and tears.

People resist many things, including assaults on our dignity, injustice, and inequality. Some of the things we resist (such as sexual harassment and hate speech) are perpetuated by individuals, while others, such as mass incarceration and de facto Jim Crow public schools, are perpetuated by authorities that have power over us through social processes and institutions that shape our lives from cradle to grave. Zamalin defines "resistance" as the act of contesting authority, but his specific focus is on *political* authority and on *unjust* uses of power. Traditionally, Hegel, Marx, Foucault, and other thinkers have fed the radical appetite for philosophies and politics of resistance—giving us tools for understanding, explaining, and defeating dominating lords, exploiting capitalists, and oppressive penal institutions.

But the canonical Western classics—works of dead white men—are not the only place to turn for radical nourishment. Black slaves resisted white masters, sometimes violently, sometimes quietly. Free blacks resisted Jim Crow. Civil-rights-era blacks resisted voter disenfranchisement. And today young black activists resist the denigration of black lives, just as their mothers and grandmothers resisted lynching. To understand these acts of resistance against unjust uses of political authority we must look to the black faces at the bottom of America's well. *Struggle on Their Minds* does this admirably, in Zamalin's words, "[by providing] an intellectual history of when resistance to racial inequality was palpable in key African American political movements."[4] By focusing on these thinkers, he skillfully shows how their work highlights the fact that slavery, segregation, lynching, black ghettos, mass incarceration, and unjust racial inequality—the evils that have occupied black resistance thinkers and movements—are perversions of American democracy.

Zamalin's concise history of the black struggle for democracy begins with a reading of David Walker's "Appeal" for black freedom in the early nineteenth century. It then excavates the antislavery philosophy of Frederick Douglass before moving on to the anti-lynching writings of Ida B. Wells, and the Black Power praxis of Huey Newton and the Black Panthers, and ending with the prison abolition activism of Angela Davis. Walker condemns tyranny and exploitation as undemocratic and argues that sowing division and discord among the voiceless and powerless is how the powerful sustain racial domination and inequality. Violence, especially extralegal violence, is another weapon for keeping the downtrodden on the ropes and violating their dignity. Douglass teaches us that we must sometimes fight back with our fists to reaffirm our dignity, and Wells says we must shine a public spotlight on illicit violence to awaken public sentiment against antidemocratic practices and inequality. Newton and the Panthers highlight the importance of community self-determination in weathering the raging storm that state violence has inflicted on black ghettos, while Davis exposes how the prison–industrial complex denigrates black lives, maintains an unequal racial order, and disenfranchises its victims.

The focus on a black politics of resistance that says "no" to antidemocratic practices and calls for direct action and critiques of the system may well be a unique site of political theory, as Zamalin insightfully tells us—one that is not a knockoff of liberalism or civil republicanism. However, the thinkers, ideas, and movements occupying this space demand a more nuanced, balanced, and, dare I say, more radical treatment than he offers us. For instance, it would have been useful to have more direct engagement with how the thinkers and movements considered in *Struggle on Their Minds*—and some of the ones overlooked—understand the role of class politics in the struggle for democracy. This would have been possible by attending to thinkers such as King, who made the dignity of labor an object of democratic struggle, or with a more serious treatment of the Panthers' Marxist critique of capitalist exploitation of labor than we get in the slim chapter on Newton.

Black resistance movements have been a permanent feature of American society, and the thinkers Zamalin discusses have all been written about before. So, what's fresh in his book? He is especially concerned with black political resistance movements "from below," or what we might call politics from the grassroots. Such movements seek democracy in the radical transformation of the basic structure of society, which is constituted by the institutions regulating the economy, law, family, education, and others that shape and order our lives. Grassroots movements also seek equitable redistribution of resources, including public goods, rights, and liberties, as well as seeking genuinely democratic political rule, as the great Ella Baker taught us. However, according to Zamalin, these thinkers are not committed to working within the system to collect on America's broken democratic promises. Thus, he supplies us with the *black radical hidden transcript*, a look at "radical" black thinkers and movements not constrained by either formal politics or politically acceptable forms of protest. This is a provocative contribution.

Black radicalism, we are told by Zamalin, can be characterized by its "uncompromising, unruly, irreverent, and militant" focus on the structural dimensions of socioeconomic and political inequality with an "intensity of pitch and commitment" absent in more moderate thinkers and gradualist movements. To be fair, Zamalin does not set out to offer us anything more than a snapshot of the history of black radical resistance, but, as he says, "my concern is with people who resisted racial inequality, which has been and still is catalyzed by the ideologies of white supremacy and racism."[5]

Placing the emphasis on this dimension of black political thought highlights one aspect of the tradition. Still, the list of figures Zamalin chooses to include and omit is instructive. The reason why there is no chapter on King, he tells us, is that King was not a black radical for much of his political life. He was more interested in abolishing legal discrimination, winning black integration, and urging Americans to love one another (as if these were not radical goals at the time, or now). And he would have us erroneously believe that King was not occupied with the pressing question we face today: "How do we address the vast racial structural and socioeconomic disparity—from jobs to income to life expectancy—that continues to create a system in which black citizens are marginalized?"[6]

The history of black struggle for democracy is full of important figures, indeed too many to feature in a short book. So, we cannot fault Zamalin for omitting King from the book. But we can take issue with this misleading reason for excluding him. Long before King entered the final years of his life calling explicitly for a "Poor People's Campaign," he appreciated the importance of both a class struggle and of mitigating racial inequality, and of linking class and race in the battle to achieve American democracy. From his early intellectual engagement with the pros and cons of Marx during his college and graduate school years, to his reflections on why positive normalcy could never be attained without economic justice during the Montgomery, Birmingham, and Selma battles, King was very radical in his efforts to shape a new world.

The question of what, and who, counts as radical is a point of contention between Zamalin and Lebron. And, as we shall see, it also informs Stanley's efforts to identify a more promising conception of integration. Yet Lebron and Stanley's books, while having other virtues, also pay insufficient attention to class matters in the black radical tradition.

In *The Making of Black Lives Matter*, Lebron makes room for King in his exposé of the black radical transcript and does so by arguing that King's call for love and nonviolence is a genuinely radical entry in the black struggle for democracy. This is an important virtue. Zamalin uncritically accepts the romantic image of Black Power advocates being more radical than King and other nonviolent civil rights warriors. But Lebron offers evidence that the "House Niggas" or "Uncle Toms" epithets leveled by these advocates do not stick because critics such as Malcolm X misunderstood the radical nature of nonviolent resistance. Lebron quotes King:

> It must be emphasized that nonviolent resistance is not a method for cowards; it does resist. If one uses this method because he is afraid or

merely because he lacks the instruments of violence, he is not truly nonviolent.... This is ultimately the way of the strong man.[7]

According to Lebron, "radicalism is the imagination and will to think and act outside the bounds of the normally acceptable."[8] And by this standard, King, Baldwin, Hurston, and Lorde were also radicals, as were Douglass, Cooper, Wells, and Hughes; they all used their imagination in claiming an authority to advocate for black lives that American society denied them.

Lebron makes clear that these eight radical black thinkers also all endorsed the ideal of democracy as a worthy aspiration while denouncing "the distortions and corruptions of *American* democracy without compromise."[9] Understanding their legacies offers hope, not despair, to those marching for black lives today. And the source of this hope, according to Lebron, is the conviction that we can awaken the moral consciousness of "good and conscientious people" (p. xiv) to assume their duties to help bend the arc of the moral universe toward justice. "Black lives matter," he tells us, "are three words often used as a lament, as a signal that our democracy has been, is, and seems likely to continue failing 12 percent of its population."[10] The radical black voices speaking from the bottom of America's well help us understand the democratic struggles of the 12 percent, why American democracy has failed them, and what they and others must do to redeem it.

As Lebron shows, the strategic use of shame, or shameful publicity, is a crucial tool used by black radicals for the moral re-education of white America. "Shame is the moral emotion or sensibility," says Lebron, "we ought to feel when we realize our actions, beliefs, or attitudes in fact conflict with some prior held principle."[11] Although Lebron dwells on the role of shameful publicity in Douglass's treatment of slavery and Wells's critique of lynching, this is arguably the same strategy we find in the other six thinkers he considers. Each thinker, in their own way, calls attention to the hypocrisy of American democracy, preaching freedom, equality, and justice for all on the one hand, while denying the promises of democracy to black folks on the other.

For example, a familiar tactic for explaining away this hypocrisy, trying to resist shame, and turning a blind eye to white supremacy and black subordination is to assume that blacks are inferior to whites in mind, body, and soul. Yet black radical artists such as Hughes and Hurston used art to push back against these derogatory and baseless portrayals of black humanity. And thinkers such as Cooper and Lorde teach us that because the 12 percent is comprised of women too, not just men, as well as persons with different sexual orientations, the democratic struggle for black lives must find common cause with struggles against domination based on gender and sexuality.

Lebron also identifies another worry about King. "The struggle in the South," said King, "is not so much the tension between white people and Negro People. The struggle is rather between justice and injustice."[12] Here King flirts with the idea that race is not central to the struggle for justice and democracy in America. It would certainly be misleading to read King as being unconcerned with race; however, it would be equally misleading to neglect his efforts to develop a politics of resistance that was able to transcend the racial divide. Not only did he appreciate the links between race and poverty, as did many other black radical thinkers, but King was also moved by Marx's critique of capitalism and the damage that it inflicted on the poor and on low-wage workers of all races. The exclusive focus on white supremacy, and the ways in which it is sustained within American democracy, neglects this penetrating analysis and obscures the need for a broader coalition between blacks and the white working class to work together in achieving our democratic promise.

Although Lebron offers us a more radical King than Zamalin, neither of them offers us a perspective on the democratic socialist King, or the King who was unwilling to adjust himself to the inequalities of an unjust economic system rigged to rob the masses so that the upper classes could live lavishly. Because Lebron's account of the black radical transcript frames the struggle for democracy too narrowly as a battle against white supremacy, we get no lessons on what the black voices of the past thought about the politics of class, and its potential to shame the nation into fulfilling its democratic promises to the 12 percent. If shaming white America in the way that Lebron hopes for were possible, and I have long had my doubts about this, perhaps the nation could finally realize an elusive goal. Still, a broader multiracial politics of class is also essential to achieving a truly democratic society.

Racial integration is typically put forward as the goal of democratic struggle in America. Yet too many people have been willing to believe that racial desegregation (allowing blacks to enter places and spaces previously reserved for whites in Jim Crow America) realizes this aim. When *Brown v. Board of Education* and post-*Brown* cases ended de jure American apartheid, a rift emerged in the courts over whether prohibiting legally mandated racial segregation was enough, or whether society also had an obligation to undo de facto segregation to achieve integration. With the emergence of a conservative Supreme Court majority, racial imbalance not mandated by law is now treated as constitutionally permissible, and what Sharon Stanley calls a minimalist approach to desegregation prevails. More aggressive legal approaches to desegregation, typically championed by liberal justices, which call for targeting historical patterns of racial imbalance not proscribed by law, have not entirely disappeared from constitutional jurisprudence. But today they are more likely to crop up in dissenting opinions. Although she prefers the latter over the former, Stanley argues that neither model of integration addresses the problem that "any worthy model of integration must dismantle":[13] the problem of white supremacy.

An Impossible Dream? places a normative concern with undoing white supremacy and black subordination at the core of a model of racial integration that we should pursue. It then asks whether achieving this ideal is wishful thinking. Focusing on racial imbalance, and seeking merely to move blacks into white spaces, as many conscientious liberals call for, is not radical enough to realize these more ambitious ends. If we take the aim of integration to be achieving racially mixed spaces and institutions, we can realize this goal while leaving the evils of white supremacy and black subordination untouched.

John L. Rury and I argue in *The Color of Mind: Why the Origins of the Achievement Gap Matter for Justice* (2018)[14] that this is precisely what we find in nominally desegregated K–12 schools today. They are racially mixed but have systemic sorting practices associated with tracking, discipline, and special education that reinforce racist ideas and white supremacy to the detriment of black student achievement. In a similar spirit, Stanley argues that "if desegregation secures physical mixing, but fails to transform either explicit and implicit racist beliefs and inclinations," then in reality "it does not fully redress the injustices or the democratic pathologies of segregation."[15] This is well said, and I certainly agree with it.

In staking out a more promising form of integration, one that does not take "proximity to white people as the goal and prize of integration,"[16] Stanley takes her cue from a notion of black radicalism that pitches a tent large enough to include Malcolm X, Martin Luther King Jr., and Stokely Carmichael. Integration worthy of our democratic struggle, she rightly reminds us, goes beyond putting blacks and whites in the same neighborhoods, churches, schools, jobs, and families. It requires changing the terms on which whites and blacks interact, aiming to make them fairer, more egalitarian, and genuinely democratic. But, as she incisively argues, achieving such radical racial integration requires two things that have proven difficult to secure in America, given its racist history and the enduring effects of historical injustice: it requires "internal transformation that achieves psychic conversion, and the redistribution of power."[17]

The central argument of her book is that because these things are so difficult to come by, blacks are justified in their pessimism, and if a new, more radical, form of integration is to be possible, whites have more work to do than blacks to bring it about. White Americans must work harder to develop a new sense of self, and a new sense of black worth that rejects the false view of white superiority and black inferiority. They must also acknowledge white privilege and take steps to undo structures of power distributing wealth, housing, education, and other resources along with rights, duties, and liberties that sustain it. Stanley concludes that "it is white privilege itself that stands as the strongest and most intransigent obstacle to true integration."[18]

Stanley's book is, in many ways, the most militant of the three under review here. It puts the onus for achieving radical racial integration squarely on the backs of whites. White people must take the steps needed to secure reparations, criminal justice reform, education reform, housing reform, and all the other reform policies needed to redistribute power and deconstruct white privilege in America. And they must do so wholeheartedly enough to convince blacks that they are serious about psychic transformation, redistribution of power, and relating to blacks as moral and social equals. But Stanley's militancy, which is rooted in taking white supremacy to be the root of all evil, comes at a cost: it leaves no room at all for us to consider a democratic politics that takes us beyond race and lays the groundwork for interracial coalitions that target those who stand to gain the most materially from democracy's discontents.

To be sure, the evidence Stanley supplies in chapter 6, "Confronting White Privilege," on whites' reluctance to take these steps, and their willingness to settle instead for demonizing blacks, paints a dismal picture of the prospects for such a politics. Nevertheless, the convergence of interests has proven a powerful motivating factor in past democratic struggles, which managed to secure such coalitions. And if things are as dismal as she suggests, with whites being virtually inseparable from their privilege, we have little reason to believe that a groundswell of white support for black reparations is on the horizon, no matter how beautifully crafted an essay Ta-Nehisi Coates can make for the case.

Each of these books dwells on the battle against white supremacy in the black radical struggle for democracy. They feature different black voices. There is some overlap and some disagreement over just how radical some of these voices are. For instance, Lebron and Stanley find evidence of a radical King, where Zamalin passes over King as insufficiently radical. Nevertheless, the irony in all three of these books is not that they fail to highlight the confrontation with white supremacy in black democratic struggles but, rather, that this focus is all-consuming. The black radical tradition is a rich one, and combating white supremacy has certainly been part of it. But fighting back against the antidemocratic tendencies of capitalism, imperialism, indifference (including elite black indifference) to poverty, and insufficient attention to intersecting types of domination has also been central to this tradition. It would have been good to get more of this story onto the table.

These timely books are thus valuable—yet narrow—contributions to political theory. They illustrate the relevance of black radical thinkers and movements to the ongoing struggle for democracy in America. While we should applaud them for this, we must also be critical of their failure to find a politics of resistance in the black voices and social movements of the past that takes us beyond a politics of race—indeed beyond a politics of white supremacy. Admittedly, this is a surprising thing to ask for in this age of Trump, where symbols of white supremacy are poisoning the American landscape, and neo-Nazis and white supremacists are on the march. But if one thinks that this age is only about race and not money, it will be very difficult to make sense of the new tax bill smuggled into law at the end of 2017 to the sound of popping corks on Wall Street.

The road beyond race is one we must travel to build a broader coalition to defeat those who are operating with stealth to save capitalism from democracy. Historian Nancy MacLean, in *Democracy in Chains: The Deep History of the Radical Right's Stealth Plan for America* (2017),[19] provides compelling evidence for why we should be worried about this. The plutocrats, and politicians on their payrolls, have relied on their own politics of resistance and hidden agenda. And combating this alchemy calls for a politics of resistance that can build productive coalitions between groups of people with different social identities, where each group—from blacks housed in inner-city ghettos, to Latinos relegated to dilapidated barrios, to poor whites corralled in rural trailer parks—is being abused by the stealth manipulation of democracy's rules to make America "great" again for the rich by making American democracy less democratic.

When democracy is under siege we must ask, who are the winners and losers? Any answer to this question that does not distinguish between the rich and the rest of us will be utterly unsatisfactory. Black radical thought clearly provides resources for appreciating this point, and in these dark days when so many are trying to achieve our country with blood, sweat, and tears, we would do well to draw lessons from the black voices in the back of America's bus urging us to save democracy from the tyranny of the rich. Unfortunately, a crucial question that each book leaves unanswered is this: How do black voices and social movements of the past, including ones from other parts of the African diaspora, provide insights for moving us beyond a black radicalism rooted in a narrow preoccupation with white supremacy to inform thinking on how to save democracy from capitalists?

The call for a politics of resistance that takes us beyond race is not naive, nor does it diminish the importance or radical nature of identity politics. On the contrary, it encourages us to take to heart points made by Ella Baker, Angela Davis, Audre Lorde, and other black democratic warriors. To achieve our country, groups must not only assert their particular interests, as the Combahee River Collective did on behalf of black feminists, but they must also form political coalitions with other groups struggling for democracy's promises. Furthermore, the distinctiveness of black women's identities, which can implicate the matrix of race, gender, sexuality, disability, and class oppression, shows the inadequacy of plotting a course to a brighter democratic future that focuses too narrowly on white supremacy.

A genuinely radical politics of resistance should indeed direct our attention to black voices and movements of the past and present. But only when it moves us beyond a narrow concern with white supremacy are we able to glimpse what kind of politics transcends black radicalism itself, why such a politics of resistance should be more central to contemporary democratic struggles, and how Alicia Garza, Patrisse Cullors, and Opal Tometi—three young black activists, following in the footsteps of democratic visionaries that came before them—courageously moved America in this direction in 2013 when they created #BlackLivesMatter. A genuinely radical politics of resistance, inspired by past and present black democratic warriors and determined to achieve a realistic blacktopia in an America under the spell of postracialism, recognizes the imperative that we must unite to fight.

Acknowledgments

I have approached this book like a recording artist who releases single after single and eventually drops an album. A lot of time has passed between writing the first chapter and the last one. And I have incurred many debts in the twelve years it took to complete this book. Unfortunately, it is impossible to acknowledge them all here, and I do not want to leave anyone out. So, a hearty thanks to everyone! I am immensely grateful for generous and insightful feedback from colleagues, students, referees, and attentive audiences on the many occasions that I presented drafts of this material in the United States and abroad.

All but one of the chapters is an abridged and modified version of work first published elsewhere. Chapter 1 is drawn from "Educational Inequality and the Science of Diversity in *Grutter*: A Lesson for the Reparations Debate in the Age of Obama," *The University of Kansas Law Review* 57 (2009): 755–793, © 2009 by the Kansas Law Review. Chapter 2 draws from "Uncovering the Voting Rights Act: The Racial Progress Argument in *Shelby County*," *Kansas Journal of Law & Public Policy* 25 (2016): 329–346, © 2016 by the Kansas Journal of Law & Public Policy. Chapter 3 draws from "Educational Inequality and the Science of Diversity in *Grutter*" and from "Reparations and Racial Inequality," *Philosophy Compass* 5 (2010): 55–66, © 2010 by John Wiley & Sons Ltd. Chapter 4 draws from "Charles Mills's Liberal Redemption Song," *Ethics* 129 (2019): 370–397, © 2019 by The University of Chicago. Chapter 5 draws from "Postracial Remedies" (with Richard E. Levy), *University of Michigan Journal of Law Reform* 50 (2017): 387–488, © 2017 by the University of Michigan Journal of Law Reform. Chapter 6 draws from "Beyond the Sins of the Fathers: Responsibility for Inequality" (with Nyla R. Branscombe), *Midwest Studies in Philosophy* 38 (2014): 121–137, © 2014 by Wiley Periodicals, Inc. Chapter 7 draws from "Du Bois's Defense of Democracy," in *Democratic Failure* NOMOS LXIII, ed. Melissa Schwartzberg & Daniel Viehoff (New York: New York University Press, 2020): 207–246, © 2020 by New York University Press.

Chapter 9 draws from "A Vindication of Voting Rights," in *To Shape A New World: Essays on the Political Philosophy of Martin Luther King, Jr.*, ed. Tommie Shelby and Brandon M. Terry (Cambridge, MA: Harvard University Press, 2018), 161–183, © 2018 by Harvard University Press. The epilogue draws from "Democracy Born of Struggle," *Perspectives on Politics* 16 (2018): 449–454, © 2018 by Cambridge University Press.

Two chapters from this book, chapter 5, "Postracial Remedies," and chapter 6, "Collective Responsibility," draw from articles that I coauthored. I have made changes to each chapter, but the substance and main arguments have been preserved. I am grateful for the opportunities to work with my coauthors, Richard E. Levy and Nyla R. Branscombe, respectively, both former University of Kansas colleagues. I owe a special debt to Rick for the massive amount of work and thought we jointly put into developing our ideas.

My sincere thanks to Kayla Jackson—my stellar graduate student research assistant at Rutgers—for editorial assistance and for insightful comments on the Introduction. She pressed me to find the best voice and angle to pitch my argument to sympathetic yet skeptical readers. Thanks also to Eduardo Martinez—my former graduate student and now colleague in the profession and coauthor—for detailed comments on the book's Introduction. I am grateful to Linda Alcoff, coeditor of the series, for inviting me to contribute a book, and for providing a model for how to do the kind of philosophy that matters to the lives of real people. My thanks to Peter Ohlin, executive editor, for eagerly embracing my book idea from the beginning and to the editorial team at Oxford University Press.

Thanks to my small group of confidants, especially Ahmed Johnson, Paul Mark Wallace, Michael Hanchard, and Christian Davenport, for always having an ear for me and being willing to rap about philosophy and life. Thanks to Tommie Shelby for being my most valuable philosophical interlocuter as well as a constant source of encouragement and support. Thanks to my beautiful family, Angela, Nastassia, and Tatiana, for love, laughter, and for making life worth living. And last but not least, thanks to the late Charles W. Mills, to whom this book is dedicated, for setting the bar high and for inspiring me to do my best work.

Notes

Introduction

1. Lawrence D. Bobo, "Somewhere between Jim Crow & Post-Racialism: Reflections on the Racial Divide in America Today," *Daedalus* 140 (2011): 11–36, 14.
2. Ibid.
3. Ibram X. Kendi, "Our New Postracial Myth," *The Atlantic*, June 22, 2021, https://www.theatlantic.com/ideas/archive/2021/06/our-new-postracial-myth/619261/.
4. Keeanga-Yamahtta Taylor, "Did Last Summer's Black Lives Matter Protests Change Anything?," *The New Yorker*, August 6, 2021, https://www.newyorker.com/news/our-columnists/did-last-summers-protests-change-anything.
5. Elizabeth A. Harris, "In Backlash to Racial Reckoning, Conservative Publishers See Gold," *The New York Times*, August 15, 2021, https://www.nytimes.com/2021/08/15/books/race-antiracism-publishing.html.
6. Alicia Garza, *The Purpose of Power: How We Come Together When We Fall Apart* (New York: One World, 2020).

Chapter 1

1. Then-senator Barack Obama, Remarks at CNN/YouTube Democratic Presidential Debate, Apr. 26, 2007; transcript available at https://www.cnn.com/2007/POLITICS/07/23/debate.transcript/ (last visited Feb. 15, 2009).
2. 539 U.S. 306 (2003).
3. Nikhil Pal Singh, *Black Is a Country: Race and the Unfinished Struggle for Democracy* (Cambridge, MA: Harvard University, 2004).
4. Ibid.
5. 60 U.S. 393, 407 (1856).
6. See Charles M. Payne, *I've Got the Light of Freedom: The Organizing Tradition and the Mississippi Freedom Struggle* (Berkeley: University of California Press, 1995), 419.
7. See David A. Hollinger, *Postethnic America: Beyond Multiculturalism* (New York: Basic Books, 1995), 171.
8. Singh, *Black Is a Country*, 10 (citing Jeffrey Rosen, "The Color-Blind Court," *The New Republic*, July 31, 1995, 23).

9. See Charles Murray, *Losing Ground: American Social Policy, 1950–1980* (New York: Basic Books, 1994), 233; Thomas Sowell, *Race and Culture: A World View* (New York: Basic Books, 1994), 177; Shelby Steele, *A Dream Deferred: A Second Betrayal of Black Freedom in America* (New York: HarperCollins, 1998), 47–48.
10. Lawrence D. Bobo, James R. Kluegel, & Ryan A. Smith, "Laissez-Faire Racism: The Crystallization of a Kinder, Gentler, Antiblack Ideology," in *Racial Attitudes in the 1990s: Continuity and Change*, ed. Steven A. Tuch & Jack K. Martin (Westport, CT, Praeger, 1997), 17.
11. Ibid., 17.
12. Ibid., 16.
13. Sowell, *Race and Culture*, chap. 4.
14. 481 U.S. 279 (1987).
15. Ibid., 287.
16. Ibid., 290–291.
17. Ibid., 294–295.
18. The University of Michigan's Law School Dean charged a faculty committee in 1992 with crafting an admissions policy that complied with the Supreme Court's ruling in *Regents of University of California v. Bakke*, 148 U.S. 265 (1978), on the use of race in university admissions. See *Grutter v. Bollinger*, 539 U.S. 306, 312 (2003).
19. *Grutter*, 315.
20. Ibid., 321.
21. Ibid., 322.
22. 515 U.S. 200, 227 (1995).
23. See *Regents of Univ. of Cal. v. Bakke* 438 U.S. 265, 270 (1978).
24. *Grutter*, 328.
25. Ibid., 344.
26. *Grutter*, 329 (quoting *Bakke*, 310).
27. Ibid., 315.
28. Ibid., 316.
29. These are, with slight modification, the same objections that Justice Powell raised in *Bakke*. See *Bakke*, 306–07, 310.
30. *Grutter*, 374.
31. See, e.g., Brief for American Educational Research Association et al., as Amici Curiae Supporting Respondents, *Grutter v. Bollinger*, 539 U.S. 306 (2003) (No. 02-241), 2003 WL 398292. This brief relied heavily upon the "Gurin Report," an expert report produced by Patricia Y. Gurin, a Professor of Psychology and Women's Studies at the University of Michigan, to demonstrate the positive effects of educational diversity. Analysis of the data leads to several major conclusions, including: "[s]tudents who experienced the most racial and ethnic diversity in classroom settings and in informal interactions with peers showed the greatest engagement in active thinking processes, growth in intellectual

engagement and motivation, and growth in intellectual and academic skills."
Ibid., 5–6. The Gurin Report found that "diversity leads to 'a learning environment that fosters conscious, effortful, deep thinking' as opposed to automatic, preconditioned responses." The Report found that diverse learning environments resulted in "more active engagement in the learning process and an increased ability to understand the perspectives of others." And the Report found that "[s]tudents educated in diverse settings are more motivated and better able to participate in an increasingly heterogeneous and complex democracy."

32. *Grutter*, 328.
33. Ibid., 330.
34. See Amici Curiae Brief, 2003 WL 398292, 1.
35. Angelo N. Ancheta, *Scientific Evidence and Equal Protection of the Law* (New Brunswick, NJ: Rutgers University Press, 2006), 2.
36. Ibid., 1.
37. Ibid., 3.
38. See William H. Tucker, *The Science and Politics of Racial Research* (Champaign: University of Illinois Press, 1994), 149.
39. Ibid.
40. Ibid., 521.
41. Ibid., 364.
42. Ibid.
43. Ibid.
44. Ibid., 364–365.
45. Ibid., 373.

Chapter 2

1. *Shelby Cty. v. Holder*, 133 S. Ct. 2612 (2013).
2. The Fifteenth Amendment to the US Constitution outlaws government discrimination in voting based on race or color; US CONST. amend. XV. The VRA of 1965 reaffirms this amendment by permanently proscribing state actions, nationwide, that result in vote denial or abridgment due to race or color. Voting Rights Act of 1965 § 2, 52 U.S.C. § 10301 (2012). Section 4(b), the "coverage formula," of the VRA singles out for special attention certain jurisdictions with egregious histories of Fifteenth Amendment violations through the use of poll taxes, literacy tests, and other devices *and* with low voter registration and turnout; see §10303. Section 5, the "preclearance requirement," provides that voting changes in covered jurisdictions must gain preapproval either from the federal district court in Washington, DC, or the US Department of Justice; see §10304. However, in the initial Act Congress understood sections 4 and 5 to

be temporary measures and set them to expire after five years, the most recent reauthorization of the VRA in 2006 extended them for an additional twenty-five years leaving the coverage formula untouched. *Compare* Voting Rights of 1965, Pub.L.89-110, §4–5, 79 Stat. 437 (1965), at 438–439 *with* §10303. This decision prompted Shelby County, Alabama, a covered jurisdiction, to seek judgment declaring the coverage formula and the preclearance requirement unconstitutional and barring their enforcement. See 133 S. Ct. 2612. The *Shelby County* ruling invalidated section 4(b) but did not rule on section 5. Ibid., 2631.

3. The Voting Rights Act of 1965, 52 U.S.C. §10303(b) (2012).
4. *Shelby Cty.*, 2623.
5. Ibid., 2622.
6. Richard A. Posner, *Supreme Court 2013: The Year in Review*, SLATE, June 26, 2013, http://www.slate.com/articles/news_and_politics/the_breakfast_table/features/2013/supreme_court_2013/the_supreme_court_and_the_voting_rights_act_striking_down_the_law_is_all.html.
7. *Dred Scott v. Sandford*, 60 U.S. 393 (1857).
8. James Blacksher & Lani Guinier, "Free at Last: Rejecting Equal Sovereignty and Restoring the Constitutional Right to Vote *Shelby County v. Holder*," *Harvard Law & Policy Review* 8 (2014): 39–69.
9. See Franita Tolson, "Reinventing Sovereignty?: Federalism as a Constraint on the Voting Rights Act," *Vanderbilt Law Review* 65 (2012): 1195–1259. The Elections Clause provides that "[t]he Times, Places and Manner of holding elections for Senators and Representatives, shall be prescribed in each state by the legislature thereof; but the Congress may at any time by law make or alter such regulations, except as to the places of choosing Senators"; US CONST. art. I, § 4.
10. See, e.g., Thomas Colby, "In Defense of the Equal Sovereignty Principle," *Duke Law Journal* 65 (2016): 1087–1171.
11. Derrick Darby and Richard E. Levy, "Postracial Remedies," *University of Michigan Journal of Law Reform* 50 (2017): 387–488.
12. Daniel P. Tokaji, "The New Vote Denial: Where Election Reform Meets the Voting Rights Act," *South Carolina Law Review* 57 (2006): 689–733. Vote denial practices also referred to as voter suppression prevent people from voting and having votes counted. Vote dilution practices weaken a group's political influence by making it harder for their political preferred candidates or issues to win. See Daniel P. Tokaji, "Responding to *Shelby County*: A Grand Election Bargain," *Harvard Law & Policy Review* 8 (2014): 71–108.
13. *Shelby Cty.*, 2628.
14. See Ellen D. Katz, "Dismissing Deterrence," *Harvard Law Review Forum* 127 (2014): 248–252, 250.
15. We should presume that these states are not seeking to enact intentionally discriminatory requirements, since these could not pass constitutional muster. However, it is also clear that these states need not worry too much about passing

voting laws that have disparate impacts on blacks, Latinos, and other voters as a constitutional matter. According to settled law, this would not suffice to invalidate them constitutionally. See *Washington v. Davis*, 426 U.S. 229 (1976). To be found unconstitutional under the Fourteenth Amendment the laws must have racially discriminatory intent or purpose, and the Supreme Court has made it very challenging to invalidate voting and other laws on this basis. Based on the rule established in *Washington*, and elaborated in subsequent decisions, e.g., *Personnel Adm'r of Mass. v. Feeney*, 442 U.S. 256, 278 (1979), petitioners must show that state legislatures "selected or reaffirmed a particular course of action at least in part, 'because of,' not merely 'in spite of,' its adverse effects upon an identifiable group." The Court applied this rule to a voting case involving the construction of electoral districts, finding facially neutral districting constitutional, even if they have the effect of diluting the black vote in at-large elections. See *Mobile v. Bolden*, 100 S. Ct. 1490 (1980). When section 2 of the VRA was amended two years later, Congress prohibited voting regulations that were discriminatory in effect regardless of whether they were designed or applied to discriminate. The Voting Rights Act of 1965, 52 U.S.C. § 10301 (2012). Some *post–Shelby County* commentators have argued that all hope is not lost for voting rights plaintiffs seeking relief from vote denial, as section 2 of the VRA provides ample power to press their claims. See, e.g., Daniel P. Tokaji, "Applying Section 2 to the New Vote Denial," *Harvard Civil Rights-Civil Liberties Law Review* 50 (2015): 439–489.

16. Justice Ginsburg takes issue with this in her dissent in *Shelby County*.
17. *Shelby Cty.*, 2624. It should be noted that this 19.4 percent number does not match the 19.3 percent figure in the chart included in the opinion, which provides voter registration numbers for 1965 and 2004 for the six originally covered states: Alabama, Georgia, Louisiana, Mississippi, South Carolina, and Virginia; Ibid., 2626. According to this data compiled from Senate and House reports, in 1965, Mississippi had the largest gap at 63.2 percent, with only 6.7 percent of blacks registered to vote compared with 69.9 percent of whites. Virginia had the smallest gap at 22.8 percent, with 38.3 percent of registered black voters compared with 61.1 percent of whites.
18. *Shelby Cty.*, 2625. In contrast to the rational basis review the Supreme Court sometimes employs in equal protection cases, the "rational relationship" test deployed here is much stronger: it requires a tight connection between uses of tools and likely consequences of such uses. And it allows the historical context to provide support for positing—or in the *Shelby County* case, for rejecting—a tight connection. The crux of the argument is that the pre-1965 and post-1965 historical contexts are different enough to render unreasonable any inferences from the use of tools by states with a past history of racial discrimination to make voting harder to the effect of racial disparities in voting trends. The most germane difference in the present context, according to the *Shelby County*

majority, is that these trends have dramatically improved, which suggests that whatever problems remain in states that had been covered by the preclearance requirement might reasonably be attributed to other causes. Ibid., 2632.
19. Ibid., 2626.
20. Ibid.
21. Ibid.
22. Ibid., 2625.
23. Ibid., 2623.
24. Conservatives have swiftly seized the opportunity to make voting more burdensome in states they control. See Tomas Lopez, "*Shelby County*: One Year Later," *Brennan Cir. For Justice* (June 24, 2014), http://www.brennancenter.org/analysis/shelby-county-one-year-later.
25. Assessment of how much racial progress there has been since the civil rights era is polarized by race as well as partisanship. See, e.g., "King's Dream Remains an Elusive Goal; Many Americans See Racial Disparities," *Pew Research Center*, Aug. 22, 2013, https://www.pewresearch.org/social-trends/2013/08/22/kings-dream-remains-an-elusive-goal-many-americans-see-racial-disparities/.
26. There is evidence that Americans in general, not just members of the High Court, remain deeply divided by race, class, and political ideology over how to assess evidence of racial inequality and racial disadvantage in political representation, voting access, and many other areas. See, e.g., Lawrence D. Bobo & Camille Z. Charles, "Race in the American Mind: From the Moynihan Report to the Obama Candidacy," *The Annals of the American Academy of Political and Social Science* 621 (2009): 243–259.
27. Jillian C. Banfield, Michael Ross, & Craig W. Blatz, "Responding to Historical Injustices: Does Group Membership Trump Liberal-Conservative Ideology?," *European Journal of Social Psychology* 44 (2014): 30–42.
28. See, e.g., Richard P. Eibach & Joyce Ehrlinger, "'Keep Your Eyes on the Prize': Reference Points and Racial Differences in Assessing Progress Toward Equality," *Personality and Social Psychology Bulletin* 32 (2006): 66–77; Amanda B. Brodish, Paige C. Brazy, & Patricia G. Devine, "More Eyes on the Prize: Variability in White Americans' Perceptions of Progress Toward Racial Equality," *Personality and Social Psychology Bulletin* 34 (2008): 513–527.
29. *Veasey v. Abbott*, 796 F.3d 487 (5th Cir. 2015), 500.
30. *Holder v. Hall*, 114 S. Ct. 2581 (1994), 2592, 2619 (J. Thomas, concurring).
31. *Shelby Cty.*, 2635 (J. Ginsburg, dissenting).
32. Ibid., 2636.
33. Here one might seek guidance from section 2 of the VRA, as amended in 1982, which assigns liability if electoral practices result in racial minorities having "less opportunity than other members of the electorate to participate in the political process and to elect representatives of their choice." Voting Rights Act of 1965 §2, 52 U.S.C. §10301 (2012). This broader interpretation came on the heels

of a Supreme Court decision in *Mobile v. Bolden*, which constituted a serious blow to second-generation voter discrimination claims. See 446 U.S. 55 (1980). The Court ruled that only intentional discrimination based on race was unconstitutional and given that section 2 of the VRA was essentially a congressional restatement of the Fifteenth Amendment, this rule applied to the statute as well; Ibid., 61. The amendment of Section 2 in 1982 placed racially disparate results in electoral outcomes alongside intentional discrimination in blocking access to the ballot as a way of falling short of the principle of equal opportunity to participate in the political process; §10301.
34. Any legal response to the decision aiming to argue that the coverage formula remains rational in theory and practice must take seriously the "basic principles" guiding the majority's review. A response strategy that I will not pursue here would be to deny that what the majority characterizes as "the fundamental principles of equal sovereignty" is really an established legal principle. This would be sufficient to derail the case for scrapping the coverage formula because the Court's concerns about respecting the equal dignity of states seem to be the only positive normative foundation it has for objecting to the unequal treatment of covered and non-covered states, and only allowing for it under what it deems truly exceptional circumstances. However, resolving this issue requires diving into a thicket of constitutional and constitutional interpretation matters that go beyond the scope of this chapter.
35. *Shelby Cty.*, 2634–35.
36. See Manning Marable, *The Great Wells of Democracy: The Meaning of Race in American Life* (New York: Civitas Books, 2002), 67–92.
37. Thom File, "U.S. Census Bureau, The Diversifying Electorate-Voting Rates by Race and Hispanic Origin in 2012 (and Other Recent Elections)," *US Census Bureau* (May 2013), https://www.census.gov/library/publications/2013/demo/p20-568.html. And as for evidence of disparate impact of current burdens on voting, this alone will not suffice to establish voter discrimination without a showing of intent. One way around this would be to find a middle-ground approach that could establish discrimination without having to show intent. But it is unclear whether this could be a winning argument before a Supreme Court with a conservative majority. For a useful analysis of the limits of disparate impact analysis, see Janai S. Nelson, "The Causal Context of Disparate Vote Denial," *Boston College Law Review* 54 (2013): 579–644.
38. Jake Rosenfeld, Becky Pettit, Jennifer Laird, & Bryan Sykes, "Incarceration and Racial Inequality in Voter Turnout," *SSRN*, http://ssrn.com/abstract=1901381 (last updated Aug. 12, 2011).
39. Christopher Uggen & Jeff Manza, "Democratic Contraction? Political Consequences of Felon Disenfranchisement in the United States," *American Sociological Review* 67 (2002): 777–803.

40. Jon C. Rogowski & Cathy J. Cohen, "Black and Latino Youth Disproportionately Affected by Voter Identification Laws in the 2012 Election," *Black Youth Project* 1–7, http://blackyouthproject.com/wp-content/uploads/2015/11/voter_id_effect_2012.pdf.
41. Even if this argument stands, it certainly does not follow that Congress was compelled to update or reshape the VRA by scrapping the coverage formula, or that the Court was justified in replacing Congress's judgment about how to reshape a revised law to address "current conditions" with its judgment, particularly if Congress found evidence of voter discrimination in the record before it notwithstanding whatever other progress there may have been. It had the authority to decide the proper remedy, which clearly involved keeping the coverage formula intact. For more on this astute criticism, see Ellen D. Katz, "What Was Wrong with the Record?," *Election Law Journal* 12 (2013): 329–331, 330.
42. Lopez, "*Shelby County:* One Year Later," 29. See also Zachary Roth, "In 2015, Hope and Fear on Voting Rights," *MSNBC* (Dec. 29, 2015), http://www.msnbc.com/msnbc/2015-hope-and-fear-voting-rights.
43. *Shelby Cty.*, 2642 (J. Ginsburg, dissenting).
44. Ibid.
45. 553 U.S. 181 (2008).
46. Joseph Fishkin, "Equal Citizenship and the Individual Right to Vote," *Indiana Law Journal* 86 (2011): 1289–1360.
47. Richard H. Pildes, "What Does the Court's Decision Mean?," *Election Law Journal* 12 (2013): 317–318.
48. See Tokaji, "Responding to *Shelby County*," 72.
49. Ibid., 73.
50. Ibid.
51. Guy-Uriel E. Charles & Luis Fuentes-Rohwer, "The Voting Rights Act in Winter: The Death of a Superstatute," *Iowa Law Review* 100 (2015): 1389–1439.
52. Martin Luther King Jr., "Address to the Hungry Club in Atlanta," Dec. 15, 1965.
53. Ibid.

Chapter 3

1. Elazar Barkan, *The Guilt of Nations: Restitution and Negotiating Historical Injustices* (New York: W. W. Norton & Company, 2000); Ruti G. Teitel, *Transitional Justice* (New York: Oxford University Press, 2000).
2. Roy L. Brooks, *When Sorry Isn't Enough: The Controversy over Apologies and Reparations for Human Injustice* (New York: N.Y.U. Press 1999); Alfred L. Brophy, *Reparations Pro & Con* (New York: Oxford University Press, 2006); Charles J. Olgetree, "Repairing the Past: New Efforts in the Reparations Debate in America," *Harvard Civil Rights - Civil Liberties Law Review* 38 (2003): 279–320.

3. Brooks, *When Sorry Isn't Enough*. See also Joe R. Feagin, "Documenting the Costs of Slavery, Segregation, and Contemporary Racism: Why Reparations Are in Order for African Americans," *Harvard BlackLetter Law Journal* 20 (2004): 49–81; David R. Williams & Chiquita Collins, "Reparations: A Viable Strategy to Address the Enigma of African American Health," *American Behavioral Science* 47 (2004): 977–1000.
4. Brophy, *Reparations Pro & Con*, 4.
5. Ibid., 5.
6. Cornel West, *Race Matters* (New York: Vintage, 1993); Howard Schuman, Charlotte Steeh, Lawrence D. Bobo, & Maria Krysan, *Racial Attitudes in America: Trends and Interpretations* (Cambridge, MA: Harvard University Press, 1997); Andrew Hacker, *Two Nations: Black and White, Separate, Hostile, and Unequal* (New York: Scribner, 2003).
7. Michael Dawson, *Black Visions: The Roots of Contemporary African-American Political Ideologies* (Chicago: University of Chicago Press, 2001).
8. Michael Hanchard, *Party/Politics: Horizons in Black Political Thought* (New York: Oxford University Press, 2006).
9. Christopher Kutz, "Justice in Reparations: The Cost of Memory and the Value of Talk," *Philosophy & Public Affairs* 32 (2004): 277–312, 283.
10. John Torpey, *Making Whole What Has Been Smashed: On Reparations Politics* (Cambridge, MA: Harvard University Press, 2006), 42.
11. Barkan, *The Guilt of Nations*.
12. Thomas McCarthy, "Coming to Terms with Our Past, Part II: On the Morality and Politics of Reparations and Slavery," *Political Theory* 32 (2004): 750–772; Bernard R. Boxill, "A Lockean Argument for Black Reparations," *The Journal of Ethics* 7 (2003): 63–91; David Lyons, Corrective Justice, Equal Opportunity, and the Legacy of Slavery and Jim Crow," *Boston University Law Review* 84 (2004): 1375–1404; Jonathan Kaplan & Andrew Valls, "Housing Discrimination as a Basis for Black Reparations," *Public Affairs Quarterly* 21 (2007): 255–273.
13. Jeremy Waldron, "Superseding Historical Injustice," *Ethics* 103 (1992): 4–28, and "Redressing Historic Injustice," *The University of Toronto Law Journal* 52 (2002): 135–160.
14. See Susan Dodds, "Justice and Indigenous Land Rights," *Inquiry* 41 (1998): 187–205; Janna Thompson, "Historical Injustice and Reparation: Justifying Claims of Descendants," *Ethics* 112 (2001): 114–135; Lukas H. Meyer, "Historical Injustice and the Right of Return," *Theoretical Inquires in Law* 5 (2004): 305–316; Paul Patton, "Historical Injustice and the Possibility of Supersession," *Journal of Intercultural Studies* 26 (2005): 255–266.
15. See McCarthy, "Coming to Terms with Our Past, Part II." See also Kaplan & Valls, "Housing Discrimination as a Basis for Black Reparations."

16. See Lauren J. Krivo & Robert L. Kaufman, "Housing and Wealth Inequality: Racial-Ethnic Differences in Home Equity in the United States," *Demography* 41 (2004): 585–605.
17. See Williams & Collins, "Reparations: A Viable Strategy to Address the Enigma of African American Health."
18. See Ruth D. Peterson & Lauren J. Krivo, "Race, Residence, and Violent Crime: A Structure of Inequality," *Kansas Law Review* 57 (2009): 903–933.
19. See Roy L. Brooks, *Atonement and Forgiveness: A New Model for Black Reparations* (Berkeley: University of California Press, 2004).
20. See Kim Forde-Mazrui, "Taking Conservatives Seriously: A Moral Justification for Affirmative Action and Reparations," *California Law Review* 92 (2004): 683–753.
21. Ibid., 703–704.
22. See Rodney C. Roberts, "The Counterfactual Conception of Compensation," 37 *Metaphilosophy* 37 (2006): 414–428.
23. Commission to Study Reparation Proposals for African Americans Act, H.R. 40, 110th Cong. (2007). At the beginning of the 111th Congress, Representative John Conyers, Jr., of Michigan reintroduced this legislation. See Commission to Study Reparations Proposals for African Americans Act, H.R. 40, 111th Cong. (2009).
24. H.R. 40, 110th Cong. (2007); H.R. 40, 111th Cong. (2009).
25. *Legacy of the Trans-Atlantic Slave Trade: Hearing before the Subcomm. on the Constitution, Civil Rights, and Civil Liberties of the House Comm. on the Judiciary*, 110th Cong. (2007) [hereinafter *Hearings*] (hearing to discuss H.R. 40, 110th Cong. [2007]), available at http://frwebgate.access.gpo.gov//cgi-bin/getdoc.cgi?dbname=110_house_hearings&docid=f:39707. pdf.
26. Ibid.
27. *Hearings*, supra, note 106, at 28, 30 (testimony of Roger Clegg).
28. Ibid., 29.
29. Ibid., 82–86 (testimony of Stephan Thernstrom).
30. Ibid., 85.
31. Ibid., 72 (testimony of Tommy Wells).
32. Ibid., 2–73.
33. Ibid., 78.
34. *Hearings*, 79.
35. See, generally, Aristotle, *Nicomachean Ethics*, 2nd ed., trans. Terence Irwin, (Indianapolis: Hackett Publishing Co., 2000).
36. See, e.g., Chandran Kukathas, "Who? Whom? Reparations and the Problem of Agency," *Journal of Social Philosophy* 37 (2006): 330–341.
37. See, e.g., Waldron, *Superseding Historic Injustice*.
38. In re African-Am. Slave Descendants Litig., 471 F.3d 754, 759 (7th Cir. 2006). Some philosophers have challenged the presumption that there can be a moral

statute of limitations on rectifying injustice. See, e.g., Rodney C. Roberts, "Another Look at a Moral Statute of Limitations on Injustice," *The Journal of Ethics* 11 (2007): 177–192.

39. See Boris I. Bittker, *The Case for Black Reparations* (Boston: Beacon Press, 1973), 93; and Emma Coleman Jordan, "A History Lesson: Reparations for What?," *New York University Annual Survey of American Law* 58 (2003): 557–613, 558.
40. See Kaplan & Valls, "Housing Discrimination as a Basis for Black Reparations," and also Roberts, "The Counterfactual Conception of Compensation."
41. Williams & Collins, "Reparations: A Viable Strategy to Address the Enigma of African American Health," 995–996.
42. Peterson and Krivo, "Race, Residence, and Violent Crime: A Structure of Inequality," 904, provide a useful way of capturing the agent-neutral versus agent-relative distinction: "Taking this perspective shows how differential patterns of violence across ethnoracial groups are products of structural relations of society rather than stemming from individual differences in propensities to engage in violent behavior." This quotation is illuminating because it shows how some social scientists draw a sharp distinction between the agent-neutral and agent-relative explanations.
43. McCarthy, "Coming to Terms with Our Past, Part II," 764.
44. See, generally, David Horowitz, *Uncivil Wars: The Controversy over Reparations for Slavery* (San Francisco, CA: Encounter Books, 2002).
45. David Austen-Smith & Roland G. Fryer Jr., "An Economic Analysis of 'Acting White,'" *The Quarterly Journal of Economics* 120 (2005): 551–583, 568–71; Signithia Fordham & John U. Ogbu, "Black Students' School Success: Coping with the 'Burden of "Acting White,"'" *The Urban Review* 18 (1986): 176–206, 177. For an important empirical assessment and criticism of this explanation, see Karolyn Tyson, William Darity Jr., & Domini R. Castellino, "It's Not 'a Black Thing': Understanding the Burden of Acting White and Other Dilemmas of High Achievement," *American Sociological Review* 70 (2005): 582–605, 583.
46. *Grutter v. Bollinger*, 539 U.S. 306 (2003).
47. Eduardo Bonilla-Silva, *Racism without Racists: Color-Blind Racism and the Persistence of Racial Inequality in America* (London: Rowman & Littlefield, 2003).

Chapter 4

1. Charles W. Mills, *Black Rights/White Wrongs: The Critique of Racial Liberalism* (New York: Oxford University Press, 2017).
2. Charles W. Mills, *The Racial Contract* (Ithaca, NY: Cornell University Press, 1997).

3. Mills, *Black Rights/White Wrongs*, 215.
4. Ibid., 5.
5. Ibid., 28.
6. See Samuel Freeman, "Illiberal Libertarians: Why Libertarianism Is Not a Liberal View," *Philosophy and Public Affairs* 30 (2001): 105–151.
7. Mills, *Black Rights/White Wrongs*, 162.
8. Because Mills puts so much emphasis on Rawls's silences on this matter, he neglects the possibility that a Rawlsian argument for reparations could be produced. It has already been shown that black reparations could be defended on Lockean grounds, and Mills situates Locke and Rawls in the same liberal camp. See Bernard R. Boxill, "A Lockean Argument for Black Reparations," *The Journal of Ethics* 7 (2003): 63–91. Furthermore, some folks, both blacks and whites, might endorse a form of reparations that is not about material wealth transfer, which is much more radical, but about rectification of the present harms being done by people because of false beliefs about race, such as the view that races are biologically real. See Naomi Zack, "Reparations and the Rectification of Race," *The Journal of Ethics* 7 (2003): 139–151. And those who find Rawls's views about the social bases of self-respect congenial may see in them a way to develop an argument for black reparations that is connected with systematically debunking beliefs about black inferiority and the role they might play in the basic structure of society, including, e.g., in the system of public education. For an account of this, see Derrick Darby & John L. Rury, *The Color of Mind: Why the Origins of the Achievement Gap Matter for Justice* (Chicago: University of Chicago Press, 2018).
9. Mills, *Black Rights/White Wrongs*, 131.
10. Ibid., 133.
11. Ibid., 243.
12. Ibid., 25–26.
13. Ibid., 243.
14. For a statement of the worry that Mills "hedges on nationalism," and that his quest to redeem liberalism is somewhat conservative, see Howard Winant, "Charles Mills for and against Liberalism," *Ethnic and Racial Studies* 41 (2017): 551–556.
15. See G. A. Cohen, "Where the Action Is: On the Site of Distributive Justice," *Philosophy & Public Affairs* 26 (1997): 3–30.
16. Mills, *Black Rights/White Wrongs*, 132.
17. Ibid.
18. Ibid.
19. One way to avoid my challenge is for Mills not to frame his case as providing a theoretical tool that radical liberals can use to achieve racial justice, instead simply arguing for the rightness or truth of his alternative backward-looking principles of justice. However, this way out is not likely, given that he is fully

invested in a partly instrumentalist defense of justice. This also explains why the question of audience matters for assessing whether the tool can serve the group that he intends for it to serve.
20. See Terry Eagleton, *Ideology: An Introduction* (New York: Verso, 1991), 2.
21. Mills, *Black Rights/White Wrongs*, 148.
22. Ibid., 156.
23. Ibid., 215.
24. See Derrick Darby & Nyla R. Branscombe, "Beyond the Sins of the Fathers: Responsibility for Inequality," *Midwest Studies in Philosophy* 38 (2014): 121–137.
25. Black Americans are not the only ones with grievances associated with the apparent contradiction between liberalism's proclamations and its practices—Native Americans, women, immigrants, poor whites, and homosexuals also have stories to tell. However, its application to, and consequences for, descendants of African slaves in the United States will be the focus here.
26. See Lucius T. Outlaw Jr., *Critical Social Theory in the Interests of Black Folks* (Washington, DC: Rowman & Littlefield Publishers, 2005).
27. See Tommie Shelby, "Race and Social Justice: Rawlsian Considerations," *Fordham Law Review* 72 (2004): 1697–1714.
28. See Anna Julia Cooper, "The Ethics of the Negro Question (1902)," in *The Voice of Anna Julia Cooper*, ed. Charles Lemert & Esme Bhan (Washington, DC: Rowman & Littlefield, 1998), 206–207.
29. This story begins with the rape of Africa and takes us from there across the Middle Passage to colonial Jamestown, the American Revolutionary War, the Constitutional Convention, and through the many years of slavery, Jim Crow segregation, the struggle for civil rights, and right up to current problems of poverty, inequality, housing and labor market discrimination, and state-sanctioned violence that disproportionately impact blacks. These problems continue to challenge the idea that America is a liberal nation governed by emancipatory ideals of freedom and equality, and that liberalism—as a political philosophy—can be a tool for eradicating racial injustice.
30. Mills, *Black Rights/White Wrongs*, 90.
31. Ibid., 157–158.
32. See Charles W. Mills, "White Time: The Chronic Injustice of Ideal Theory," *Du Bois Review* 11 (2014): 27–42, 36. According to Mills, the best attempt to deploy the "Rawlsian apparatus," unmodified, to address racial injustice can be found in Shelby, "Race and Social Justice." Mills argues that Shelby fails to show that a principle of corrective justice can be derived from Rawls; see Charles W. Mills, "Retrieving Rawls for Racial Justice? A Critique of Tommie Shelby," *Critical Philosophy of Race* 1 (2013): 1–27. On my reading of Shelby, he does not try to establish this. Instead, he argues that applying Rawls's existing principles may suffice to address many of the most pressing concerns of racial injustice. For

instance, if we applied the fair equality of opportunity principle fairly, this may be enough to address many of the socioeconomic disadvantages that blacks suffer today owing to past racial injustice. Shelby further argues that if we successfully addressed material disadvantage, then perhaps claims for material reparations of the kind associated with rectificatory justice may diminish. For Shelby's replies to Mills, see Tommie Shelby, "Racial Realities and Corrective Justice: A Reply to Charles Mills," *Critical Philosophy of Race* 1 (2013): 145–162.
33. Mills, *Black Rights/White Wrongs*, 214.
34. To make his positive conception of justice as rectification more precise and compelling, Mills will have to tackle obvious questions, especially given his strategic decision to modify rather than totally reject the liberal social contract framework. In what sense do principles 1, 2, and 3 constitute "principles" of justice? Would a fully worked-out conception of justice as rectification include all of Rawls's current principles with the addition of Mills's principles of rectificatory justice? If so, how would the resulting plurality of principles be weighted, and would he follow Rawls's way of proceeding here, which aims to minimize the role of intuition in settling conflict between them? Alternatively, would Mills's resulting conception of justice remove, modify, or demote in importance one or more of the existing principles while adding principles of rectificatory justice to the mix?
35. See John Rawls, *A Theory of Justice* (Cambridge, MA: Belknap Press, 1971), 455.
36. See John Rawls, *Justice as Fairness: A Restatement*, ed. Erin Kelly (Cambridge, MA: Belknap Press, 2005), 5.
37. See Rawls, *A Theory of Justice*, 6.
38. This point is related to an argument Mills makes for why social movements should rely on liberalism; see *Black Rights/White Wrongs*, 14. Presumably, one of the things that holds such movement together is that its participants are bound to it and to one another by shared normative principles. Of course, this is not the only thing that binds them.
39. See John Rawls, "The Sense of Justice," *The Philosophical Review* 72 (1963): 281–305, 285.
40. Ibid., 281.
41. See Martha C. Nussbaum, *Political Emotions: Why Love Matters for Justice* (Cambridge, MA: Belknap Press, 2013).
42. I say "especially" nonideal theorists because they make a big deal of painting a picture of what the world actually looks like, how people behave, and what moves them in thinking about the demands of justice. This is certainly a significant part of what makes Mills's work so appealing—he does not ignore the messy history and social psychology. I am also a racial realist, and thus I believe that it is important to attend to as much of the evidence as we can about racial in-group and out-group psychology. But this opens up the possibility of disagreement between nonideal theorists not only about just how messy

things are but also about the implications of the mess. For an illuminating statement of this point, see Harry Brighouse, "Nonideal Theorizing in Education," *Educational Theory* 65 (2015): 215–231, 218.

43. However, elsewhere Mills appeals to this framework to argue that if contractors knew certain facts about a racist society, governed by relations of domination, they would recognize the prudence of choosing principles of rectificatory justice. See Carole Pateman & Charles Mills, *Contract and Domination* (Cambridge: Polity, 2007), chaps. 3 and 4.
44. See Matthew O. Hunt, "African American, Hispanic, and White Beliefs about Black / White Inequality, 1977–2004," *American Sociological Review* 72 (2007): 390–415.
45. See Lawrence D. Bobo et al., "The *Real* Record on Racial Attitudes," in *Social Trends in American Life: Finding from the General Society Survey since 1972*, ed. Peter V. Marsden (Princeton, NJ; Princeton University Press, 2012), 38–83.
46. See Derrick Darby, "Reparations and Racial Inequality," *Philosophy Compass* 5 (2010): 55–66.
47. See Tracie L. Stewart & Nyla R. Branscombe, "The Costs of Privilege and Dividends of Privilege Awareness: The Social Psychology of Confronting Inequality," in *"I Don't See Color": Personal and Critical Perspectives on White Privilege*, ed. Bettina Bergo & Tracey Nicholls (University Park: Penn State University Press, 2014), 136; see also Adam A. Powell, Nyla R. Branscombe, & Michael T. Schmitt, "Inequality as Ingroup Privilege or Outgroup Disadvantage: The Impact of Group Focus on Collective Guilt and Interracial Attitudes," *Personality and Social Psychology Bulletin* 31 (2005): 508–521.
48. See Nyla R. Branscombe, Michael T. Schmitt, & Richard D. Harvey, "Perceiving Pervasive Discrimination among African Americans: Implications for Group Identification and Well-Being," *Journal of Personality and Social Psychology* 77 (1999): 135–149.
49. See Jessica C. Nelson, Glenn Adams, & Nyla R. Branscombe, "The Role of Historical Knowledge in Perception of Race-Based Conspiracies," *Race and Social Problems* 2 (2010): 69–80.
50. See Jean Halley, Amy Eshleman, & Ramya M. Vijaya, *Seeing White: An Introduction to White Privilege and Race* (Washington, DC: Rowman & Littlefield Publishers, 2011).
51. See Stewart & Branscombe, "The Costs of Privilege and Dividends of Privilege Awareness."
52. See Nyla R. Branscombe, Bertjan Doosje, & Craig McGarty, "Antecedents and Consequences of Collective Guilt," in *From Prejudice to Intergroup Emotions: Differentiated Reactions to Social Groups*, ed. Diane M. Mackie & Eliot R. Smith (Philadelphia: Psychology Press, 2002), 49–66; see also Anca M. Miron, Nyla R. Branscombe, & Michael T. Schmitt, "Collective Guilt as Distress

over Illegitimate Intergroup Inequality," *Group Processes & Intergroup Relations* 9 (2006): 163–180.
53. See Nyla R. Branscombe, Michael T. Schmitt, & Kristin Schiffhauer, "Racial Attitudes in Response to Thoughts of White Privilege," *European Journal of Social Psychology* 37 (2007): 203–215; see also Michael M. Unzueta & Brian S. Lowery, "Defining Racism Safely: The Role of Self-Image Maintenance on White Americans' Conceptions of Racism," *Journal of Experimental Social Psychology* 44 (2008): 1491–1497.
54. See Darby & Branscombe, "Beyond the Sins of the Fathers."
55. See Stewart & Branscombe, "Costs of Privilege," 137.
56. See Branscombe, Schmitt, & Schiffhauer, "Racial Attitudes."
57. See Amy Ansell & James Statman, "I've Never Owned Slaves," in *The Global Color Line: Racial and Ethnic Inequality and Struggle from a Global Perspective*, ed. Pinar Batur-VanderLippe & Joe Feagin (New York: JAI Press, 1999), 151–173.
58. For an argument as to why appealing to the sins of the past is not an attractive way to ground collective responsibility for racial inequality under nonideal circumstances, see Darby and Branscombe, "Beyond the Sins of the Fathers."
59. Researchers have found evidence of this form of distancing at work in accounting for racial group differences in support for reparations in post-apartheid South Africa. See Bert Klandermans, Merel Werner, & Majorka van Doorn, "Redeeming Apartheid's Legacy: Collective Guilt, Political Ideology, and Compensation," *Political Psychology* 29 (2008): 331–349.
60. See Shannon Sullivan, *Good White People: The Problem with Middle-Class White Anti-Racism* (Bingley, UK: Emerald Publishing Limited, 2014).
61. See Aarti Iyer, Colin Wayne Leach, & Faye J. Crosby, "White Guilt and Racial Compensation: The Benefits and Limits of Self-Focus," *Personality and Social Psychology Bulletin* 29 (2003): 117–129.
62. See Brian S. Lowery, Eric D. Knowles, & Miguel M. Unzueta, "Framing Inequality Safely: Whites' Motivated Perceptions of Racial Privilege," *Personality and Social Psychology Bulletin* 33 (2007): 1237–1250.
63. See Tracie L. Stewart, Iona M. Latu, Nyla R. Branscombe, Nia L. Phillips, & Ted H. Denney, "White Privilege Awareness and Efficacy to Reduce Racial Inequality Improve White American's Attitudes toward African Americans," *Journal of Social Issues* 68 (2012): 11–27; see also Janet K. Swim & Deborah L. Miller, "White Guilt; Its Antecedents and Consequences for Attitudes toward Affirmative Action," *Personality and Social Psychology Bulletin* 25 (1999): 500–514.
64. See Iyer, Leach, & Crosby, "White Guilt and Racial Compensation"; Aarti Iyer, Colin W. Leach, & Anne Pederson, "Racial Wrongs and Restitutions: The Role of Guilt and Other Group-Based Emotions," in *Collective Guilt: International*

Perspectives, ed. Nyla R. Branscombe & Bertjan Doosje (Cambridge: Cambridge University Press, 2004), 262–283.

65. See Charles W. Mills, "Under Class under Standings," *Ethics* 104 (1994): 855–881, 873–874.
66. Mills, *Black Rights/White Wrongs*, 134.
67. Ibid., 201.
68. Apparently, according to a recent study, these considerations were also more relevant than economic interests to explaining why many whites voted for Trump in the 2016 election. See Diana C. Mutz, "Status Threat, Not Economic Hardship, Explains the 2016 Presidential Vote," *Proceedings of the National Academy of Sciences* 115 (2018): E4330–E4339.
69. Mills, *Black Rights/White Wrongs*, 134–135.
70. To offer us a more realistic solution to the race problem, Mills may need to decide between being a black radical and being a radical liberal, and if he opts for the latter, the distance between him and Rawls may not be as great as he has made it out to be. Either way, he needs to give us a more definitive account of the primary white audience that needs his message of liberal redemption so that we can accurately identify the barriers that must be overcome in getting them to be moved—in sufficient numbers—to end white supremacy and racial exploitations.

Chapter 5

1. This chapter is an abridged version of an article coauthored with Richard E. Levy.
2. We use the terms "race specific" and "race sensitive" to avoid confusion with other commonly used terms, such as "race conscious" or "race targeted," which have connotations we wish to avoid.
3. See, e.g., Sheryll Cashin, *Place, Not Race: A New Vision of Opportunity in America* (Boston: Beacon Press, 2014).
4. NYC Dept. of Educ., "Chancellor Fariña Announced New Initiatives to Increase Diversity in Schools," Nov. 20, 2015, https://www.harlemworldmagazine.com/chancellor-farina-announced-new-initiatives-to-increase-diversity-in-schools/.
5. Postracial remedies resemble so-called universalist remedies, which eschew targeting specific groups of individuals, whether defined by race, ethnicity, class, disability, or some other classification. See Samuel R. Bagenstos, "Universalism and Civil Rights (with Notes on Voting Rights after *Shelby*)," *The Yale Law Journal* 123 (2014): 2838–2876.
6. See Reva B. Siegel, "From Colorblindness to Antibalkanization: An Emerging Ground of Decision in Race Equality Cases," *The Yale Law Journal* 120 (2011): 1278–1366. Although Siegel is focused on the jurisprudence of Justice

Kennedy, who seems to occupy the middle ground on a divided Court, he is representative of a broader group whose views on race are mixed. In addition, we are concerned with both the political and legal manifestations of postracialism and so seek an approach that both facilitates coalition building across racial lines *and* is capable of surviving constitutional scrutiny.

7. See, generally, David Theo Goldberg, *Are We All Postracial Yet?* (Cambridge: Polity, 2015); Ta-Nehisi Coates, "There Is No Post-Racial America: The United States Needs More than a Good President to Erase Centuries of Violence," *The Atlantic*, Aug. 2015, https://www.theatlantic.com/magazine/archive/2015/07/post-racial-society-distant-dream/395255/.

8. See, generally, Alan B. Krueger, "Economic Scene; Sticks and Stones Can Break Bones, but the Wrong Name Can Make a Job Hard to Find," *The New York Times*, Dec. 12, 2002, http://www.nytimes.com/2002/12/12/business/economic-scene-sticks-stones-can-break-bones-but-wrong-namecan-make-job-hard.html; William A. Darity Jr. & Patrick L. Mason, "Evidence on Discrimination in Employment: Codes of Color, Codes of Gender," *The Journal of Economic Perspectives* 12 (1998): 63–90; Marianne Bertrand & Sendhil Mullainathan, "Are Emily and Greg More Employable than Lakisha and Jamal? A Field Experiment on Labor Market Discrimination," *The American Economic Review* 94 (2004): 991–1013; Devah Pager, Bruce Western, and Bart Bonikoswki, "Discrimination in a Low-Wage Labor Market: A Field Experiment," *American Sociological Review* 74 (2009): 777–799.

9. Rachel L. Swarns, "Biased Lending Evolves, and Blacks Face Trouble Getting Mortgages," *The New York Times*, Oct. 30, 2015, http://www.nytimes.com/2015/10/31/nyregion/hudson-city-bank-settlement.html?hp&actionclick&pgtypehomepage&modulesecond-column-region&region=top-news&WT.nav=top-news&_r=0.

10. Martin Luther King Jr., "Address to Hungry Club of Atlanta Speech," May 10, 1967.

11. 551 U.S. 701 (2007), at 748.

12. For an illuminating conversation between Jon Stewart and Bill O'Reilly on the "Daily Show" that highlights these competing perspectives, see "The Daily Show—Bill O'Reilly Extended Interview," *Youtube*, Oct. 16, 2014, https://www.youtube.com/watch?v=8raaT7SRx18.

13. See, generally, Darren Lenard Hutchinson, "Racial Exhaustion," *Washington University Law Review* 86 (2009): 917–974.

14. See, e.g., McCleskey v. Kemp, 481 U.S. 279 (1987); Washington v. Davis, 426 U.S. 229 (1976).

15. See, e.g., City of Richmond v. J.A. Croson Co., 488 U.S. 469 (1989); see also Adarand Constructors, Inc. v. Peña, 515 U.S. 200 (1995).

16. See, e.g., Bd. of Educ. of Oklahoma City Pub. Schs., Indep. Sch. Dist. No. 89 v. Dowell, 498 U.S. 237 (1991); Freeman v. Pitts, 503 U.S. 467 (1992).

17. See Shelby Cty. v. Holder, 133 S. Ct. 2612 (2013).
18. Similarly, nongovernmental actors—such as employers—are also limited by the Court's postracial premises to the extent that these premises permeate the construction and application of civil rights statutes that prohibit private racial discrimination.
19. See Thomas F. Jackson, *From Civil Rights to Human Rights: Martin Luther King, Jr., And the Struggle for Economic Justice* (Philadelphia: University of Pennsylvania Press, 2007), 365.
20. Similar disagreements appear along ideological lines. A recent Pew Center survey, for example, reports that 58 percent of white Republicans compared to 40 percent of white Democrats think that the nation has made significant progress on race matters. Michael Dimock et al., "King's Dream Remains an Elusive Goal; Many Americans See Racial Disparities," *Pew Research Center* (2013), 8.
21. Lawrence D. Bobo, "Somewhere between Jim Crow & Post-Racialism: Reflections on the Racial Divide in America Today," *Daedalus* 140 (2011): 11–36, 29.
22. Ibid., 30.
23. Ibid.
24. A recent survey showed that, although Americans remained divided along racial lines, a higher percentage of both whites and blacks thought that the Michael Brown shooting raised important issues about race than thought same thing about the Trayvon Martin shooting, and, conversely, a smaller percentage of both whites and blacks thought that race was getting too much attention. See "Stark Racial Divisions in Reactions to Ferguson Police Shooting," *Pew Research Center*, August 18, 2014, 4, https://www.pewresearch.org/politics/2014/08/18/stark-racial-divisions-in-reactions-to-ferguson-police-shooting/#:~:text=Fully%2065%25%20of%20African%20Americans,while%2035%25%20of fer%20no%20response.
25. Ibid., 1.
26. See "Across Racial Lines, More Say Nation Needs to Make Changes to Achieve Racial Equality," *Pew Research Center*, August 5, 2015, http://www.people-press.org/2015/08/05/across-racial-lines-more-say-nation-needs-to-make-changes-to-achieve-racial-equality. This poll is the source of the data throughout the paragraph.
27. Mario Barnes, Erwin Chemerinsky, & Trina Jones, "A Post-Race Equal Protection?," *The Georgetown Law Journal* 98 (2010): 967–1004, 1001.
28. There is a rich philosophical tradition of pragmatist thought with both methodological and substantive elements. Reviewing this tradition and staking out a detailed version of pragmatism is not necessary to our project, which is consistent with the general principles of pragmatism and need not conform to any particular version of it. To be sure, there have been many players on this terrain. See, generally, William James, *Pragmatism: A New Name for Some Old Ways*

of Thinking (New York: Barnes & Noble, 1907); John Dewey, *The Public and Its Problems* (Athens, OH: Swallow Press, 1927); John Dewey, *Liberalism and Social Action* (New York: Prometheus, 1935). For an application of pragmatism to race matters, see Cornel West, *The American Evasion of Philosophy: A Genealogy of Pragmatism* (Madison, WI: University of Wisconsin Press, 1989). Most pragmatists, even those like West whose left-leaning politics take them outside the mainstream of American politics, nonetheless recognize the virtue of pragmatism in building consensus and coalitions to solve problems that advance the cause of justice.

29. This is typically the focus of legal pragmatism. See, generally, Richard A. Posner, *Law, Pragmatism, and Democracy* (Cambridge, MA: Harvard University Press, 2003); Sydney A. Shapiro & Joseph P. Tomain, *Achieving Democracy: The Future of Progressive Regulation* (New York: Oxford University Press, 2014).

30. See, e.g., PA. Ass'n of Sch. Bds., Educ. Research & Policy Ctr., "Raising Achievement in Underperforming Schools (2011), https://www.psba.org/wp-content/uploads/2014/09/raising_achievement_in_underperforming_schools-10102011.pdf (identifying a variety of "research-grounded school improvement strategies" for underperforming schools).

31. See, e.g., New State Ice Co. v. Liebmann, 285 U.S. 262 (1932), 311 (Justice Brandeis, dissenting, observing that a "state may, if its citizens choose, serve as a laboratory; and try novel social and economic experiments without risk to the rest of the country").

32. See, generally, Calvin K. Lai et al., "Reducing Implicit Racial Preferences: I. A Comparative Investigation of 17 Interventions," *Journal of Experimental Psychology* 143 (2014): 1–21.

33. For example, the National Center for State Courts has suggested seven strategies for reducing implicit bias in the courts, including (1) "[r]aise awareness of implicit bias," (2) "identify and consciously acknowledge real group and individual differences," (3) "check thought processes and decisions for possible bias," (4) "[i]dentify distractions and sources of stress in the decision-making environment and remove or reduce them," (5) "[i]dentify sources of ambiguity in the decisionmaking context and establish more concrete standards before engaging in the decision-making process," (6) "[i]nstitute feedback mechanisms," and (7) "[i]ncrease exposure to stigmatized group members and counter-stereotypes and reduce exposure to stereotypes." See Nat'l Ctr. of State Courts, "Strategies to Reduce the Influence of Implicit Bias," https://horsley.yale.edu/sites/default/files/files/IB_Strategies_033012.pdf.

34. See, e.g., Kimberly West-Faulcon, "More Intelligent Design: Testing Measures of Merit," *University of Pennsylvania Journal of Constitutional Law* 13 (2011): 1235–1298.

35. See, generally, Germine H. Awad, "Does Policy Name Matter? The Effect of Framing on the Evaluations of African American Applicants," *Journal of Applied Social Psychology* 43 (2013): E379–E387.
36. See, e.g., Destiny Peery, "Implicit Bias Training for Police May Help, but It's Not Enough," *Huffington Post*, Mar. 14, 2016, 9:29 PM, ("Mandatory diversity trainings can lead to backlash effects that increase, rather than decrease, bias and sour participants on diversity as a goal.").
37. 136 S. Ct. 2198 (2016).
38. See Daria Roithmayr, "Direct Measures: An Alternative Form of Affirmative Action," *Michigan Journal of Race and Law* 7 (2001): 1–32.
39. This may be one problem with Professor Roithmayr's suggestion that admissions policies focus on whether (1) applicants or their families have experienced discrimination, (2) applicants would offer underrepresented perspectives on racial injustice, and (3) applicants are likely to serve underserved populations; ibid., 8–9. To the extent that these criteria are self-consciously adopted to achieve the goals of affirmative action without expressly incorporating race and might tend to overwhelmingly favor blacks and other racial minorities, they might be vulnerable to the argument that these nominally race-neutral criteria are a pretext for racial preferences.
40. See, e.g., Sharon L. Harlan & Edward J. Hackett, "Federal Job Training Programs and Employment Outcomes—Effects by Sex and Race of Participants," *Population Research and Policy Review* 4 (1985): 235–265; Peter Z. Schochet, John Burghardt, & Sheena McConnell, "Does Job Corps Work? Impact Findings from the National Job Corps Study," *American Economic Review* 98 (2008): 1864–1886.
41. There is some evidence of increased interest by some conservatives in the economic plight of the lower classes. See Jackie Calmes, "They Want Trump to Make the G.O.P. a Workers' Party," *The New York Times*, Aug. 5, 2016, http://www.nytimes.com/2016/08/06/us/politics/as-trump-rises-reformocons-see-chance-to-update-gops-economic-views.html?_r=0. These efforts could provide the basis for postracial remedies, such as tax breaks for "low- and middle-income workers through tax credits for children, the earned-income tax credit or a new wage subsidy," or "help[ing] displaced workers" affected by free trade agreements.
42. For an overview of the program, see WeCARE, FedCap, https://fedcapinc.org/wecare-iii-rehabilitation-and-employment-ny/.
43. WeCARE has been touted by the American Conservative Union because "[it] is unique among TANF programs in its laser focus on workforce readiness training and job placement." See "Grant Collins Testifies about the Future of SNAP," *The ACU Foundation*, Aug. 29, 2015, https://fedcapgroup.org/fedcap-group-senior-vp-grant-collins-testifies-before-u-s-house-committee/.

Although WeCARE is focused on clients with disabilities, it could be adapted to address other barriers to employment.

44. Cf. Opening Statement of J. Michael Conaway, "House Committee on Agriculture Public Hearing: Past, Present, & Future of SNAP," June 10, 2015, http:agriculture.house.gov/news/documentsingle.aspx?DocumentID=1087 (observing that "it is important to have a realistic view of what it takes for many Americans to get back on their feet," that "[s]teady employment makes it possible to climb the economic ladder and rise out of poverty," and that "a greater level of engagement is needed between SNAP and recipients").

45. For example, the Republican Party Platform proclaims, "We will encourage investments in small businesses." See "Republican Platform: Restoring the American Dream: Economy & Jobs," https://www.gop.com/platform/restoring-the-american-dream/ (last visited Nov. 19, 2016), (https://web.archive.org/web/20160806223918/https://www.gop.com/platform/re-   storing-the-american-dream/).

46. Thus, for example, greater pay transparency might deter pay discrimination. See Gowri Racmachandran, "Pay Transparency," *Penn State Law Review* 116 (2012): 1043–1080.

47. Katie R. Eyer, "That's Not Discrimination: American Beliefs and the Limits of Anti-Discrimination Law," *Minnesota Law Review* 96 (2012): 1275–1362; see also Ann C. McGinley, "Rethinking Civil Rights and Employment at Will: Toward a Coherent National Discharge Policy," *Ohio State Law Journal* 57 (1996): 1443–1524.

48. See Mark Kelman, "Concepts of Discrimination in "General Ability" Job Testing," *Harvard Law Review* 104 (1991): 1157–1247.

49. See, e.g., Tristin K. Green, "A Structural Approach as Antidiscrimination Mandate: Locating Employer Wrong," *Vanderbilt Law Review* 60 (2007): 849–904; Susan Sturm, "Second Generation Employment Discrimination: A Structural Approach," *Columbia Law Review* 101 (2001): 458–568.

50. See Matthew Feeney, "Watching the Watchmen: Best Practices for Police Body Cameras," *CATO Institute Policy Analysis* no. 782, Oct. 27, 2015, https://www.cato.org/policy-analysis/watching-watchmen-best-practices-police-body-cameras.

51. Ibid., 17.

52. See, generally, Derrick Darby & John L. Rury, *The Color of Mind: Why the Origins of the Achievement Gap Matter for Justice* (Chicago: University of Chicago Press, 2018).

53. See, e.g., Cecilia E. Rouse & Lisa Barrow, "Student Vouchers and Student Achievement: Recent Evidence and Remaining Questions," *Annual Review of Economics* 1 (2009): 17–42.

54. See, e.g., Michael A. Rebell, "Poverty, 'Meaningful' Educational Opportunity, and the Necessary Role of the Courts," *North Carolina Law Review* 85 (2007): 1467–1544.
55. See, e.g., Darby and Rury, *The Color of Mind*, chap. 8.
56. See, e.g., Michael Henry Adams, "The End of Black Harlem," *N.Y. Times*, May 27, 2016, http://www.nytimes.com/2016/05/29/opinion/sunday/the-end-of-black-harlem.html.
57. Siegel, "From Colorblindness to Antibalkanization," 1302.
58. Bagenstos, "Universalism and Civil Rights," 2840.
59. Ibid., 2852.
60. Ibid., 2853.
61. See Kenji Yoshino, "The New Equal Protection," *Harvard Law Review* 124 (2011): 747–803, 748.
62. The extent to which this sort of result is a cause for concern is unclear. In practice, for example, programs to promote "diversity" are often perceived as "code" for affirmative action. Notwithstanding this phenomenon, employment programs to promote diversity have proven to be more effective in practice than affirmative action programs.
63. Bagenstos, "Universalism and Civil Rights," 2849.
64. Thus, for example, a recent article examines the practical effect of pursuing universalistic remedies under the Fair Labor Standards Act (FLSA), as opposed to remedies for racial discrimination under Title VII. See Charlotte S. Alexander, Zev J. Eigen, & Camille Gear Rich, "Post-Racial Hydraulics: The Hidden Dangers of the Universal Turn," *New York University Law Review* 91 (2016): 1–58. The authors argue that this turn to universalistic remedies has unfortunate side effects that include the ossification of Title VII law, reinforcing the courts' acceptance of the postracial narrative, lack of attorney availability for race-based claims that do not implicate the FLSA, and suppression of the clients' ability to voice their claims in terms of racial discrimination. While such concerns cannot be completely discounted, the side effects of particular litigation strategies are not necessarily transferable to other contexts. More broadly, these criticisms help to highlight the differences between our approach and universalism: our approach does not demand the acceptance of postracial assumptions or the abandonment of racial discrimination claims, and the remedies we advocate are race sensitive and not limited to universalistic ones.
65. We note, for example, that affirmative action programs did not necessarily help the truly disadvantaged blacks, including those who lived in poverty, attended failing schools in impoverished neighborhoods, and were embroiled in the criminal justice system.
66. See Kimberlé Williams Crenshaw, "Twenty Years of Critical Race Theory: Looking Back to Move Forward," *Connecticut Law Review* 43 (2011): 1253–1354, 1314. Later we will address Crenshaw's broader concern that our approach

would concede victory to the postracial narrative and undermine advocacy for racial justice.
67. West, *The American Evasion of Philosophy*, 5.
68. Cornel West, *Prophesy Deliverance! An Afro-American Revolutionary Christianity* (Louisville, KY: Westminster John Knox Press, 2002).
69. Siegel, "From Colorblindness to Antibalkanization."
70. Parents Involved in Cmty. Sch. v. Seattle Sch. Dist. No. 1, 551 U. S. 701 (2007), 787.
71. Siegel, "From Colorblindness to Antibalkanization," 1294.
72. Ibid., 1308.
73. Coming from the right, the criticism would argue that any attention to racial inequality is unnecessary and counterproductive. As we stated earlier, however, we start from a different premise—that racial inequality is a problem that must be addressed. Because we doubt the possibility of building coalitions with those who deny that racial inequality is a problem but regard the left as a necessary partner in these efforts, we will focus on the purity objection as it would be advanced from that perspective.
74. Crenshaw, "Twenty Years of Critical Race Theory," 1333.
75. The Overton window describes the range of policies that the public regards as politically acceptable. See, generally, Joseph G. Lehman, "An Introduction to the Overton Window of Political Possibility," *Mackinac Ctr. For Pub. Policy*, Apr. 8, 2010, http://www.mackinac.org/12481.
76. Crenshaw, "Twenty Years of Critical Race Theory," 1314.
77. The concern about stigma clearly cuts both ways. If it is problematic to stigmatize race consciousness, it is equally problematic to stigmatize pragmatists as sellouts or capitulators to racial inequality and injustice.

Chapter 6

1. Hannah Arendt, *Responsibility and Judgment* (New York: Schocken, 2003).
2. William Julius Wilson, *More than Just Race: Being Black and Poor in the Inner City* (New York: W. W. Norton & Company 2009).
3. This chapter is an edited version of an article coauthored with Nyla R. Branscombe.
4. See Arendt, *Responsibility and Judgment*.
5. Iris Marion Young, *Responsibility for Justice* (New York: Oxford University Press, 2011).
6. Derrick Darby & Nyla R. Branscombe, "Egalitarianism and Perceptions of Inequality," *Philosophical Topics* 40 (2012): 7–25.

7. Daniel Sullivan, Mark J. Landau, Nyla R. Branscombe, & Zachary K. Rothschild, "Competitive Victimhood as a Response to Accusations of Ingroup Harm Doing," *Journal of Personality and Social Psychology* 102 (2012): 778–95.
8. Adam A. Powell, Nyla R. Branscombe, & Michael T. Schmitt, "Inequality as Ingroup Privilege or Outgroup Disadvantage: The Impact of Group Focus on Collective Guilt and Interracial Attitudes," *Personality and Social Psychology Bulletin* 31 (2005): 508–521.
9. Emina Subašic, Katherine J. Reynolds, & John C. Turner, "The Political Solidarity Model of Social Change: Dynamics of Self-Categorization in Intergroup Power Relations," *Personality and Social Psychology Review* 12 (2008): 330–52.
10. Nyla R. Branscombe, "A Social Psychological Process Perspective on Collective Guilt," in *Collective Guilt: International Perspectives*, ed. Nyla R. Branscombe & Bertjan Doosje (Cambridge: Cambridge University Press, 2004), 320–334.
11. Nyla A. Branscombe, Ben Slugoski, & Diane M. Kappen, "The Measurement of Collective Guilt: What It Is and What It Is Not," in *Collective Guilt: International Perspectives*, ed. Nyla R. Branscombe & Bertjan Doosje (Cambridge: Cambridge University Press, 2004), 16–34; Bertjan Doosje, Nyla R. Branscombe, Russell Spears, & Anthony S. R. Manstead, "Guilty by Association: When One's Group Has a Negative History," *Journal of Personality and Social Psychology* 75 (1998): 872–886; Aarti Iyer, Colin W. Leach, & Faye J. Crosby, "White Guilt and Racial Compensation: The Benefits and Limits of Self-Focus," *Personality and Social Psychology Bulletin* 29 (2003): 117–129; Craig McGarty & Ana-Maria Bliuc, *Refining the Meaning of the "Collective,"* in Branscombe & Doosje, *Collective Guilt*.
12. See Powell et al., "Inequality as Ingroup Privilege or Outgroup Disadvantage."
13. Harry C. Triandis, *Individualism and Collectivism* (Oxfordshire, UK: Routledge, 1995).
14. Albert Bandura, "Selective Activation and Disengagement of Moral Control," *Journal of Social Issues* 46 (1990): 27–46.
15. Nyla R. Branscombe & Anca M. Miron, *Interpreting the Ingroup's Negative Actions toward Another Group: Emotional Reactions to Appraised Harm*, in *The Social Life of Emotions*, ed. Larissa Z. Tiedens & C. W. Leach (Cambridge: Cambridge University Press, 2004).
16. James D. Johnson, Carolyn Simmons, Sophie Trawalter, Tara Ferguson, & William Reed William, "Variation in Black Anti-White Bias and Target Distancing Cues: Factors that Influence Perceptions of 'Ambiguously Racist' Behavior," *Personality and Social Psychology Bulletin* 29 (2003): 609–622; Anca M. Miron, Ruth H. Warner, & Nyla R. Branscombe, "Accounting for Group Differences in Appraisals of Social Inequality: Differential Injustice Standards," *British Journal of Social Psychology* 50 (2011): 342–353; Lee Sigelman & Susan Welch, *Black Americans' Views of Racial Inequality: The Dream Deferred* (Cambridge: Cambridge University Press, 1991).

17. Anca M. Miron, Nyla R. Branscombe, & Michael T. Schmitt, "Collective Guilt as Distress over Illegitimate Intergroup Inequality," *Group Processes Intergroup Relations* 9 (2006): 163–180.
18. Michael T. Schmitt, David A. Miller, Nyla R. Branscombe, & Jack W. Brehm, "The Difficulty of Making Reparations Affects the Intensity of Collective Guilt," *Group Processes & Intergroup Relations* 11 (2008): 267–279.
19. Roy L. Brooks, *When Sorry Isn't Enough: The Controversy over Apologies and Reparations for Human Injustice* (New York: N.Y.U. Press, 1999).
20. Jillian C. Banfield, Michael Ross, & Craig W. Blatz, "Responding to Historical Injustices: Does Group Membership Trump Liberal-Conservative Ideology?," *European Journal of Social Psychology* 44 (2014): 30–42.
21. William Julius Wilson, *The Bridge over the Racial Divide: Racial Inequality and Coalition Politics* (Berkeley: University of California Press, 1999).
22. Margaret Gilbert, "Who's to Blame? Collective Moral Responsibility and Its Implications for Group Members," *Midwest Studies in Philosophy* 30 (2006): 94–114.
23. Jonathan Kaplan & Andrew Valls, "Housing Discrimination as a Basis for Black Reparations," *Public Affairs Quarterly* 21 (2007): 255–273; Thomas A. McCarthy, "Coming to Terms with Our Past, Part II: On the Morality and Politics of Reparations for Slavery," *Political Theory* 32 (2004): 750–772; David R. Williams & Chiquita Collins, "Reparations: A Viable Strategy to Address the Enigma of African American Health," *The American Behavioral Scientist* 47 (2004): 977–1000.
24. Derrick Darby, "Educational Inequality and the Science of Diversity in *Grutter*: A Lesson for the Reparations Debate in the Age of Obama," *The University of Kansas Law Review* 57 (2009): 755–793; see also Derrick Darby, "Reparations and Racial Inequality," *Philosophy Compass* 5 (2010): 55–66.
25. Ricard Wilkinson & Kate Pickett, *The Spirit Level: Why Greater Equality Makes Societies Stronger* (New York: Bloomsbury Press, 2010).
26. See Darby & Branscombe, "Egalitarianism and Perceptions of Inequality."
27. Lawrence D. Bobo, "Somewhere between Jim Crow & Post-Racialism: Reflections on the Racial Divide in America Today," *Daedalus* 140 (2012): 11–36.
28. Derrick Darby & Argun Saatcioglu, "Race, Justice, and Desegregation," *Du Bois Review* 40 (2014): 87–108.
29. Lawrence D. Bobo, Camille Z. Charles, Maria Krysan, and Alicia D. Simmons, "The *Real* Record on Racial Attitudes," in *Social Trends in American Life: Finding from the General Social Survey since 1972*, ed. Peter V. Marsden (Princeton, NJ: Princeton University Press, 2012), 38–83.
30. See Powell et al., "Inequality as Ingroup Privilege or Outgroup Disadvantage."
31. Jim Sidanius & Felicia Pratto, *Social Dominance: An Intergroup Theory of Social Hierarchy and Oppression* (Cambridge: Cambridge University Press, 1999);

William Julius Wilson, *The Bridge over the Racial Divide: Racial Inequality and Coalition Politics* (Berkeley: University of California Press, 2009).
32. See Subašić et al., "The Political Solidarity Model of Social Change."
33. David Horowitz, *Uncivil Wars: The Controversy over Reparations for Slavery* (San Francisco, CA: Encounter Books, 2002).
34. See Joe R. Feagin, *Racist America: Roots, Current Realities, and Future Reparations* (New York: Routledge, 2000); see also Sidanius & Pratto, *Social Dominance*.
35. Nyla R. Branscombe & Tracey Cronin, "Confronting the Past to Create a Better Future: The Antecedents and Benefits of Intergroup Forgiveness," in *Identity and Participation in Culturally Diverse Societies*, ed. Assad Azzi, Xenia Chryssochoou, Bert Klandermans, & Bernd Simon (Malden, MA: Wiley-Blackwell, 2010).
36. Desmond Tutu, *No Future without Forgiveness* (New York: Image Books, 1999).
37. Thomas J. Epenshade & Alexandria W. Radford, *No Longer Separate, Not Yet Equal: Race and Class in Elite College Admission and Campus Life* (Princeton, NJ: Princeton University Press, 2009).
38. Daniel Sullivan, Mark J. Landau, Nyla R. Branscombe, and Zachary K. Rothschild, "Competitive Victimhood as a Response to Accusations of Ingroup Harm Doing," *Journal of Personality and Social Psychology* 102 (2012): 778–795.
39. Yuen J. Huo & Ludwin E. Molina, "Is Pluralism a Viable Model of Diversity? The Benefits and Limits of Subgroup Respect," *Group Processes and Intergroup Relations* 9 (2006): 359–376.
40. See John Rawls, *A Theory of Justice* (Cambridge, MA: Belknap Press, 1971), 7.
41. Ibid.
42. Young, *Responsibility for Justice*, 70.
43. Wilson, *The Bridge over the Racial Divide*, 98.
44. Young, *Responsibility for Justice*, 34.
45. Wilson, *The Bridge over the Racial Divide*, 98.
46. See John Rawls, *Political Liberalism* (New York: Columbia University Press, 2005), 270.
47. See Young, *Responsibility for Justice*.
48. Ibid., 52.
49. Ibid., 55.
50. Rawls, *Political Liberalism*, 269.
51. Glenn Adams, Monica Biernat, Nyla R. Branscombe, Christian S. Crandall, and Lawrence S. Wrightsman, "Beyond Prejudice: Toward a Sociocultural Psychology of Racism and Oppression," in *Commemorating Brown: The Social Psychology of Racism and Discrimination*, ed. Glenn Adams, Monica Biernat, Nyla R. Branscombe, Christian S. Crandall, & Lawrence S. Wrightsman (Washington, DC: American Psychological Association, 2008).

52. Young, *Responsibility for Justice*, 117.
53. Ibid.
54. See Wilson, *The Bridge over the Racial Divide*.
55. Margaret Gilbert, "Who's to Blame? Collective Moral Responsibility and Its Implications for Group Members," *Midwest Studies in Philosophy* 30 (2006): 94–114.
56. Janna Thompson, "Collective Responsibility for Historic Injustices," *Midwest Studies in Philosophy* 30 (2006): 154–167.

Chapter 7

1. W. E. B. Du Bois, "Democracy Fails in America, June 1954," 1. *W. E. B. Du Bois Papers*. Special Collections and University Archives, University of Massachusetts Amherst Libraries, http://credo.library.umass.edu.
2. W. E. B. Du Bois, "No Second-Class Citizens," in *Writings by W. E. B. Du Bois in Periodicals Edited by Others*, vol. 4: 1945–1961, ed. Herbert Aptheker (Millwood, NY: Kraus-Thomson, 1982), 51.
3. W. E. B. Du Bois, *Darkwater: Voices from Within the Veil* (New York: Dover, 1999).
4. What explains my preference is that Du Bois himself concedes that despite the negative effect race has had on the American soul, when compared with older European forms of political rule, the nation managed to realize key elements of a democratic society, though it was limited by color caste. See W. E. B. Du Bois, "Black America," in *Writings by W. E. B. Du Bois in Non-Periodical Literature Edited by Others*, ed. Herbert Aptheker (Millwood, NY: Kraus-Thomson, 1982), 170.
5. Admittedly, my reading of him as a champion of broadly inclusive democratic rule is somewhat surprising given Du Bois's elitist leanings associated with his doctrine of the Talented Tenth, his fascination with antidemocratic rulers (e.g., Chairman Mao) and nations (e.g., Russia), and his patriarchal practical dealings with black women leaders and intellectuals. For a useful summary of these criticisms, see Marable, supra note 9, Introduction. I will not pursue these tensions between Du Bois's antidemocratic affinities and his pro-democracy argument in *Darkwater*. The seriousness with which he defends democracy against an exclusive type of epistocracy is, in my view, all the more interesting given these tensions. I believe that Du Bois was indeed a "radical democrat," where this amounts to having a deep, thorough, and consistent commitment to pursuing the broadest measure of justice for all by removing obstacles to voting and political empowerment faced by the masses. So, I agree with Bernard Boxill, who held that Du Bois was an "uncompromising democrat" by the time he wrote *Darkwater*. See Bernard R. Boxill, "Du Bois on Cultural Pluralism," in *W. E. B. Du Bois on Race and Culture: Philosophy, Politics, and Poetics*, ed. Bernard W.

Bell, Emily Grosholz, & James B. Stewart (New York: Routledge, 1996), 85n74. And I disagree with Robert Gooding-Williams, who believes that Du Bois's vanguardist strains complicate this interpretation. See his book *In the Shadow of Du Bois: Afro-Modern Political Thought* (Cambridge, MA: Harvard University Press, 2010), 273n114, where Gooding-Williams writes, "Notwithstanding his democratic commitment, Du Bois persistently worried that the masses lacked the wherewithal (e.g., the intelligence, the knowledge, and the experience) for competent democratic citizenship." My interpretation of *Darkwater*, and supporting evidence from other works, concedes that this was a real worry for Du Bois. However, my argument is that he uses the problem of ignorance to double down on the importance of democratic rule on the broadest possible terms.

6. Although Du Bois placed great emphasis on voting, one should not think that participating in electoral politics through voting is the only way to have a voice that counts in politics. Indeed, looking at the political practices of black youth reveals the rich variety of ways that citizens can make their voices heard politically. For an insightful study, which examines politics beyond the voting booth, see Cathy J. Cohen, *Democracy Remixed: Black Youth and the Future of American Politics* (New York: Oxford University Press, 2010).

7. W. E. B. Du Bois, "Negro Ideals Described," in *Writings by W. E. B. Du Bois in Periodicals Edited by Others*, vol. 1: 1891–1909, ed. Herbert Aptheker (Millwood, NY: Kraus-Thomson, 1982), 361.

8. W. E. B. Du Bois, "Democracy, November 6, 1950," 1 and 6. *W. E. B. Du Bois Papers*. Special Collections and University Archives, University of Massachusetts Amherst Libraries, http://credo.library.umass.edu/.

9. Nancy MacLean, *Democracy in Chains: The Deep History of the Radical Right's Stealth Plan for America* (New York: Viking, 2017).

10. Du Bois, *Darkwater*, 84.

11. Ibid.

12. Ibid., 82.

13. Ibid., 84.

14. W. E. B. Du Bois, Letter to W. P. Robinson dated January 26, 1939, in *The Correspondence of W. E. B. Du Bois*, vol. II: 1934–1944, ed. Herbert Aptheker (Amherst: University of Massachusetts Press, 1976), 184.

15. Du Bois, *Darkwater*, 78.

16. Ibid., 81.

17. Du Bois does not spend time theorizing about the distinction between instrumental and noninstrumental goods. My reading of what he has in mind by the latter category of goods, however, is that he believes that popular sovereignty allows us to partake of certain things that are arguably valuable for their own sake, including individual self-development, self-knowledge, culture, and civilization. He might say that these are valuable regardless of whether popular sovereignty leads to justice.

18. W. E. B. Du Bois, "The Possibility of Democracy in America," in *Writings in Periodicals Edited by W. E. B. Du Bois, Selections from the Crisis*, vol. 2: 1926–1934, ed. Herbert Aptheker (Amherst: University of Massachusetts Press, 1976), 521.
19. Although it would be interesting to distinguish different conceptions of ignorance in Du Bois's work, I will not pursue this task in the text. Nothing in my reconstruction of his defense of democracy turns on doing so. Some of what he says pertains to ignorance of what is taught in schools. Some of it has to do with ignorance of the workings of industry, social problems, policy matters, race privilege, and, in the case of the white and black masses, ignorance of what is needed to build a larger coalition to confront plutocrats and political elites who benefit from exclusionary democracy.
20. W. E. B. Du Bois, "The Study of the Negro Problems," in *Writings by W. E. B. Du Bois in Periodicals Edited by Others*, vol. 1: 1891–1909, ed. Herbert Aptheker (Millwood, NY: Kraus-Thomson, 1982), 44. Historian John Rury and I argue that schooling in America was designed to produce black ignorance, stamping blacks with a stigmatizing badge of inferiority, which was then used to reinforce their separate and inferior schooling during and long after slavery's demise. See Derrick Darby and John L. Rury, *The Color of Mind: Why the Origins of the Achievement Gap Matter for Justice* (Chicago: University of Chicago Press, 2018).
21. In keeping with Du Bois's usage, I will use "Negroes" and "blacks," and "Negro" and "black" interchangeably throughout this chapter, though the former uses are no longer common in public discourse.
22. W. E. B. Du Bois, "The Present Outlook for the Dark Races of Mankind," in *Writings by W. E. B. Du Bois in Periodicals Edited by Others*, vol. 1: 1891–1909, ed. Herbert Aptheker (Millwood, NY: Kraus-Thomson, 1982), 79.
23. Du Bois, *Darkwater*, 79.
24. As Du Bois writes, "The laws of the Southern states for generations forbade us to learn and even today when it is assumed that the Negro is receiving too much education for his good, not one Negro child in three is attending regularly the public schools or having any reasonable chance to learn how to read and write. Not only are the Negro schools bad but save in some few cities they are worse today than they were ten years ago and there is no sign of their getting better." See Du Bois, "Negro Ideals Described," 360.
25. W. E. B. Du Bois, "The Training of Negroes for Social Power," in *Writings by W. E. B. Du Bois in Periodicals Edited by Others*, vol. 1: 1891–1909, ed. Herbert Aptheker (Millwood, NY: Kraus-Thomson, 1982), 180.
26. Du Bois, *Darkwater*, 78.
27. Du Bois, "No Second-Class Citizens," 47.
28. Du Bois, *Darkwater*, 81.

29. All the quotes in this paragraph are located here: W. E. B. Du Bois, "The Economic Aspects of Race Prejudice," in *Writings by W. E. B. Du Bois in Periodicals Edited by Others*, vol. 2: 1910–1934, ed. Herbert Aptheker (Millwood, NY: Kraus-Thomson, 1982), 1.
30. Du Bois, "The South and a Third Party," in *Writings by W. E. B. Du Bois in Periodicals Edited by Others*, vol. 2: 1910–1934, ed. Herbert Aptheker (Millwood, NY: Kraus-Thomson, 1982), 172.
31. Du Bois identifies tribalism, selfishness, and ignorance as individual factors that could undermine efforts at moral suasion. However, one could argue that they are related in ways that reinforce this effect. For example, tribalism might explain why white workers do not process information about how white elites exploit them, resulting in a certain kind of motivated ignorance that makes them impervious to arguments that joining with black workers is the right thing to do.
32. Recent evidence suggests that status threat to whites was a greater factor than economic hardship in explaining Trump's victory. See Diana C. Mutz, "Status Threat, Not Economic Hardship, Explains the 2016 Presidential Vote," *Proceedings of the National Academy of Sciences* 115 (2018): E4330–E4339. For criticism of this view, see Stephen L. Morgan, "Fake News: Status Threat Does Not Explain the 2016 Presidential Vote," May 10, 2018, https://osf.io.
33. W. E. B. Du Bois, "The Economic Aspects of Race Prejudice," in *Writings by W. E. B. Du Bois in Periodicals Edited by Others*, vol. 2: 1910–1934, ed. Herbert Aptheker (Millwood, NY: Kraus-Thomson, 1982), 2.
34. Labor movements, especially those that emerge from the grassroots, constitute an insurgency seeking to realize a broader measure of justice. They play a vital role in working out the meaning of democracy in ways that counter the exclusive visions of it that have given us slavery, Jim Crow, and plutocracy. Part of this meaning making involves countering myths that support unjust social arrangements, thereby challenging these arrangements. It also involves giving us commonsense perspectives on the nature of more just arrangements and the constellation of rights and duties that they entail. Furthermore, it involves identifying the problems, e.g., poor wages, working conditions, and worker safety and health protections, that contravene America's claim of being a just and democratic nation. So, as Du Bois fully understood, labor movements and other social movements seeking broader justice help us better understand not only why democracies fail but also how they flourish. For a recent analysis of how social movements like the one for a living wage have contributed to transformative meaning making, see Deva R. Woodly, *The Politics of Common Sense: How Social Movements Use Public Discourse to Change Politics and Win Acceptance* (New York: Oxford University Press, 2015).
35. This point puts Du Bois into conversation with contemporary political theorists thinking about epistemic democracy and its challenges. See, for example,

Melissa Schwartzberg, "Epistemic Democracy and Its Challenges," *Annual Review of Political Science* 18 (2015): 187–203. Du Bois's point was *not* that the masses will make the correct decisions; in fact, he believed they often would not. Nevertheless, he thought that they were an indispensable source of wisdom for securing the broadest measure of justice for all. And he relies on history as his primary evidence to support this claim. On my reading of Du Bois, this epistemic claim plays a pivotal role in his defense of democracy.

36. W. E. B. Du Bois, "Reconstruction and Its Benefits," in *Writings by W. E. B. Du Bois in Periodicals Edited by Others*, vol. 2: 1910–1934, ed. Herbert Aptheker (Millwood, NY: Kraus-Thomson, 1982), 16.
37. Du Bois, "Socialism and the Negro Problem," in *Writings by W. E. B. Du Bois in Periodicals Edited by Others*, vol. 2: 1910–1934, ed. Herbert Aptheker (Millwood, NY: Kraus-Thomson, 1982), 86.
38. W. E. B. Du Bois, "Diuturni Silenti," in *The Education of Black People, Ten Critiques, 1906–1960*, ed. Herbert Aptheker (New York: Monthly Review, 1973), 74.
39. Du Bois, *Darkwater*, 83.
40. Ibid., 84.
41. Ibid., 85. He also very briefly touches on excluding the wisdom of darker nations from international federations of democratic countries, which is, of course, a prominent theme in Du Bois's post–World War II book *Color and Democracy: Colonies and Peace* (New York: Harcourt, Brace and Co., 1945).
42. Du Bois, *Darkwater*, 84.
43. Many years after Du Bois made this point, John Dewey expressed a similar sentiment in a 1937 speech, arguing that no person was wise enough to rule others without their consent. Dewey argued that this form of coercion fails to account for important knowledge possessed by the masses. He writes, "The individuals of the submerged mass may not be very wise. But there is one thing they are wiser about than anybody else can be, and that is where the shoe pinches, the troubles they suffer from." See John Dewey, "Democracy and Educational Administration," in *The Later Works of John Dewey*, vol. II: 1935–1937, ed. Jo Ann Boydston (Carbondale: Southern Illinois University Press, 1987), 219. His use of this metaphor appears in an earlier writing, though still after Du Bois's observation. See John Dewey, *The Public and Its Problems* (Athens, OH: Swallow Press, 2016), 224, where he writes: "The man who wears the shoe knows best that it pinches and where it pinches, even if the expert shoemaker is the best judge of how the trouble is to be remedied."
44. W. E. B. Du Bois, "I Won't Vote," in *Writings by W. E. B. Du Bois in Periodicals Edited by Others*, vol. 4: 1945–1961, ed. Herbert Aptheker (Millwood, N.Y.: Kraus-Thomson, 1982), 271.

45. W. E. B. Du Bois, "Third Party," in *Writings in Periodicals Edited by W. E. B. Du Bois, Selections from the Crisis*, vol. 2: 1926–1934, ed. Herbert Aptheker (Amherst: University of Massachusetts Press, 1976).
46. John Wagner, "'No Person in America Should Be Too Poor to Live': Ocasio-Cortez Explains Democratic Socialism to Colbert," *Washington Post*, June, 29, 2018, https://www.washingtonpost.com/politics/no-person-in-america-should-be-too-poor-to-live-ocasio-cortez-explains-democratic-socialism-to-colbert/2018/06/29/d6752050-7b8d-11e8-aeee-4d04c8ac6158_story.html.
47. Others have appreciated this point. For instance, see Sheri Berman, "Against the Technocrats," *Dissent*, Winter 2018, https://www.dissentmagazine.org/article/against-technocrats-liberal-democracy-history, who sees a connection between voter dissatisfaction with elite rule and their willingness to elect politicians determined to bring down elites and democratic institutions. She writes, "That many Americans, in short, view democratic institutions and elites as fundamentally corrupt and unaccountable to them and are therefore willing to vote for politicians and parties who promise to blow them all up is not, unfortunately, all that hard to understand."
48. Du Bois, "Negro Ideals Described," 361.
49. Reinhold Niebuhr, *The Children of Light and the Children of Darkness: A Vindication of Democracy and a Critique of Its Traditional Defenders* (Chicago: University of Chicago Press, 1944).
50. Du Bois, "The Possibility of Democracy in America," 521.
51. Ibid.
52. Du Bois, "The Training of Negroes for Social Power," 182.
53. There is, of course, the philosophical question of how to think about the nature of this duty, particularly when we have white voters in mind. But remember that Du Bois was addressing an audience at the beginning of the 1900s. During that time one could more plausibly ground this duty to support black voting rights in the idea that whites were in some sense causally responsible for the legacy of black slavery and its aftermath and therefore had a backward-looking responsibility to act as saving democracy would require. And one could also say, somewhat more weakly, that even if whites were not causally responsible for black disadvantage, they benefited from it and also suffered from it. Today, these arguments are still being made, but they are a much tougher sell.
54. Du Bois, "The Training of Negroes for Social Power," 183.
55. W. E. B. Du Bois, "Votes for Women," in *Writings in Periodicals Edited by W. E. B. Du Bois, Selections from the Crisis*, vol. 1: 1911–1925, ed. Herbert Aptheker (Millwood, NY: Kraus-Thomson, 1983), 79–80.
56. Ibid., 80.
57. For example, see Du Bois, *Darkwater*, 85, where he writes, "Every white Southerner, who wants peons beneath him, who believes in hereditary menials

and a privileged aristocracy, or who hates certain races because of their characteristics, would resent this."
58. Du Bois, "Democracy Fails in America, June 1954," 1.
59. All the quotes in this paragraph are located here: W. E. B. Du Bois, "The Negro Citizen," in *Writings by W. E. B. Du Bois in Non-Periodical Literature Edited by Others*, ed. Herbert Aptheker (Millwood, NY: Kraus-Thomson, 1982), 159.
60. W. E. B. Du Bois, "How Should Negroes Vote? Be Intelligently Selfish at Polls," in *Writings by W. E. B. Du Bois in Periodicals Edited by Others*, vol. 3: 1935–1944, ed. Herbert Aptheker (Millwood, NY: Kraus-Thomson, 1982), 212.
61. Ibid., 212–13.
62. My view is that the solution to racial inequality in contemporary America, given the profound impact of race and the myth that America is "postracial," lies in remedies that are race sensitive but not race specific. I take Du Bois's insights about how democracy survives to support the kind of *principled pragmatic realism* that I advance in chapter 5. Furthermore, to the extent that there is a substantive difference between "democratic socialism" and "social democracy," the latter is more determined to operate *within* democracy to make it more inclusive by finding workable just solutions to social problems that cut across race, gender, class, and other intersecting identities. The latter is a more apt characterization of my perspective and, I believe, Du Bois's as well. For a perspective on this way of drawing the distinction, see Sheri Berman, "Democratic Socialists Are Conquering the Left. But Do They Believe in Democracy?," *Washington Post*, Aug. 10, 2018, https://www.washingtonpost.com/outlook/democratic-socialists-are-conquering-the-left-but-do-they-believe-in-democracy/2018/08/10/5bf58392-9b90-11e8-b60b-1c897f17e185_story.html.

Chapter 8

1. Shelby County v. Holder 133 S. Ct. 2612 (2013).
2. The Fifteenth Amendment to the US Constitution outlaws government discrimination in voting based on race or color. Section 2 of the VRA reaffirms this amendment by permanently proscribing state actions, nationwide, that result in vote denial or abridgement due to race or color. Section 4, the "coverage formula," of the VRA singles out for special attention certain jurisdictions with egregious histories of Fifteenth Amendment violations through the use of poll taxes, literacy tests, and other devices *and* with low voter registration and turnout. Section 5, the "preclearance requirement," provides that voting changes in covered jurisdictions must gain federal preapproval. Although in the initial Act, Congress understood sections 4 and 5 to be temporary measures and set them to expire after five years, the most recent reauthorization of the VRA in 2006 extended them for an additional twenty-five years, leaving the

coverage formula untouched. This decision prompted Shelby County, Alabama, a covered jurisdiction, to seek judgment declaring the coverage formula and the preclearance requirement unconstitutional and barring their enforcement. The Shelby County ruling invalidated section 4 but did not rule on section 5.
3. Assessment of how much racial progress there has been since the civil rights era is polarized by race as well as partisanship. For example, see Pew Research Center, "King's Dream Remains an Elusive Goal; Many Americans See Racial Disparities," Aug. 22, 2013, available at (http://www.pewsocialtrends.org/2013/08/22/kings-dream-remains-an-elusive-goal-many-americans-see-racial-disparities).
4. Jillian C. Banfield, Michael Ross, & Craig W. Blatz, "Responding to Historical Injustices: Does Group Membership Trump Liberal-Conservative Ideology?," *European Journal of Social Psychology* 44 (2014): 30–42.
5. There is also evidence that Americans in general, not just members of the High Court, remain deeply divided by race, class, and political ideology over how to assess evidence of racial inequality and racial disadvantage in political representation, voting access, and in many other areas. See, for example, Lawrence D. Bobo & Camille Z. Charles, "Race in the American Mind: From the Moynihan Report to the Obama Candidacy," ANNALS, AAPSS 621 (2009): 243–259.
6. See Richard P. Eibach & Joyce Ehrlinger, "'Keep Your Eyes on the Prize': Reference Points and Racial Differences in Assessing Progress Toward Equality," *Personality and Social Psychological Bulletin* 32 (2006): 66–77; and Amanda B. Brodish, Paige C. Brazy, and Patricia G. Devine, "More Eyes on the Prize: Variability in White Americans' Perceptions of Progress Toward Racial Equality," *Personality and Social Psychological Bulletin* 34 (2008): 513–527.
7. John Rawls, "The Basic Liberties and Their Priority," in *The Tanner Lectures on Human Values*, vol. III, ed. Sterling McMurrin (Salt Lake City: University of Utah Press, 1982), reprinted in John Rawls, *Political Liberalism* (New York: Columbia University Press, 1996).
8. See Brennan Center for Justice at NYU School of Law, "The Truth about Voter Fraud," 2007, available at http://www.brennancenter.org/sites/default/files/legacy/The%20Truth%20About%20Voter%20Fraud.pdf.
9. Niko Kolodny, "Rule over None I: What Justifies Democracy?," *Philosophy and Public Affairs* 42 (2014): 195–229.
10. Harry Brighouse, "Political Equality in Justice as Fairness," *Philosophical Studies* 86 (1997): 155–184.
11. Rawls, *A Theory of Justice*, 195. While this may not be enough, or compelling enough, to justify adding political liberties to this list, it seems to offer some support. If the equal right to participate was *not* a basic liberty, and the principle of equal basic liberties is, as Rawls supposes, lexically prior to the other principles, then citizens excluded from the rule-making process would not have as powerful grounds for complaint. Moreover, the justification he uses to

compensate for the influence of gross economic disparities on political participation could not get off the ground.

12. Ibid., 200. This is the core normative ideal undergirding my fair-value defense of voting rights. It is, in effect, the ideal that accounts for why it is not merely a strategic defense but one with a firm normative foundation. Although I will not fully explicate this ideal and its value, I am very sympathetic to a recent attempt to do so. See Niko Kolodny, "Rule over None II: Social Equality and the Justification of Democracy," *Philosophy and Public Affairs* 42 (2014): 287–336. Also see chapter 9.

13. Rawls, *A Theory of Justice*, 197.

14. See ibid., 206. When the Founders of the United States of America affirmed, "We hold these truths to be self-evident, that all men are created equal," they signaled their belief in the intrinsic value of equality. We know, however, that historically their commitment to equality was insufficiently realized. Voting was a way of recognizing this commitment in the political realm, but early on access to the ballot was restricted to property-owning white males of a certain age. And later, wealth, religion, race, and gender differences were used to diminish the usefulness of voting for some and to enhance it for others.

15. Brighouse also observes that Rawls gives both a non-instrumental justification (rooted in political equality) and an instrumental justification for singling our political liberties for special treatment, though his exposition of the latter differs from mine. See Brighouse, "Political Equality in Justice as Fairness," 158–159. But this is not a problem. There are several instrumental justifications on offer in Rawls's discussion of this issue. Another one has to do with this facilitating the exercise of one of what Rawls describes as our two moral powers, namely, to form, pursue, and rationally revise a conception of the good, and to acquire, apply, and be motivated to act on a sense of justice. Here the argument is that guaranteeing the fair value of political liberties is instrumental for assisting persons in developing their capacity for a sense of justice. For a critical discussion of this argument, see Steven Wall, "Rawls and the Status of Political Liberty," *Pacific Philosophical Quarterly* 87 (2006): 245–270.

16. Rawls, *A Theory of Justice*, p. 198. The Supreme Court has offered a similar justification for viewing the right to vote as fundamental by taking it to be "preservative of all rights." See, for instance, Reynolds v. Sims 377 U.S. 533, 562 (1964), and Harper v. Virginia State Bd. of Elections 383 U.S. 663, 667 (1966).

17. One might suggest adding the qualification that seeking to offset inequalities in political influence, which stem from failure to guarantee the worth of political liberty, takes account of the purposes of this influence and how it is transmitted with the aim of equalizing rational or reasonable influence. Brighouse, "Political Equality in Justice as Fairness," makes this point in defending "influence as mediated through rationality-respecting mechanisms" (160–162). However, this aim seems less relevant if we are specifically interested in offsetting the way

resource disparities can impact access to the ballot. In this case, "influence" is simply about being able to vote, and the rationality or reasonableness of one's reason for voting need not be open for inspection or debate to appreciate the importance of enhancing the worth of a person's basic liberty to vote. If social equality has the kind of noninstrumental value that Rawls, Kolodny, and others claim for it, and guaranteeing voting rights their fair value is a way of realizing this ideal in the "manifest constitution of society," as Rawls puts it, this further makes sense of my point about the irrelevance of ensuring rational or reasonable influence. What really matters is that we instantiate the possibility of relating to one another as social equals.

18. Rawls, "The Basic Liberties and Their Priority," 42.
19. Recent research shows that this worry is not unfounded; see Martin Gilens, *Affluence and Influence: Economic Inequality and Political Power in America* (Princeton, NJ: Princeton University Press, 2014).
20. Rawls deployed this argument to criticize the Supreme Court's ruling in *Buckley v. Valeo* 424 U.S. 1 (1976), where the Court ruled that congressional measures to limit political campaign contributions were unconstitutional.
21. Moreover, in Rawls's view, insisting upon securing the fair value of political liberties with such steps is also a concrete way to respond to the worry that equal political liberties are merely formal rather than substantive, that is, that they are liberties in name only but not in practice for some citizens. For this criticism, see Norman Daniels, "Equal Liberty and Unequal Worth of Liberty," in *Reading Rawls: Critical Studies of A Theory of Justice*, ed. Norman Daniels (New York: Basic Books, 1975), 253–281.
22. There has been a good deal of discussion of Rawls's fair value thesis in connection with campaign finance and free speech issues, but relatively little work on it in connection with focused attention on the right to vote.
23. Alexander Keyssar, *The Right to Vote: The Contested History of Democracy in the United States* (New York: Basic Books, 2000).
24. For an elaboration on this point with reference to basic liberties in general, see Rawls, *Political Liberalism*, 324–331.
25. Thomas Pogge, *John Rawls: His Life and Theory of Justice*, trans. Michelle Kosch (New York: Oxford University Press, 2007), 92.
26. Rawls, *A Theory of Justice*, 198.
27. See, for example, J. Morgan Kousser, *Colorblind Injustice: Minority Voting Rights and the Undoing of the Second Reconstruction* (Chapel Hill: The University of North Carolina Press, 1999); and Richard Valelly, *The Two Reconstructions: The Struggle for Black Enfranchisement* (Chicago: University of Chicago Press, 2004). Of course, blacks are not the only group of persons that have been disenfranchised in the United States. Well into the twentieth century, in some states, white males without property could not vote. Women could not vote until the passage of the Nineteenth Amendment, and Native Americans had

to wait until passage of the 1924 Indian Citizenship Act to vote. However, what was distinctive about black disenfranchisement, historically, was its connection to a racial ideology that represented blacks as inferior and thus unfit to rule with whites as equal participants in democratic governance. In 1905–1906, Hoke Smith successfully campaigned for governor of Georgia on the platform of imposing educational qualifications on voting with the intent to keep blacks from the ballot box on grounds that "[t]he negro is inferior mentally to the white man," and "[b]ecause [whites] are the superior race and do not intend to be ruled by our semi-barbaric inferiors." This is but one example of a perspective that was widely held at this time and held well into the twentieth century; see Laughlin McDonald, *A Voting Rights Odyssey: Black Enfranchisement in Georgia* (Cambridge: Cambridge University Press, 2003), 40.

28. One of the bills most effective at making it virtually impossible for blacks to vote was Georgia's *Disfranchising Act* of 1908, which combined various tests and devices into a single law. The only males who could register to vote in Georgia back then were required to be sane; have no criminal background; be caught up on poll taxes since 1877; meet residency requirements; and either be a war veteran, descended from one, able to pass a good character and understanding tests, or a literacy test, or own at least forty acres of land or real property valued at $500 or greater. See McDonald, *A Voting Rights Odyssey*, 41.

29. The Supreme Court declared these exemptions unconstitutional in Guinn v. United States 238 U.S. 347 (1915). But this was merely a bump in the road of state efforts to disenfranchise black voters. Well into the twentieth century, indeed up until the VRA was passed in 1965, states were allowed to use literacy tests for voter qualification, and the Court sanctioned this practice, only requiring that these tests be applied equally to all races; see Lassiter v. Northampton County Board of Elections 360 U.S. 45 (1959).

30. Two especially significant cases in addition to Lassiter are United States v. Reese 92 U.S. 214 (1876), in which the Court cleared a path for states to disenfranchise blacks from voting by denying that the Fifteenth Amendment recognized a right to vote, and Breedlove v. Suttles 302 U.S. 277 (1937), in which the Court ruled poll taxes constitutional. The poll tax, one of several popular methods of denying blacks the fair value of the right to vote, was eventually abolished with the passage of the Twenty-Fourth Amendment and was declared unconstitutional with the reversal of Breedlove in Harper v. Virginia State Board of Elections 383 U.S. 663 (1966).

31. Supreme Court justices on opposite ends of the liberal–conservative ideological divide have endorsed strict scrutiny of laws that burden fundamental rights. For instance, Thurgood Marshall applies this standard to the right of the mentally challenged to "establish a home" to argue that an ordinance requiring a special use permit for a group home for them should have been rejected by applying the more searching standard of review merited when

fundamental liberties are burdened. See City of Cleburne, Texas v. Cleburne Living Center, Inc.105 S. Ct. 3249, 3265 (1985). And dissenting in Lawrence v. Texas 123 S. Ct. 2472, 2489 (2003), Scalia, Thomas, and Rehnquist contend that *only* fundamental rights merit strict scrutiny. They add that only liberty interests deeply rooted in the history and tradition of the United States count as fundamental. Hence, they would have upheld the Texas statute making consensual same-sex sodomy illegal on grounds that the asserted that liberty interest was not fundamental.
32. 128 S. Ct. 1610 (2008).
33. I am very grateful to Richard Levy for instructive conversations about the Supreme Court's voting rights jurisprudence.
34. Some scholars have argued that there is a basis in law, connected with the Privileges and Immunities Clause of the Article IV, section 2 of the US Constitution, for recognizing the right to vote as fundamental. Moreover, they have argued that America's dark racial past and steadfastness to maintain white supremacy and black subordination (under the guise of "equal state sovereignty") explain why congressional action is more likely to elevate this basic liberty to its proper place in the pantheon of fundamental rights than judicial review. See Blacksher & Guinier, "Free at Last: Rejecting Equal Sovereignty and Restoring the Constitutional Right to Vote *Shelby County v. Holder.*"
35. The Court denies the right to vote is absolute and exempt from restrictions. See Burdick v. Takushi 504 U.S. 428 (1992). According to the Court, a state's interests in realizing values such as integrity, efficiency, and equity in elections can suffice to justify imposing certain burdens on the right to vote.
36. Rawls, *A Theory of Justice*, 196.
37. Richard Sobel, "The High Cost of 'Free' Photo Voter Identification Cards," Charles Hamilton Houston Institute for Race & Justice 2014 report, Harvard Law School, Cambridge, MA, available at http://today.law.harvard.edu/wp-content/uploads/2014/06/FullReportVoterIDJune20141.pdf.
38. There is a question of whether the principle of equal participation requires merely offsetting inequalities in resources or, more strongly, providing equal resources to exercise political influence (pace Brighouse, p. 161). And there is a question of whether Rawls holds the former (weaker view) or the latter (stronger view). I think the weaker view is more consistent with his understanding of the difference principle, and that the stronger view would make democracy too expensive.
39. Brennan Center for Justice at NYU School of Law, "The Challenge of Obtaining Voter Identification," 2012, available at (https://www.brennancenter.org/sites/default/files/legacy/Democracy/VRE/Challenge_of_Obtaining_Voter_ID.pdf).
40. For philosophical reflection on some of the questions and concerns raised by race in a "postracial" epoch, see the essays in *Du Bois Review* 11(1) (2014).

41. See Lorraine C. Minnite, *The Myth of Voter Fraud* (Ithaca, NY: Cornell University Press, 2011); and David Schultz, "Less than Fundamental: The Myth of Voter Fraud and the Coming of the Second Great Disenfranchisement," *William Mitchell Law Review* 34 (2008): 483–532.
42. In Texas, before its strict voter ID law (SB 14) was passed in 2011, just two cases of in-person voter impersonation fraud cases were successfully prosecuted during a period of time when twenty million votes were cast. See Veasey v. Perry 71 F. Supp. 3d 627, 640 (S.D. Tex. 2014). This lengthy decision also contains a useful discussion of the legal disposition of voter ID laws in other state jurisdictions, comparing and contrasting them with the Texas law.
43. Some critics have suggested that Rawls devalues political liberties because priority is given to personal liberties when they conflict. See, for example, Amy Gutmann, "Rawls on the Relationship between Liberalism and Democracy," in *The Cambridge Companion to Rawls*, ed. Samuel Freeman (New York: Cambridge University Press, 2003): 168–199. I do not find this criticism convincing, however. Adjustments made to secure the fair value of political liberties, including the right to vote, in a way that can be squared with the central range of application of personal liberties, including the liberty of thought and expression, cannot be dismissed merely because these adjustments undermine or conflict with them. As Rawls says, these personal liberties are no more absolute than are the political ones. See John Rawls, *Justice as Fairness: A Restatement*, ed. Erin Kelly (Cambridge: Harvard University Press, 2003), 149–150. Curiously, Gutmann acknowledges this point (p. 184) but does not retract the criticism.
44. For the view that there are no rights without social recognition of ways of acting and being treated, see my book: Derrick Darby, *Rights, Race, and Recognition* (Cambridge: Cambridge University Press, 2009).
45. Demonstrating the pragmatic benefit of my race-neutral normative argument for voting rights is a nod to "racial realists," who have long argued for facing up to the pervasiveness and enduring character of the belief that blacks are, in all kinds of ways, inferior to whites. I find racial realism compelling. And the argument of this chapter is in line with my other work, which registers the value of theorizing about the demands of justice, as well as the prospects for achieving it in our nonideal circumstances, by working from more realistic premises regarding the beliefs of persons whose social cooperation is necessary to move us toward a more well-ordered society. For an important source on racial realism, see Derrick Bell, *And We Are Not Saved: The Elusive Quest for Racial Justice* (New York: Basic Books, Inc., 1987). And for an account of what we stand to lose by not taking the divisiveness of racial divisions seriously, see William Julius Wilson, *The Bridge over the Racial Divide: Rising Inequality and Coalition Politics* (Berkeley: University of California Press, 2001).

46. Andrew Altman, "Race and Democracy: The Controversy over Racial Vote Dilution," *Philosophy and Public Affairs* 27 (1998): 175–201.
47. Derrick Darby, "Uncovering the Voting Rights Act: The Racial Progress Argument in Shelby County," *Kansas Journal of Law & Public Policy* 25 (2016): 329–346. Also see chapter 2.

Chapter 9

1. Kant, *Anthropology from a Pragmatic Point of View*, 7:127. I will follow common practice of using the Academy volume and page numbers for references to Kant. My source for this work is Immanuel Kant, *Anthropology, History, and Education*, ed. Günter Zöller & Robert B. Louden (Cambridge: Cambridge University Press, 2007).
2. For an account of Kant's infamous contribution these legacies, see Thomas McCarthy, *Race, Empire, and the Idea of Human Development* (Cambridge: Cambridge University Press, 2009), chap. 2.
3. Martin Luther King, Jr., *Strength to Love* (Minneapolis, MN: Fortress Press, 2010), 29.
4. Jeremy Waldron, *Dignity, Rank, and Rights* (New York: Oxford University Press, 2012), 33.
5. To put this distinction another way, the former alternative suggests that specific rights can be inferred from a conception of dignity, whereas the latter alternative suggests that an existing system of rights tells us something about what we mean by dignity and how strongly we value it. I think that the latter alternative is a more modest position, but one that can also do some critical normative work.
6. See Cornel West, *The Radical King: Martin Luther King, Jr.* (Boston: Beacon Press, 2015).
7. For criticism of the view that particular rights can be inferred from a conception of dignity, see Charles R. Beitz, "Human Dignity in the Theory of Human Rights: Nothing but a Phrase?," *Philosophy & Public Affairs* 41 (2013): 259–290.
8. See Gary May, *Bending toward Justice: The Voting Rights Act and the Transformation of American Democracy* (New York: Basic Books, 2013), xix.
9. Martin Luther King, Jr., *Where Do We Go from Here: Chaos or Community?* (Boston: Beacon Press, 2010), 145.
10. See Martha C. Nussbaum, *Political Emotions: Why Love Matters for Justice* (Cambridge, MA: Belknap Press of Harvard University Press, 2013).
11. King, *Where Do We Go from Here*, 145.
12. A craving for normalcy arguably compelled Shelby County, Alabama, to appeal to the US Supreme Court to lift the heavy burden placed on it and other jurisdictions for their shameful histories of voting rights abuses. They won their day in court in Shelby County v. Holder (2013). For discussion, see Derrick

Darby, "Uncovering the Voting Rights Act: The Racial Progress Argument in *Shelby County*," *Kansas Journal of Law & Public Policy* 25 (2016): 329–346; also see chapter 2. As King might have predicted, the enactment, following Shelby County, of voter ID laws that made it harder for blacks and other citizens to vote suggests that some version of negative normalcy is what they were after all along. To be sure, it was not the kind of "normalcy in the state of Mississippi which made it possible for authorities to say that a Negro must starve if he wanted to vote" (Martin Luther King, Jr., "People to People: Civil Rights and Negative Normalcy," *New York Amsterdam News*, March 12, 1988). Nor was it the kind of normalcy they had in Alabama under Governor George Wallace, where blacks had to withstand the brutal force of Sheriff Jim Clark if they wanted to vote and then pass a literary test if they made it to the ballot box. Nevertheless, it clearly is a kind of negative normalcy in which just being an American citizen of voting age is not enough. To procure the documents needed to vote, one must also have ample time and money, both of which are resources that are unequally distributed across the population of eligible voters and in disproportionately short supply for black Americans in particular.

13. King, "People to People." King uses the phrase "new birth of democracy" in letter to Laura R. Daly, April 19, 1966, thanking her for a financial contribution to the Southern Christian Leadership Conference voting rights campaign.
14. King, "People to People."
15. As quoted in Martin Luther King, Jr., *All Labor Has Dignity*, ed. Michael K. Honey (Boston: Beacon Press, 1963), 97.
16. Ibid., 97–98.
17. King, "People to People."
18. King, *All Labor Has Dignity*, 98.
19. Ibid.
20. Ibid., 91.
21. Ibid., 90.
22. King, *Where Do We Go from Here*, 3–4. For a rich historical account of what was at stake in this phase of struggle, and how it advanced long-standing radical agendas, see Thomas F. Jackson, *From Civil Rights to Human Rights: Martin Luther King, Jr., and the Struggle for Economic Justice* (Philadelphia: University of Pennsylvania Press, 2007).
23. King, *Where Do We Go from Here*, 4.
24. Ibid., 5.
25. King, *Where Do We Go from Here*, 20.
26. Martin Luther King Jr., "Draft of an Article on the Status of Civil Rights Movement during 1965," Martin Luther King, Jr., Papers, Speeches, Sermons, Etc., box 7, King Center Archive in Atlanta (hereafter cited as King Papers, King Center Archive), 2.
27. King, *Strength to Love*, 150.

28. Ibid.
29. Martin Luther King, Jr., *Stride toward Freedom: The Montgomery Story* (Boston: Beacon Press, 2010), 31.
30. Bernard R. Boxill, *Blacks and Social Justice*, rev. ed. (Lanham, MD: Rowman and Littlefield, 1992), 193–194.
31. Ibid., 194.
32. Kant, *Groundwork of the Metaphysics of Morals*, 4:435. My source for his moral works is Immanuel Kant, *Practical Philosophy*, ed. Mary J. Gregor (Cambridge: Cambridge University Press, 1996).
33. In some cases, the sanctions might be legal ones, imposed by laws that proscribe ways of acting. Or being treated that are deemed undignified. Laws against dwarf tossing, wearing a burka, pornography, and prostitution can be located within this category. In these cases, a community conception of respect for the dignity, holiness, or sacredness of humanity is enshrined within a legal system of rights.
34. Kant, *The Metaphysics of Morals*, 6:436.
35. Martin Luther King, Jr., "Speech before the Youth March for Integrated Schools," in *A Testament of Hope: The Essential Writings and Speeches of Martin Luther King, Jr.*, ed. James M. Washington (New York: Harper Collins, 1991), 22.
36. King, *Where Do We Go from Here*, 103, 104.
37. Ibid., 102.
38. Ibid., 104.
39. Martin Luther King, Jr., "How Modern Christians Should Think of Man," *King Papers*, box 1, King Center Archive, 3.
40. King, *Where Do We Go from Here*, 102.
41. One philosopher puts the point this way: "The worst evil-doers have human dignity despite their atrocious acts, for this basic dignity is a moral status that is not earned and cannot be forfeited." See Thomas E. Hill, Jr., "Human Dignity and Tragic Choices," *Proceedings and Addresses of the American Philosophical Association* 89 (2015): 74–97, 86.
42. King credits his studies at Boston University for giving him "a metaphysical basis for the dignity and worth of all human personality" (King, *Stride toward Freedom*, 88). For a historical treatment of the philosophical influences on King's racial justice activism, see David Levering Lewis, *King: A Biography*, 3rd ed. (Urbana: University of Illinois Press, 2013).
43. It is commonly held that human beings are the only animals with dignity in this sense of inherent worth. But some philosophers have taken issue with this by offering a more inclusive reading of what makes a creature a Kantian end in itself. See, for instance, Christine M. Korsgaard, "Fellow Creatures: Kantian Ethics and Our Duties to Animals," in *The Tanner Lectures on Human Values*, vol. 5, ed. Grethe B. Peterson (Salt Lake City: Utah University Press, 2005).
44. King, *Strength to Love*, 29.

45. Ibid., 79.
46. King, "Draft of an Article," 12, 14.
47. Martin Luther King, Jr., "Press Statement 10/5/57 re Crusade for Citizenship SCLC Memphis, Tennessee," King Papers, box 1, ca. early 1950s, King Center Archive.
48. King, *All Labor Has Dignity*, 92.
49. Ibid., 93.
50. Ibid., 78.
51. Martin Luther King, Jr., *Why We Can't Wait* (Boston: Beacon Press, 2010), 93.
52. King, *All Labor Has Dignity*, 92. It is important to add, however, that blacks are not the only ones bound by chains here. In a draft of a speech on the passage of the 1965 Voting Rights Act, King says, "For white people in our nation have been enslaved to the ideal of racial superiority and we cannot free ourselves without freeing them."
53. King's admonishment of rank, sorting persons into higher and lower rank, also shows up in his sharp criticism of churches that fail to "recognize that worship at its best is a social experience in which people from all levels of life come together to affirm their oneness and unity under God" (King, *Strength to Love*, 60).
54. King, *All Labor Has Dignity*, 129.
55. King, *Where Do We Go from Here*, 44.
56. My reading of King on honor, and on its bearing on yet another use of dignity in his work, is inspired and informed by Waldron's insightful treatment of dignity's relationship to honor and rank, though in this chapter I cannot give his views the careful attention they deserve. I am also struck by the many parallels between this approach to dignity and the one I take to rights in Derrick Darby, *Rights, Race, and Recognition* (Cambridge: Cambridge University Press, 2009). There I treat being a bearer of rights as a social status rooted in practices of recognition, taking seriously the reality that this status is not guaranteed by the nature of our being but must be fought for and can be won or lost. I suspect that much of what I say there can be adapted to a socially grounded analysis of dignity.
57. Kant, *Anthropology from a Pragmatic Point of View*, 7:137.
58. Martin Luther King, Jr., "Address at Selma State Capitol in Montgomery, Alabama on 3/25/195," at 5, King Papers, box 8, King Center Archive.
59. King, *Why We Can't Wait*, 94, 99.
60. Public Statement at the Mississippi Freedom Democratic Party, July 22, 1964; Statement before the Credentials Committee, Democratic National Committee, August 22, 1964, King Papers, box 8, King Center Archive.
61. Martin Luther King, Jr., "The Right to Vote, the Quest for Jobs 3/65," at 7, King Papers, box 8, King Center Archive. In the annotated copy, King crosses out this passage; however, his remark is insightful and a point worth making.

62. Keesha Gaskins & Sundeep Iver, "The Challenge of Obtaining Voter Identification," Brennan Center for Justice at New York University School of Law, July 29, 2012, available at http://brennancenter.org/publication/challenge-obtaining-voter-identification.
63. Martin Luther King, Jr., "Give Us the Ballot—We Will Transform the South," in *A Testament of Hope*, 197.
64. Ibid.
65. For an influential account of nondomination as a political ideal, see Phillip Pettit, *Republicanism: A Theory of Freedom and Government* (New York: Oxford University Press, 1997), chap. 3.
66. King also discusses the consequences of the political domination involved in denying blacks the vote: such domination erodes democracy and puts democracy on trial. No one can govern or respect people as well as they can represent or govern themselves, he argues, and therefore when they are subject to political domination, they face pressure to flee their circumstances if they cannot change them within the legal systems of rights. They might flee the Iron Curtain from East to West, says King, or the Cotton Curtain from South to North. He laments how mass Northern migration, prompted partly by political domination, depleted the South of blacks and how it burdened Northern dark ghettos. He observes that it also depressed economic development in the South and left congressional power in the hands of the most reactionary bloc, which made national social welfare and education bills difficult to pass, and which put American democracy on trial on the global stage. See King, "Draft of an Article."
67. This argument can be generalized to cover many of the evil monsters or racial injustice that King highlights. Our national commitment to dignity can be enhanced by a legal system of rights that includes rights and duties that vanquish or guard against the ways in which evil monsters assail our dignity. But I shall keep the focus squarely on voting rights in expounding the argument.
68. Beitz, "Human Dignity," 288.
69. For a very insightful and detailed overview of the modern struggle for voting rights, see Ari Berman, *Give Us the Ballot: The Modern Struggle for Voting Rights in America* (New York: Farrar, Straus and Giroux, 2015).
70. Beitz, "Human Dignity," 288.
71. Waldron, *Dignity, Rank, and Rights*, 145.

Chapter 10

1. Christopher J. Lebron, *The Making of Black Lives Matter: A Brief History of an Idea* (New York: Oxford University Press, 2017).

2. Sharon A. Stanley, *An Impossible Dream? Racial Integration in the United States* (New York: Oxford University Press, 2017).
3. Alex Zamalin, *Struggle on Their Minds: The Political Thought of African American Resistance* (New York: Columbia University Press, 2017).
4. Ibid., 6.
5. Ibid., 7.
6. Ibid., 168–169.
7. Lebron, *The Making of Black Lives Matter*, 120.
8. Ibid., xx.
9. Ibid., xxi.
10. Ibid., xiv.
11. Ibid., 132.
12. Ibid., 122.
13. Stanley, *An Impossible Dream?*, 16.
14. Derrick Darby and John L. Rury, *The Color of Mind: Why the Origins of the Achievement Gap Matter for Justice* (Chicago: University of Chicago Press, 2018).
15. Stanley, *An Impossible Dream?*, 38.
16. Ibid., 35.
17. Ibid., 42.
18. Ibid., 143.
19. Nancy MacLean, *Democracy in Chains: The Deep History of the Radical Right's Stealth Plan for America* (New York: Viking, 2017).

Index

For the benefit of digital users, indexed terms that span two pages (e.g., 52–53) may, on occasion, appear on only one of those pages.

Adarand Constructors, Inc. v. Peña, 23–24
admissions, in higher education, 16, 22–26, 28, 67, 118–19. *See also* affirmative action
affirmative action, 15–31. *See also* admissions, in higher education
   challenges of, 18
   limitations of, 16
   origin of term, 18
   in postracial era, 18–26
   as small-tent remedy, 15–16
   social science research and, 27–31
   University of Michigan Law School and, 22–26
   whites' attitude toward, 96–97
African Americans. *See also* black radical liberalism; disparities, racial; racial differences
   alleged inferiority of, 17, 19–20, 85, 196, 205, 226, 227, 233, 242, 244, 289–90n.27
   dignity of, 208–34
   disrespect of, 85
   educational underachievement of, 15–16, 66–67
   marginalized populations' needs/ wants homologous to those of, 3–4, 7, 12, 242
   postracialist myth about, 4–7
   small-tent remedies for, 1–3
Alito, Samuel, 198
alliances/coalitions
   building, 109, 113, 115–16, 125–26, 247
   class-based, 126
   with liberals, 3, 71–72, 76–79, 86, 100–1
   with marginalized populations, 3–4, 7, 12
   psychological barriers to, 140
   with whites during civil rights movement, 217–18
American Bar Association, 59
antibalkanization, 105, 123–24, 125, 132
Arendt, Hannah, 136, 151
Aristotle, 52–53

Bagenstos, Samuel, 124, 126–27
Baker, Ella, 11, 239, 247
Bakke decision, 23, 24–25, 29
Baldwin, James, 236, 241
Bandura, Albert, 139
Barkan, Elazar, 51–52
baseline problem, 204
Bell, Derrick, 10
big-tent remedies. *See also* postracial remedies
   advocates and opponents of, 10–11
   collective responsibility for, 136–58
   cooperation and coalition as keys to, 7, 11
   issues addressed by, 7, 12, 116–17, 118
   for the 99 percent, 11–12
   in postracial era, 103–35
   precursors of, 11
   small-tent remedies subsumed in, 7
black activist tradition, 11

black liberalism, 3. *See also* black radical liberalism
#BlackLivesMatter, 11, 247
black nationalism, 3
Black Panthers, 238
Black Power, 78, 212, 238, 240
black radicalism, 239–47
black radical liberalism, 3, 74–75, 76–77, 79, 80–81, 82, 83–84, 100–2
bling laws, 227–28, 229
Bobo, Lawrence D., 4–5
Boxill, Bernard, 220–21
Brown, Michael, C.P60, 111–12
Brown v. Board of Education, 15, 18, 27–29, 106–7, 110, 121–22, 144–45, 243
Buber, Martin, 226

Carmichael, Stokely, 244
Carson, Ben, 75
CATO Institute, 121
citizenship, 17–18, 85
Citizens United decision, 202
Civil Rights Act (1964), 18, 216–17
Clark, Jim, 219, 220–21
class ("place"), as substitute for racial categories, 104, 119, 124, 126
Clegg, Roger, 58–59
clothing. *See* bling laws
coalitions. *See* alliances/coalitions
Coates, Ta-Nehisi, 74, 245
Cohen, G. A., 72–74, 78, 86
Colbert, Stephen, 182
collective guilt/responsibility
  elicitation of, 92–93, 97, 136–37
  forward- vs. backward-looking, 137–38, 140–46, 150–58
  issues in, 136–37, 141
  joint commitment and, 155–57
  positive social benefits from, 138–39
  psychological resistance to, 94–96, 97–98, 107–8, 137–38, 139–41, 145–46, 151–52
Combahee River Collective, 247

Committee on Equal Employment Opportunity, 18
Conaway, J. Michael, 120
conservatives
  justifications of, for voting restrictions, 191, 201
  on link between past discrimination and present disparities, 37–38
  and postracial era, 4, 5–6
  and racial progress argument, 32–33, 37, 41, 44, 189–90
  on Supreme Court, 25, 32–33, 37, 38, 40, 46, 243
  and VRA, 37, 38
Conyers, John, 58
Cooper, Anna Julia, 82–83, 236, 241, 242
Cooper, Annie Lee, 220–21
corrective justice argument
  basis of, 52–53
  and government complicity, 55–56
  limitations of, 65–67
  objections to, 53, 60–65
coverage formula, 32, 33–35, 36, 40, 41, 42–44, 45, 255–56n.2
Crawford v. Marion County Election Board, 44, 198, 201
Crenshaw, Kimberlé Williams, 131, 133
criminal justice system
  racial disparities in, 59–60, 115
  reform of, 120–21
critical race theory, 5–6
Crowley, Joseph, 182
Cullors, Patrisse, 247

Davis, Angela, 11, 236, 238, 247
democracy. *See also* voting rights
  capacity/knowledge of citizens for, 161–62, 168–77
  commitment to processes of, 107, 125, 131–33, 153–54, 162
  Du Bois and, 161–88, 280n.5
  failures of, 161–62, 163, 181–88
  fully inclusive, 5–6, 163, 166, 184–85, 186

perfect vs. imperfect, 165, 168, 186–88
popular sovereignty model of, 164–65, 166–67, 172, 178, 187
racial justice linked to, 12
restrictions on, 9, 41, 43
role of money and business in, 164–65, 170–71, 172–73, 175–77, 184–85, 188, 193–94, 246–47
threats to, from the voting masses, 161–62, 182
Trump's effect on, 235–36
universal good as object of, 165–66, 178–79

Dewey, John, 179

dignity
capacity for deliberate choice as source of, 209, 211, 222, 223, 226, 227, 231–34
conducting oneself with, 209, 218–22, 223
as fundamental American value, 209, 215–16, 229–30, 232, 234
as innate human property, 209, 218–19, 221–23, 226
meanings of, 209, 218–19, 223
nondomination linked to, 231–32
positive normalcy linked to, 215–16
racial justice linked to, 216–18, 224–30
rank associated with, 209–10, 216, 228–30, 232, 233–34
rights as public expression of, 210–11, 214–15
voting rights linked to, 45, 209–11, 214–15, 218–19, 222, 224–25, 230–34

discrimination. *See also* implicit bias; racism
conflicting views on, 37–38
difficulties of proving effects of, 20–21, 24–25, 64–67, 68, 110, 139–40, 144–45
first-generation vs. second-generation, in voting rights, 40, 41
government complicity in, 53–54, 55–56
housing, 55, 64, 121–23
judicial thought about, 24–26, 243, 256–57n.15
race-specific remedies for, 16–17
short- vs. long-term view of, 38

disparities, racial. *See also* systemic racial barriers
agent-neutral explanations of, 60, 263n.42
agent-relative explanations of, 18–21, 58–59, 67–68, 106–7, 263n.42
controversies over causes of, 19–20, 60–61, 106–7, 110, 114, 116, 143–44, 154–55
in criminal justice system, 59–60, 115
in education, 58, 66
in health, 64
as hindrance to equal opportunity, 18
King on, 225–26
King's campaign to erase, 216–18
linking of past discrimination to current, 20–21, 24–25, 52, 55, 56–57, 63–65, 139–40, 144–45
persistence of, 56
postracial approaches to, 16–17, 18–19, 106–7, 109–10, 143
postracial remedies for, 113–19
public opinion on, 125–26
reparations justified by appeal to, 53–57
social science research on, 57–60, 65–67

diversity
as admissions criterion, 22–26
social science research on, 27–31

Douglass, Frederick, 215–16, 233, 236, 238, 241

Dred Scott v. Sandford, 17, 33

Du Bois, W. E. B., 161–88
on capacity/knowledge of citizens for democracy, 161–62, 168–77
Darkwater, 163, 168, 179–80

Du Bois, W. E. B. (cont.)
"Diuturni Silenti," 179
on failures of democracy, 161–62, 163, 181–88
on nature and value of democracy, 163–68
The Negro, 235
"Of the Ruling of Men," 163, 165–66, 168, 177–78, 179, 183–84
Dunn v. Blumstein, 189
Dworkin, Ronald, 73–74, 86, 143

Eagleton, Terry, 79
education. *See also* admissions, in higher education; affirmative action
initiatives for ameliorating racial disparities in, 104, 121–22
racial disparities in, 15–16, 66–67
election officials, 9
Emancipation Proclamation, 215–16
employment programs, 120
Enlightenment, 169, 172
equal opportunity, 39
equal participation, 191–94, 197, 200, 206, 291n.38. *See also* voting rights
equal protection jurisprudence
in current judicial thought, 21, 23–25, 29, 33, 108–9, 112–13, 115–16, 118, 124
individuals, not groups, as subject of, 24–25
postracial narrative underlying, 105, 108–9, 112–13
race-specific remedies proscribed by, 24–25, 29, 118
social science research used in, 27–28
equal sovereignty, 32–33, 36–37
Executive Order 10925, 18
expressive relationship, of rights, 210–11, 214–15
Eyer, Katie, 120

Fair Housing Act (1968), 18

fatigue
compassion, 126–27
identity, 124–25
race, 205–6, 212–13
Fifteenth Amendment, 215–16, 233–34, 255–56n.2, 286–87n.2
Fisher v. Texas, 118–19
Floyd, George, 5–6, 8
Foucault, Michel, 237
Fourteenth Amendment, 23, 24–25, 28, 215–16

Garza, Alicia, 11–12, 247
Georgia, voting restrictions in, 9–10, 189
Gilbert, Margaret, 155–56
Ginsburg, Ruth Bader, 38–39, 40, 42, 44, 59, 198
Great Society programs, 18, 25, 52, 111, 144–45
grounding relationship, of rights, 210–11, 232–33
Grutter, Barbara, 23
Grutter v. Bollinger, 16, 23–25, 27–31, 59, 67
Gurin Report, 254–55n.31

Hamer, Fannie Lou, 11
Harper, Frances Ellen Watkins, 215–16
Harvard Education Review, 29–30
Hegel, G.W.F., 237
Hobbes, Thomas, 147–48
Holocaust, 47, 51–52
honor, 227–29, 233–34
housing discrimination/segregation, 55, 64, 121–23
H.R. 40, 58–60
Hughes, Langston, 236, 241, 242
Hurston, Zora Neale, 236, 241, 242

ideology, 79
implicit bias. *See also* discrimination; racism
in criminal justice system, 121
difficulty of combating, 115
exposure of, 96

initiatives to remove, 114–15, 117–18
postracial downplaying of, 106–7, 110
racial injustice resulting from, 106
resistance to addressing, 117–18
systemic barriers related to, 115
unavailability of legal remedies for, 108
in the workplace, 120
Indiana, voting restrictions in, 198, 201
inequalities. *See* disparities, racial

Jefferson, Thomas, 214–15
Jim Crow racism
collective memory of, 51
enactment of, 8–9
end of, 10, 16–17, 18, 19–20, 57, 103, 110, 243
laissez-faire racism's supplanting of, 21
racial disparities attributed to, 20–21, 48, 50, 52, 58–59, 60–61, 63–64, 95, 110, 142–43, 144–45, 184
J-Live, 225–26
Johnson, Lyndon B., 18, 144–45, 211–14, 216, 218
joint commitment, 155–57
Journal of College Student Development, 29–30
judicial thought. *See* US Supreme Court
Juneteenth, 5–6
justice. *See also* corrective justice argument
as fairness, 77, 80–81, 87–88, 190–91
feelings associated with, 87–89, 93, 98
forward- vs. backward-looking prescriptions for, 79, 80–81
ideal theory vs. nonideal theory, 90, 266–67n.42
psychological obstacles to realizing, 3, 80–81, 85
Rawlsian conception of, 85–86, 87–88

as rectification, 74, 79, 80–81, 84, 85, 86–87, 90, 98, 99–100, 266n.34
stability as essential factor for, 87–90

Kant, Immanuel, 209, 218–19, 221–22, 223, 227–28, 233–34
Kendi, Ibram X., 5
Kennedy, Anthony, 25–26, 32–33, 59, 132–33, 198
Kennedy, John F., 18
King, Martin Luther, Jr., 17–18, 45, 46, 78, 105–6, 109, 138–39, 206–7, 208–34, 236, 238, 239–41, 242–43, 244, 245–46
"Letter from Birmingham Jail," 226

labor, and democracy, 169, 171, 173, 175–77, 283n.34
laissez-faire racism, 19–20, 21, 67–68
Lebron, Christopher, J., *The Making of Black Lives Matter*, 236–37, 240–43, 245–46
liberals/liberalism. *See also* black radical liberalism; whites
as allies for racial justice, 3, 71–72, 76–79, 86, 100–1
black philosophers' approaches to, 83
classical vs. contemporary, 73
deracialization of, 82–84, 101
exclusionary vs. inclusive, 73–74
ideal theory vs. nonideal theory, 81–82, 83, 84–85
and individualism, 72–73
on link between past discrimination and present disparities, 37–38
Mills on race problem of, 71–83, 84, 90, 101–2
popular conception of, 73
and postracial era, 4
and racial progress argument, 33, 37, 39, 41, 44, 189–90
and VRA, 37, 38–39
Lincoln, Abraham, 215–16
Lippmann, Walter, 179
Lorde, Audre, 236, 241, 242, 247

MacLean, Nancy, 164–65, 246
Mandela, Nelson, 144–45
Marable, Manning, 41
March on Washington, DC (1963), 17
marginalized populations
  big-tent remedies inclusive of, 7
  building alliances with, 3–4, 7, 12, 242
Marley, Bob, 71
Martin, Trayvon, 111–12
Marx, Karl, 237, 240, 242
mature realism, 212
McCleskey, Warren, 21
McCleskey v. Kemp, 21
Mills, Charles W.
  approach to racial justice, 78–79, 80, 81–90
  critique of, 3, 73–81, 87, 100, 101–2
  critique of Rawls and white liberalism, 71–83, 84–85, 90
  on white psychology, 98–99, 100

Native Americans, 1–2
Newton, Huey P., 225–26, 236, 238
Niebuhr, Reinhold, 183
NIMBY (not-in-my-backyard), 122–23
nondomination, 231–32
normalcy
  dignity linked to, 215–16
  negative, 213–14, 216, 220–21, 224, 293–94n.12
  positive, 214–16
  social benefits from, 229–30
  whites' desire for return to, 211–14, 216–17, 293–94n.12
Nozick, Robert, 72–74, 77

Obama, Barack, 4, 15–16, 48, 51–52, 74, 109–10
Ocasio-Cortez, Alexandria, 182
O'Connor, Sandra Day, 27
Overton window, 133–34, 276n.75

Parents Involved in Community Schools v. Seattle School District. No. 1, 106–7

Parks, Rosa, 220
partisan differences
  concerning racial injustice, 111–12
  on voting rights, 45
personal responsibility. *See also* collective guilt/responsibility
  as postracial theme, 18–20, 91, 106–7, 143
  racial disparities attributed to, 18–20, 58–59, 91, 106–7, 143–44
polarization
  political despair in response to, 125–26
  political strategies in face of, 45, 46, 103–4, 105, 107–8, 109, 112, 127, 197, 205–6
  on racial disparities, 106–7
  on racial progress, 37–39, 111–12
police accountability and reform, 8, 104–5, 121
police discretion, 115, 121
police violence, 8, 92, 105–6, 111–12, 115–16
popular sovereignty, 164–65, 166–67, 172, 178, 187
postracial era
  affirmative action in, 18–26
  America's belief in, 4–7, 12, 16–22, 68, 103, 108–10, 111
  attractiveness of, 5
  characteristics of, 19, 111
  citizenship and, 17–18
  counternarratives to, 5–6
  dangers of concept of, 5–7
  evidence against, 105–6
  in judicial thought, 115–16
  judicial thought in, 24–26, 33, 103, 108, 118, 124
  personal responsibility as theme in, 91
  voting rights in, 32–46
postracial remedies. *See also* big-tent remedies
  application of, 119–23
  cost of, 129
  criticized as appeasement, 133–35

criticized as impractical, 125–30
criticized as unprincipled, 130–33
current social and psychological conditions for, 104–5, 112–13, 115–16, 123–35, 157
defined, 103–4
as disguised race-specific remedies, 127–28
effectiveness of, 104–5, 114, 128–30
experimenting with, 114
incremental, 116–17, 128–29
motivations for supporting, 103–5, 116–17, 125, 131
objections to, 125–35
political, 116–17, 118
pragmatism of, 12, 103–5, 113, 115–16, 123–24, 125–30, 131–32
race-sensitive vs. race-specific character of, 103–4, 107–8, 114, 118–19, 124, 128, 132–33
for racial inequality, 113–19
social cohesion as goal of, 104–5, 125, 131, 132–33
types of, 104
universalistic approaches compared to, 104, 124–25
Powell, Lewis, 23, 24–25, 29
preclearance requirement, 32, 34, 35–37, 108, 189, 255–56n.2
progress. *See* racial progress
psychological considerations. *See also* collective guilt
collective guilt/responsibility, 137–38, 139–41, 145–46, 151–52
forward- vs. backward-looking responsibility, 140–46
postracial remedies tailored to, 112–13, 115–16, 123–24
racial differences in perception of racism, 91–92
resistance to claims of racism or racial injustice, 3, 78–79, 80–81, 85, 87, 90–99, 101–2, 116, 218
roots of racial narratives, 107, 112–13, 114

public opinion
racial disparities, 125–26
racism, 106–7, 111–12

race-first initiatives. *See* racial remedies
race moderates, 105, 125, 130, 132
race-sensitive remedies, 103–4, 107–8, 114, 118–19, 124, 128, 132–33
race-specific remedies
attractiveness of, 127
effectiveness of, 129–30
judicial antipathy to, 108
Left's promotion of, 2–3, 10–11, 106, 124, 130
nonviability of, 3, 7–8, 10–11, 12, 16–17, 107–9, 111, 112–13, 116–17
postracial criticisms of, 103–4, 106–7
postracial remedies accused of being covert, 127–28
race-sensitive vs., 103–4, 107–8, 114, 118–19, 124, 128
racial contract, 76, 81, 84–85, 92–96
racial differences
concerning racial inequality, 109–10, 111, 217–18
concerning racial injustice, 91–92, 111–12
concerning reparations, 48–50
racial disparities. *See* disparities, racial
racial exploitation, 74–76, 78–79, 85
racial progress. *See also* racial progress argument
big-tent remedies for, 7, 12
conflicting views on, 37–38, 189–90
postracialism as obstacle to, 1, 6–7
realistic evaluation of, 15–16, 46
small-tent (race-first) remedies for, 1–3
substantive, 3–4
symbolic, 3–4, 5–6, 7–8
undoing/retreat/backlash after, 5–6, 8–10, 15–16
racial progress argument
critics of, 37, 40–41
danger of arguing against, 41–43

racial progress argument (*cont.*)
　difficulties in countering, 40–44, 45
　empirical data on, 42
　in *Shelby County*, 32–46
racial realism, 78–79, 80–81, 98, 190, 292n.45
racial remedies (race-first initiatives). *See also* small-tent remedies
　advocacy of, 1–3
　limitations of, 3, 7–8, 12, 33
　Thomas's views on, 29
racism. *See also* discrimination; implicit bias; Jim Crow racism; laissez-faire racism; postracial era
　hard-eyed view of, 7–8, 10, 190
　persistence of, 1, 20–21
　psychological resistance to claims of, 3, 71–72, 78–79, 80–81, 115–16
　public opinion about, 106–7, 111–12
　racial differences in perception of, 91–92
Rand, Ayn, 73
Rawls, John
　and basic social structure, 78, 146–47, 148–49
　on guilt's role in society, 88–89
　and justice, 77, 80–81, 84–86, 87–88, 98, 99–100, 190–91, 265–66n.32
　liberalism of, 72–73, 76–77, 78, 79–80, 81–82
　Mills's critique of, 71–72, 73–74, 76–77, 78, 79–82, 84–85
　and political liberties, 153–54, 189, 191–94, 195–96, 198–99, 200–1
　and social inequality, 150
realistic blacktopia
　big-tent remedies as path to, 12
　defined, 11
rectification
　instability of justice as, 91–98
　Mills's conception of justice as, 79, 80–81, 84, 85, 86–87, 90, 98, 99–100, 266n.34

　without redemption, 98–102
rectificatory ideal, 80
redemption, of liberalism, 83–84
Rehnquist, William, 25–26
reparations, 47–68
　corrective justice argument, 52–53, 55–56
　criticisms of, 51–52, 53–54, 58–59, 60–65
　debate over, 47–50
　establishing collective memory as task of, 51
　government complicity as factor in, 53–54, 55–56
　monetary, 48–49
　racial disparities as argument for, 53–57
　racial divide over, 48–50, 97–98
　social science research as evidence for, 57–60, 65–67
　symbolic, 48–49
　temporal factors in, 54–55, 62
Republicans, 43–44. *See also* partisan differences
resistance, political, 237–40, 247
responsibility. *See* collective guilt/responsibility; personal responsibility
Rice, Condoleezza, 75
Roberts, John, 32–33, 34–37, 40, 41, 42, 106–7, 198
Robinson, Amelia Boynton, 219, 221–23
Rorty, Richard, 236
Rousseau, Jean-Jacques, 87–88
Rury, John L., *The Color of Mind* (with Derrick Darby), 244

Sanders, Bernie, 74
Santayana, George, 44
Scalia, Antonin, 17–18, 25–26, 198
segregation. *See* housing discrimination/segregation
Selma (film), 220–21
Selma, Alabama, 35, 92, 212–13, 216–17, 218–19, 228–29

Shakespeare, William, 44
Shelby, Tommie, 265–66n.32
Shelby County v. Holder, 32–46, 110, 189
Siegel, Reva, 123–24, 132–33
small-tent remedies. *See also* racial remedies
  advocacy of, 1–2
  affirmative action as example of, 15–16
  big-tent remedies inclusive of, 7
  limitations of, 1–2, 12
  racial remedies as, 1–3
social contract tradition
  and basic social structure, 147–48, 154
  Mills's critique of, 81, 83–84, 87, 88, 92–93
social institutions, 147–58
social science research
  and affirmative action, 27–31
  on diversity, 27–31
  in judicial thought, 27–31
  on racial disparities, 57–60, 65–67
  reparations claims based on, 57–60, 65–67
Souter, David, 198
South Africa, 144–45, 146
Stanley, Sharon A., *An Impossible Dream?* 236–37, 240, 243–46
states, authority over voting regulations, 32, 33, 36, 198–99, 203
Stevens, John Paul, 198
sumptuary laws. *See* bling laws
Supplemental Nutrition Assistance Program (SNAP), 120
systemic racial barriers
  basic social structure and, 147–58
  exposure of, 64–65, 93
  implicit bias related to, 115
  initiatives to remove, 114, 115, 117–18
  postracial downplaying of, 106–7, 110

racial injustice grounded in, 66, 106, 155
resistance to addressing, 117–18
unavailability of legal remedies for, 108
in the workplace, 120

Taylor, Breonna, 3–4, 5–6
Taylor, Keeanga-Yamahtta, 5
Tenth Amendment, 36, 198–99, 203
Thernstrom, Stephan, 59
third parties, in US politics, 181–82
Thirteenth Amendment, 8–9, 47, 215–16
Thomas, Clarence, 25–26, 29–31, 38, 67–68, 75, 198
Tometi, Opal, 247
Torpey, John, 51–52
Trump, Donald, 174–75, 235–36, 246
Tutu, Desmond, 144–45

universalistic approaches, to social ills, 104, 124–25
University of Michigan Law School, 22–26, 67–68
US Constitution, 29, 108, 191–92, 196, 198–99
US Declaration of Independence, 215–16
US Fifth Circuit Court of Appeals, 38
US government, discriminatory actions of, 53–54, 55–56
US Seventh Circuit Court of Appeals, 62–63, 198
US Supreme Court
  on admissions policies, 16, 23–31
  on discrimination, 24–26, 243
  in postracial era, 24–26, 33, 103, 108, 115–16, 118, 124
  use of social science research by, 27–31
  on voting rights, 32–46, 189, 197–99, 201, 202, 291n.35

voter fraud, 37, 191, 199, 201

voter ID laws, 34, 38, 42, 44, 191, 198, 199–200, 203–4
voting rights, 32–46, 189–207. *See also* equal participation
  burden of proof for restrictions on, 198, 201
  conflicts over access to, 37
  dignity linked to, 45, 209–11, 214–15, 218–19, 222, 224–25, 230–34
  Du Bois on, 166
  fairness as justification for, 190–91
  fair-value defense of, 195, 202, 205, 288n.12
  first-generation vs. second-generation discrimination in, 40, 41
  judicial thought on, 32–46, 189, 197–99, 201, 202
  obstacles to, 5–6, 9, 38, 39, 40, 41, 44, 46, 189–90, 196–97, 199–200, 214
  political liberties linked to, 191–94, 195–96, 200–2
  in postracial era, 32–46
  qualifications of, 197–99, 202–3
  race-neutral defense of, 197–200, 204–7
  racial progress argument on, 32–46
  self-protection as justification for, 177–78, 182–83, 186, 230
  state sovereignty and, 32–33
  unencumbered, 190–91, 194–97, 200–1, 204–6
Voting Rights Act (VRA) [1965], 18, 32–46, 108, 189, 211–12, 216–17, 218, 233–34, 286–87n.2

Waldron, Jeremy, 54–55, 216, 234
Walker, David, 236, 238
Wallace, George, 211–12
war on drugs, 120–21

Warren, Earl, 27–28
WeCARE program, 120
Wells, Ida B., 236, 238, 241
Wells, Tommy, 59–60
West, Cornel, 131, 236
white privilege, 91, 92–93, 94–96, 97–99, 244, 245
whites. *See also* disparities, racial; racial differences; white privilege; white supremacy
  collective guilt of, 92–96, 97–98, 107–8, 136–37
  King's civil rights initiatives and, 217–18
  Mills's critique of, 3, 71–83, 84–85, 100–1
  opinions on reparations, 48–49
  positive group image maintained by, 94–96
  psychological resistance to racial justice, 3, 78–79, 80–81, 85, 87, 90–99, 101–2, 116, 218
  and struggle for democratic power, 171, 173–75
  victimhood expressed by, 145–46
white supremacy, 2–3, 73–74, 75, 77–78, 84, 99, 176, 242–44, 245–46, 247
Wilson, William Julius, 136, 140, 149–50, 152, 155
Winfrey, Oprah, 220–21
women, voting rights of, 166, 177–78, 180, 184–86

X, Malcolm, 225–26, 240, 244

Young, Iris, 148–49, 151–53, 155

Zamalin, Alex, *Struggle on Their Minds*, 236–40, 245–46